IBM Data Power Handbook

Second Edition
Volume IV: DataPower B2B and File Transfer

Richard Kinard

Andre Manriquez

Steven Koehler

Charlie Sumner

Wild Lake Press

Also available or coming soon! Volumes on DataPower Intro/Setup, Networking, and Development.

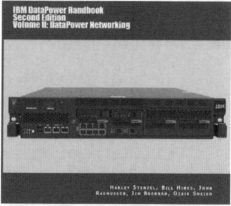

IBM DataPower Appliance Handbook, Second Edition, Volume IV: DataPower B2B and File Transfer

Version 1.0

ISBN: 0990907635

ISBN-13: 978-0990907633

Wild Lake Press

Lake Hopatcong, NJ, USA

www.wildlakepress.com

Please send questions to info@wildlakepress.com and errors/corrections to errata@wildlakepress.com and include the book title and page. Code listings and other resources in this book can be downloaded from http://wildlakepress.com/books/15-information-technology/18-datapower-handbook-resources

To my wife, Tammie and my children, Jade, Hayley and Trevor for their unconditional love and support over the past year; sacrificing many evenings and weekends to make this book possible. To my mother Nancy Kinard who taught me to have a strong work ethic and to never give up. To David Bennett who introduced me to the world of B2B many years ago and who has been a tremendous inspiration and mentor throughout the years. I also want to dedicate this to the memory of my late grandfather, John Perrotta, whose curiosity about technology and his perseverance to teach himself was imprinted on me at an early age, starting me down a path of continued success. Additionally, I would like to thank Gregory Vesper for teaching me what it means to be a truly exceptional Product Manager and finally, many thanks to John Mesberg for bringing me to IBM and for his support when Steve Koehler and I came up with the crazy idea of using DataPower for B2B. —Richard Kinard

I'd like to extend a big thank you to my wife Robbin and my kids, Megan, Bryan, and Shawn. Without their patience, support, and understanding writing this book would have been impossible. I'd like to thank Rich Kinard and Steve Koehler who have been mentors to me in my career at both Cyclone Commerce and IBM. I had the privilege of seeing their vision of B2B on DataPower one evening while at dinner, literally written on a napkin. I'd like to extend my gratitude to Brian Derby and Mike Mauss. These gentlemen were my managers at the start of my career at Premenos Corp. and helped mentor me not only on B2B but also taught me everything about professionalism, dedication, and the meaning of being a team player. —Andre Manriquez

I would like to dedicate this book to my wife, Paula. She endured many a nights of me in my home office working late on the computer. I would also like to thank my mom and dad for giving me my first computer that got me started in programming. — Steven Koehler

To my wife, BJ, for her love and support over the past 30 years in helping me to become all that I can be, and, as a technical communicator, guiding me to become a better writer and editor. And to my son, Michael Chas, who is working hard in his graduate studies for his future in cell developmental biology. —Charlie Sumner

Contents

4 IBM DataPower Handbook, 2nd Ed Vol IV

Preface: B2B and APIs, Oh My!

Just about a year ago Bill Hines came to me and explained a new approach he was taking with the next edition of the DataPower Handbook. This approach involved publishing separate volumes, making it easier for our readers to find the information they need and easier for the authors to update information to keep up with DataPower's rapid rate of evolution. I was instantly sold on the idea and honored that Bill wanted me to lead the effort on writing a volume dedicated to DataPower B2B and file transfer.

When the first edition of the Handbook was released in 2008, B2B on DataPower was in its infancy and only got a brief introduction in the book. Now, seven years later, DataPower B2B appliances have evolved from a hardware only solution to a modular deployment model that can run on DataPower hardware, as a virtual appliance, or in a cloud environment. IBM has had great success with B2B on DataPower with hundreds of customers using DataPower's B2B Gateway in the DMZ. Customers are truly seeing the value of separating B2B connectivity and B2B document processing by moving B2B governance and security closer to the edge of the network where they can reject unwanted or malicious connections prior to passing any information into the trusted network. Once the data is in the trusted network it can then be processed by the customer's integration platform. DataPower can send data to any downstream system that supports the same standards based transport protocols it does (HTTP(S), FTP(S), NFS, MQ, etc.).

This volume builds on the DataPower Handbook volumes that came before it; in *Volume I: DataPower Intro & Setup*, you learned what DataPower was all about and how easy it is to configure. In *Volume II: DataPower Networking* you learned how DataPower's advanced networking capabilities gives you the ability to drop the appliance into your existing environments with ease, how to fine tune and configure all of the networking services of the solution, and in Volume III: DataPower Development you learned how to configure DataPower programmatically and extend DataPower with its support for GatewayScript and XLST. In this volume you learn how to add B2B and Managed File Transfer capabilities on top of the base platform, taking advantage of DataPower's ease of deployment, ease of use, exceptional security and networking capabilities, as well as its ability to be expanded to add functionality that meets your specialized B2B requirements.

A very important and pertinent question that I would like to address before you even begin this book is whether the emerging API technology and standards will kill traditional B2B Standards.

Over the past several years web and mobile APIs have been evolving and have quickly become the new buzz. With the popularity of both public and private APIs being used to make data more accessible to consumers and business partners, one has to wonder if traditional B2B is even still relevant. This question has been open for debate for a few years now and before I give my opinion on the subject, let me first define what

I mean by traditional B2B. Traditional B2B encompasses exchanging files with trading partners over B2B Messaging protocols like AS1, AS2, AS3, ebMS, RNIF and AS4 (newly adopted B2B protocol); this can also include exchanging files over transport protocols like FTP, SFTP, HTTP, SMTP or MQ. The file types (B2B Document Standards) used in these exchanges can be anything, but are most commonly a B2B document standard like EDI-X12, EDIFACT, ACORD, RosettaNet, HL7, HIPAA and many more; some of these standards have been around for over 35 years and are well adopted.

I was first introduced to world of B2B a little more than fifteen years ago. Even back then, one theme I kept hearing was EDI is a dying standard that is going to quickly evolve into XML based standards. The same was said about the EDIINT protocols (AS1, AS2, AS3)—they were to be replaced with RosettaNet, ebXML and/or Web Services.

Of course, today we see EDI documents and EDIINT are not dead but are still being very widely used by many companies around the globe. There are many reasons that contributed to the slow adoption of new standards; one key issue was due to the heavy investment in EDI infrastructure by large companies in industries like retail, manufacturing and banking making it very costly to move off of the EDI standards. Another issue was the realization that many of the companies had several thousands of trading partners who were not ready to make that costly leap to new technologies, forcing companies to continue to support EDI for those partners. This has led to a hybrid approach for B2B where companies use a combination of XML based and EDI based B2B data flows using multiple specialized B2B gateway and integration products.

Companies may develop APIs that have the potential of replacing some of the B2B messaging standards over time, allowing the real-time instant access and response to REST or SOAP based requests and in theory could replace some of the file based B2B interactions they use with partners. There are many benefits in doing so; however, replacing all of their file based interactions is not going to happen overnight or maybe not even at all.

To do so typically takes several years and significant funding for a full migration. For this reason, companies who are looking at using APIs to expose data to customers and partners will want to create an API development and management environment that can handle their mobile and web APIs securely, and will also integrate well with B2B standards. This also has the capability to allow the incremental creation of B2B APIs while also having the capability to integrate to traditional B2B systems. I also believe the use of micro services will be needed to add some B2B process to the APIs in use.

Over the years, it has become clear to me that traditional B2B standards still have a very long life and APIs will only serve to extend and improve how we access and use traditional B2B systems. So, are APIs going to kill traditional B2B standards and file based transfer between trading partners? In my opinion it is unlikely to happen in the next ten years and even then we will see companies using extensible and flexible

API development and management platforms like IBM's API Economy framework to not only support their future requirements around APIs but also providing them with full support for integrating to their legacy integration systems.

On behalf of me and my fellow authors we are pleased to finally present to you the now completed B2B volume of the DataPower Handbook, 2nd Edition. I have three very talented co-authors on this book; between the four of us we bring well over a combined 50 years of B2B integration experience to the pages that follow.

—*Richard Kinard, Cave Creek, AZ, USA December 7, 2015*

Chapter 1 Introduction to DataPower B2B

This chapter presents a history of B2B on DataPower and how the DataPower Appliance uses B2B messaging to optimize and secure data, followed by a brief history of business-to-business (B2B) technologies. Additionally, it covers certain aspects of B2B security including how B2B messaging standards are used to ensure the data itself is secure and identity of each trading partner is verified. Finally, we will take a look at how DataPower B2B complements other IBM B2B Products.

B2B on DataPower

The DataPower B2B Appliance was conceived by two IBM Software Services for WebSphere (ISSW) B2B subject matter experts (Rich Kinard and Steven Koehler, both of whom are authors of this book) in late 2006 shortly after IBM's acquisition of DataPower.

The concept of using DataPower's advanced data and network security capabilities on a firmware based hardware appliance made for a perfect platform to allow B2B Gateway functionality to be moved securely into the DMZ. Placing the platform in the DMZ allows for the rejection of unwanted connections and malicious data prior to passing through the inner firewall into the trusted network. Up to this point all B2B software required a proxy server in the DMZ to perform rudimentary routing and IP/Port filtering before forwarding files to the downstream systems. Proxy servers only provide basic security, where most customers are now looking for gateways to provide much more advanced security functions like authentication, authorization and auditing (AAA), web services security, mobile API security, XML and JSON threat protection, tight integration to anti-virus solutions for in-line file scanning, rules based content routing, advanced error handling, etc. This also keeps traffic from outside your intranet safely in the DMZ, where it should be. You may trust your business partners, but not trust them that much! If their environments are compromised, and you allow their connections into your trusted zone, those compromises could well bleed into your enterprise as well.

In 2008 IBM released the world's first firmware based DMZ deployable B2B appliance called the DataPower B2B Appliance XB60. In 2011, IBM came out with an even more powerful DataPower hardware platform; the DataPower B2B Appliance XB62. The DataPower B2B Appliance has evolved over the past several years to include support for the most well adopted B2B messaging protocols. It is now available on even more powerful hardware with the new IBM DataPower Gateway (IDG) and the DataPower B2B Module. The new DataPower B2B Module can also run on IBM's DataPower IDG Virtual Edition as well as the XG45 and XI52 hardware appliances if they are running firmware version 7.1 or beyond.

The DataPower B2B appliance's great success over the years can not only be attributed to the overall success of DataPower, but also to a strategy that allows the B2B appliance to be dropped seamlessly into the DMZ in front of any application that supports the same standards-based protocols as DataPower. For many customers this means they can decrease their footprint on existing B2B and Application-to-Application (A2A) Integration solutions by separating the partner connections, security, and B2B message processing away from their downstream systems. This allows the applications inside the trusted zone to just process the payloads. This decreases the overall complexity and cost of the customer's DMZ architecture by providing consolidation of DMZ deployed proxy servers, including FTP servers in some cases. Maintenance costs related to the heavy loads are also reduced on downstream systems. Figure 1-1 shows how the B2B Module provides not only B2B specific functions, but also integration functions needed for connecting and integrating to trading partner's systems.

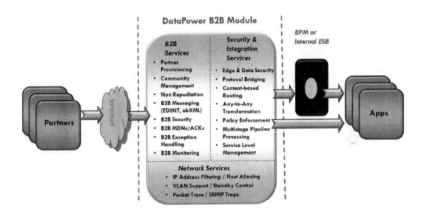

Figure 1-1 DataPower B2B Module Functionality.

DataPower with the B2B Module is also well positioned to bridge the gap between traditional file based B2B interactions and using APIs for a more real-time and manageable type of interaction between companies. Many companies are starting to expose APIs to allow partners to access downstream systems of record for things like checking inventory from their mobile phone before placing an order, checking on order status or verifying prices and discounts. The benefit of using APIs for B2B is endless and the market is still at the very early stages of adoption. Protocols like EDI and XML and file transfer of B2B messages over AS protocols will still dominate the B2B market for quite some time but DataPower B2B can future-proof your architecture making sure you are ready when APIs and the mobile channel become a reality for you.

This is why the appliance has evolved over time to become more than just a SOA Appliance; it is now a multi-channel appliance capable of addressing all of your channel security needs. Organizations need a single solution, a security and integration gateway that is capable of handling all types of application workloads with a policy-driven interface. This will promote consistent security policy enforcement and provide end-to-end security for transactional workloads, regardless of the business channel that they are coming in through. Figure 1-2 depicts IBM's Multi-channel Gateway reference architecture.

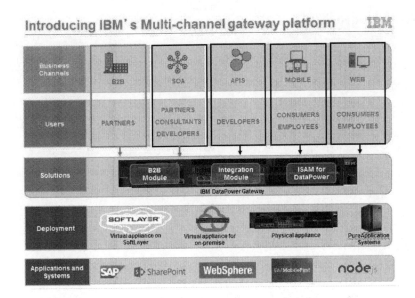

Figure 1-2 Multi-channel Gateway Reference Architecture.

The key benefits of the new multi-channel approach to IBM DataPower are depicted in Figure 1-3.

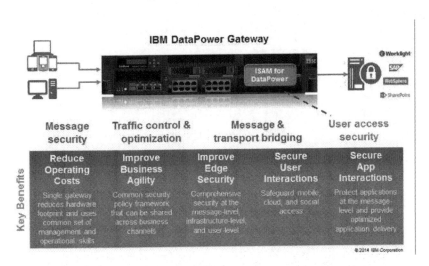

Figure 1-3 DataPower Multi-channel Gateway Benefits.

Brief History of B2B Technologies

We have come a long way since the early days of E-commerce, which was used in trading products and services over computer networks long before the Internet was available to the general public. Some companies used point-to-point connections using modems and protocols like X, Y and Z modem over telephone networks, while others used a single high speed telecom connection to a Value Added Network (VAN). A VAN functions as an intermediary between companies and thousands of trading partners who also subscribe to the same service.

NOTE—E-Commerce Sub-Categories

There are two primary sub-categories of E-Commerce; business to consumer (B2C) and business to business (B2B). For the purpose of this book we are only discussing B2B and how it applies to IBM DataPower.

Today there are very few companies still using modems to communicate point-to-point with their trading partners. However, the concept of a VAN still exists and could be thought of as the great-grandfather to the public cloud environment. For many years VANs dominated the marketplace, transporting documents like purchase orders, invoices, shipping notices, catalogs and manifests between buyers and suppliers. Due to the high cost of leased telecommunication lines and value added services from the

VAN, like EDI validation, transformation and analytics, these services became very expensive to use.

Connecting with trading partners is one thing, but what is communicated is equally as important. A standard document format for exchanging data was needed to allow a common language for each partner to follow. The earliest of these standards is Electronic Data Interchange (EDI) which has a basis dating back to the late 1940's.   EDI is the most widely adopted B2B document standard in existence and is used in almost every industry. It is still used today by many companies, either over a public cloud environment like a VAN or directly with their trading partners.

In the early to mid-1990's, companies started realizing the value of point-to-point communications over the Internet, which could save them a lot of money by moving their top tier trading partners off of the VANs. With the popularity of the Internet, new document formats for B2B also started to emerge and many were based on the XML standard.

The big benefit of direct partner to partner connections over a dedicated line and use of a VAN was that companies always knew who they were receiving their documents from. Since the connection was dedicated, they were sure no one changed, looked at or tampered with the documents they were exchanging. Trading documents over the Internet solved the issue related to costly telecommunication and VAN fees, however, this opened companies up to other issues like security and reliability of the connection, security of the data that was transferred and making sure the trading partners were who they claimed to be.

The Internet provided companies with open protocols to use for transporting files, with HTTP and FTP being the most popular. The transport protocols provide some level of connection security using X.509 certificates with Secure Sockets Layer (SSL) and Transport Layer Security (TLS) methods. These provide data integrity and connection identity assurance 'on the wire', while the messages are en-route to and from their destinations, but no protection for messages 'at rest' at their source or destination. The messages may be stored for some brief period of time, and the systems that process them often require assurance as well that they have come from a trusted, expected source, and have not been tampered with after they left that source.

To meet this need the Electronic Data Interchange – Internet Integration (EDIINT) standards were created. These standards allowed companies to use X.509 certificates to encrypt the payload and sign messages before they are transmitted to trading partners. Additionally, the standard provided the option to use a Message Disposition Notification (MDN). An MDN is a return receipt or acknowledgement to notify the sender that the files were successfully or unsuccessfully received. There are three early standards for EDIINT called Applicability Statements (AS) and each are defined in a Request for Comment (RFC) specification published by the Internet Engineering Task Force (IETF). AS1 is described in RFC3335 and uses SMTP (email) as the underlying transport protocol, AS2 is described in RFC4130 and uses HTTP as the underlying transport protocol and AS3 is described in RFC4823 and uses FTP as the underlying transport protocol. These standards were originally designed to securely transport EDI data over the Internet but over time have become payload agnostic and are used to transport any type of file.

The most widely used EDIINT protocol today is AS2. Over twenty AS2 products, which include the DataPower B2B appliance, are tested for interoperability through a vendor agnostic B2B communications interoperability company called The Drummond Group. More information on B2B interoperability testing can be found on the Drummond Group web site at http://www.drummondgroup.com/b2b-home.

Over the past 10 years Web Services have proven to be the mechanism of choice for request/response types of data exchange. Web Services have also emerged as a viable mechanism to transfer B2B documents between partners. In an effort to lessen the complexity of Web Services and make transferring B2B documents over Web Services easier to understand, a new standard called AS4 was approved as a conformance profile of the OASIS ebMS V3.0 specification in 2013. This profile is based on the functional requirements of the AS2 specification which constrains the ebMS v3.0 to support transporting files over Web Services using XML security.

More recently we have seen a paradigm shift in the market and customers are adopting APIs as a viable mechanism for meeting their B2B and B2C requirements. APIs can simplify your channel interactions by allowing you to use the same API gateway for multiple channels like mobile, web, SOA, and B2B to securely access the same systems of record inside your network.

B2B Security

When Deploying a B2B solution there are many aspects of security that need to be taken into consideration including deployment security, access control, connection security, document security, virus protection, Web and mobile threat protection. Figure 1-4 is a good representation of how DataPower can be deployed in a variety of scenarios including functioning as a security gateway. The first volume in this book series, *IBM DataPower Handbook, Second Edition, Volume 1: DataPower Intro & Setup* covers these use cases in more detail.

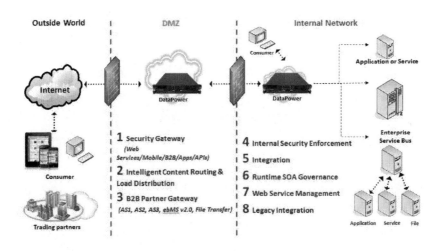

Figure 1-4 IBM DataPower Gateway Scenarios.

Deployment security

Deployment security relates to more than just the B2B gateway. It encompasses other network equipment like firewalls, routers, proxy servers, load balancers, plus downstream servers used for integration, B2B, accounting, and databases. All of these devices and applications need to be deployed in such a manner that ensures that no one who is not explicitly authorized to access the systems can get to them. DataPower can be deployed in the DMZ to provide secured access to and from external applications and trading partners; it can securely connect through the inner firewall over isolated and dedicated Ethernet connections. DataPower can also be deployed in the trusted zone to provided fine grained secured access to internal applications.

A typical deployment architecture using the IBM DataPower Gateway in both the DMZ and Trusted Network is depicted in figure 1-5. The B2B Module is being used in the DMZ to integrate and secure connections to external trading partners and the Integration Module is being used in the Trusted Network to integrate and secure connections between internal applications. The available modules are covered in the first volume in this book series, *IBM DataPower Handbook, Second Edition, Volume I: DataPower Intro & Setup.*

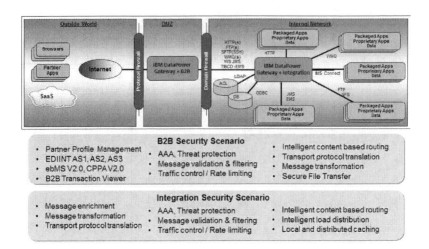

Figure 1-5 DataPower IDG deployment architecture example.

Access Control

Access control can be done at many layers and in many ways. It can be done with regard to network connections, where access can be restricted or granted based on the IP address of the sending party. This method is not completely reliable, since IP addresses can be easily spoofed. It can also be done by restricting access based on authenticated identities, using authorization policies.

DataPower B2B supports both methods of controlling access to the device. IP filtering and fine grained access and authorization is configured in DataPower's Front-side Protocol Handlers in the Access Control field and in the Password and/or certificate AAA Policy field. We will demonstrate how AAA is used for B2B to restrict access when using FTP in Chapter 5 of this book. The AAA policy can define user credentials on the device or integrate with many third party access managers to extract the information. DataPower's AAA policies are very robust and can be used to support many different methods of securing access to data and systems as seen in figure 1-6.

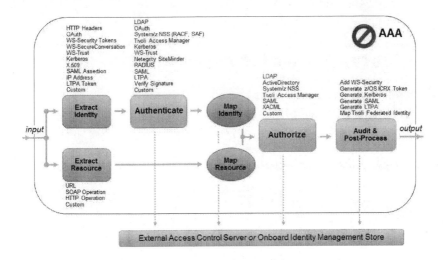

Figure 1-6 DataPower AAA Security Policy.

Connection Security

Connection security provides companies with the ability to secure data on the Internet while in transit using SSL and/or TLS. As described before, these protocols provide privacy, message integrity and authentication 'on the wire'. Unfortunately, connection security does not provide data integrity or nonrepudiation, nor can it continue to secure the data after it is transported to its final destination.

DataPower stores and manages X.509 certificates on its encrypted flash file system, or they can be stored in a FIPS 140-2 Level 3 compliant Hardware Security Module (HSM) that can optionally be installed in IBM DataPower Gateway physical appliances.

NOTE—SSL and TLS Primer

A great overview of SSL and TLS can be found in Volume II, "DataPower Networking" of this DataPower Handbook series.

Document Security

Document security is achieved using X.509 digital certificates to provide document-level encryption and to digitally sign the documents. Signatures are calculated and associated to the document and signer in such a way that prevents reproduction of the signature or tampering with the document (integrity). It also ensures the receiving party can verify the sender is who they say they are (non-repudiation).

Document security provides privacy, integrity and non-repudiation. DataPower provides document security for B2B messages using EDIINT AS1, AS2, AS3 and ebMS v2.0 protocols. For file transfer, DataPower can use a processing policy to encrypt and sign the document or decrypt and verify the signature. DataPower supports both S/MIME and XML security methods. Additionally, a processing policy can be used to be sure the payloads are encrypted before writing them to the downstream systems which is an important part of Payment Card Industry (PCI) compliance for credit card transactions. DataPower provides robust support for PCI compliance with a simple configuration model that saves you time and money. Figure 1-7 demonstrates how the DataPower B2B Module uses AS2 to secure documents between trading partners.

NOTE—Field Level Security

Field Level Security typically applies when using XML based standards. In those cases some fields inside the document require extra security and need to be encrypted individually; information like social security numbers, account numbers and credit card numbers. Typically these are encrypted before the file is packaged in a B2B Messaging protocol and decrypted after the files reach the intended application.

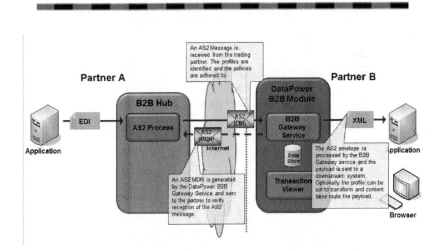

Figure 1-7 – Securing documents using AS2.

Virus Protection

Virus protection provides companies with the ability to prevent, detect, and remove malicious computer viruses that may exist inside files that are being transferred between systems. Over the years virus software vendors has evolved to provide many additional and more advanced Internet security functions such as the ability to detect spam, scam and phishing related attacks.

DataPower provides the ability to integrate to a company's existing enterprise anti-virus software using a standards-based protocol called Internet Content Adaptation Protocol (ICAP). This HTTP-like protocol allows DataPower to make a call out to the virus scanning application and instruct it to inspect the file and verify it is safe before allowing it to pass out of the gateway. An excellent article describing how DataPower integrates with anti-virus applications can be found on IBM Developer Works at the following URL:

http://www.ibm.com/developerworks/websphere/library/tech articles/1004_trucchia/1004_trucchia.html

Web and Mobile Threat Protection

Threat protection for SOA, legacy, API, Web and mobile provides a company with the ability to identify and react to threats that can be present in both request and response documents.

DataPower provides robust XML and JSON threat protection. DataPower is also a leader in PCI compliance and protection against the Open web Application Security Project (OWASP) top ten web application risks. When using the IBM

Security Access Manager (ISAM) Proxy Module on DataPower in conjunction with ISAM for Web or ISAM for Mobile, IBM expands DataPower's access control and allows companies to integrate tightly with products like QRADAR, IBM Mobile First Platform, and Trusteer Mobile SDK, providing more advanced security architectures.

There is some excellent reading material on IBM Developer Works on this subject at the following URLs:

http://www.ibm.com/developerworks/websphere/techjournal/0603_col_hines/0603_col_hines.html

http://www.ibm.com/developerworks/websphere/library/techarticles/1210_srinivasan/1210_srinivasan.html

For information regarding OWASP and PCI Compliance the following URLs are useful:

https://www.owasp.org/index.php/Category:OWASP_Top_Ten_Project

https://www.pcisecuritystandards.org/

Summary

In this chapter you learned what the DataPower B2B Module is and how it uses B2B Standards and the award winning security capabilities of DataPower to move B2B Security and Governance closer to edge of the network, allowing rejection of unauthorized users and malicious data before it gets into the trusted network.

Chapter 2 B2B Configuration Object Overview

This chapter presents a detailed description of each configuration object used in the DataPower B2B Module. Since the B2B functionality is built on top of the functionality that exists in the Integration Module we will not go into detail on the Integration Module objects, as they will be covered in other volumes of this book series. This chapter does not describe how to use each service or object; that information is presented in other chapters in this B2B book.

What is the DataPower B2B Module?

The DataPower B2B Module is a set of Services and Objects that can be used for B2B and MFT transaction exchange between two or more companies. This module takes advantage of and inherits from the integration capabilities that exist in the Integration Module; the only exception is IMS Connect and IMS Callout do not exist in the B2B Module (IMS is used to connect and integrate to mainframe environments).

At the highest level we have a B2B Gateway Service which is essentially the nerve center of B2B transaction processing; you can think of each B2B Gateway as an instance of a B2B hub and DataPower lets you have as many as you like. The next level consists of objects that need to be associated with a B2B Gateway Service, so we can provide inputs into the service;

Front-Side Protocol Handlers, and outputs from the service in the form of partner destinations.

Partner Destinations are one of many attributes of a B2B Partner Profile. B2B Partner Profiles exist so that all data that passes through a B2B Gateway Service can be governed by a set of rules defined in a partner policy; these rules define how data is handled when exchanged between two trading partners. These profiles are associated with any number of B2B Gateway Services and there is no hard limit to the number of partner profiles you can have.

In addition to the Service, Front-Side Handlers and Partner Profiles, there is an underlying architecture to support the standards that govern how B2B Messaging must be adhered to and to assure delivery of B2B messages and/or files. This architecture consists of a very fast and efficient embedded database to house transactional metadata and the state of B2B Messages. Additionally, the B2B Module has an AES encrypted hard drive partition to house off-the-wire payloads to be used for legal non-repudiation of files and for automatic resend of the B2B messages in the event a valid MDN/ACK is not received in the specified amount of time. Since the B2B Gateway Service captures and persists all of this information a B2B Transaction Viewer is provided to give you an at-a-glance view of the state of any transaction that passes through the B2B Gateway Service.

Figure 2-1 depicts the B2B Module component architecture and shows how processing policy can be applied at the partner level. This particular policy checks each file for viruses and then transforms the payload before sending it to the internal system.

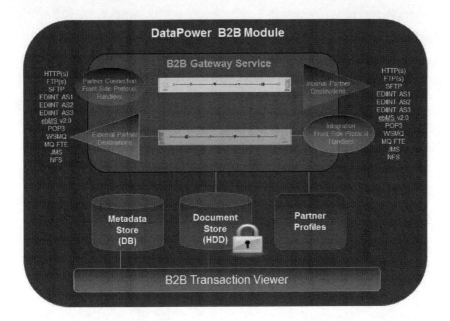

Figure 2-1 B2B Module Component Architecture.

B2B Partner Profiles

B2B Partner Profiles are configuration objects that contain all of the information needed to identify valid partners and is used to store information used to enforce partner policies. B2B Partner Profiles are defined as either internal or external, where internal partner profiles are a representation of the lines of business or applications that exist inside your network and external partner profiles represent the companies outside of your network that you do business with. There is no limit to how many partner profiles you can configure in the B2B Module; however, if you run out of space on the flash drive of the hardware appliance for the configuration, you will need to consider storing your configuration files off device.

B2B Partner Profiles can be created using the B2B Partner Profile icon on the Control Panel screen or by clicking on the link in the left navigation menu for Services→B2B Services→B2B Partner Profile (Figure 2-2).

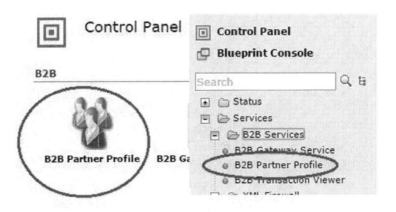

Figure 2-2 Launch B2B Partner Profile Configuration.

When you click on the B2B Partner Profile icon or link you will be presented with either a blank list (if you have not yet configured any profiles) or a list of the profiles you have already configured. Figure 2-3 is an example of a list that contains configured profiles.

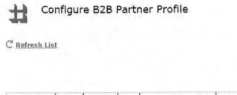

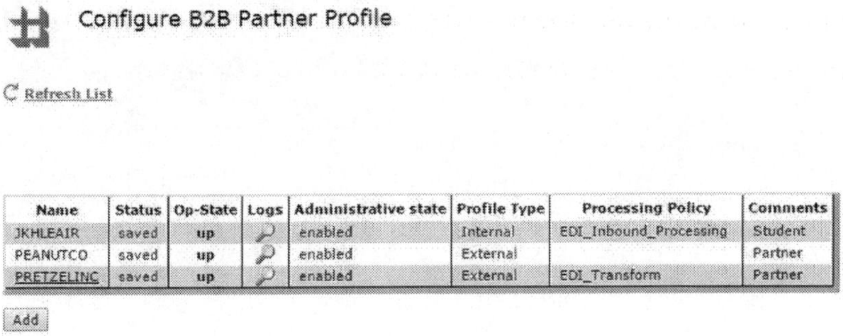

Configure B2B Partner Profile

C Refresh List

Name	Status	Op-State	Logs	Administrative state	Profile Type	Processing Policy	Comments
JKHLEAIR	saved	up		enabled	Internal	EDI_Inbound_Processing	Student
PEANUTCO	saved	up		enabled	External		Partner
PRETZELINC	saved	up		enabled	External	EDI_Transform	Partner

Add

Figure 2-3 B2B Partner Profile List View.

When you click on the Add button to create a new profile you are presented with a detailed profile configuration screen which contains several tabs with fields that hold the specific information about the trading partner. The information that follows describes each tab and field in detail.

NOTE—Bulk Loading Partner Profiles

It is a common practice to bulk load partner profiles using DataPower's SOAP Management (SOMA) Interface. You would simply create a SOMA XML script file to create all of your partner profiles at once.

B2B Partner Profile Main Tab

The Main tab contains several fields that can be populated with information about the partner; a brief description of each field is provided in this section. Figure 2-4 shows the Main tab of a sample partner profile.

Figure 2-4 B2B Partner Profile – Main Tab.

Name: This field is a mandatory field that contains a unique name for this profile. It is recommended to use descriptive names such as the partner's company and line of business name when using the external profile type or the name of the internal line of business and/or the application name when using the internal profile type.

Administrative State: The field is a mandatory field and is used to enable or disable this profile. You may wish to disable instead of deleting a profile when a partner is no longer actively trading with you. This enables you to re-enable the profile if their status changes rather than having to re-create it.

Comments: This field is an optional field and is used to give a descriptive comment about this profile.

Profile Type: This field is a mandatory field and is used to designate a profile as internal or external. Internal profiles contain private keys for encryption and signing of data when using AS or ebMS protocols while external profiles only contain public certificates provide by the partner.

Partner Business IDs: This field is used to house the free-form business IDs the partner uses for identity when exchanging B2B documents. B2B document formats/standards like EDI-X12, EDIFACT and XML typically contain a sender ID and receiver ID that is globally unique. This field is only mandatory when not using one of the other Business ID fields.

Partner Business IDs (DUNS), (DUNS+4): If the customer is using their DUNS or DUNS+4 number for identity, the ID can be entered into one of these two fields. This is mostly used for ebXML where the ID Type is used for document processing. These fields are only mandatory when not using one of the other Business ID fields.

Processing Policy: This field is used to designate a processing policy to be used in the profile. Processing policies are used to apply a broad set of rules to the data flow. It is important to note that since every data flow is between two partners, the policy that gets executed (internal vs. external) is governed by the direction of the flow. E.g. if the flow is inbound then the policy in the internal profile's policy will be executed, if the flow is outbound then the policy in the external profile will be executed. For B2B, processing policies are most commonly used to dynamically route documents or extract metadata and then send it to downstream systems that require specific metadata to trigger internal business process.

NOTE—Processing Policy and Services

Processing policy and services are described at a high level in "Volume 1, DataPower Intro and Setup" of this handbook series. B2B Policies differ in that they are contained in the partner profile instead of the service and they do not include a route action as routing in partner profiles is governed by partner destinations.

Response Traffic Type: This field characterizes the traffic that originates from the receiving partner when responding from a processing policy. For inbound flows this is the response from the internal partner; for outbound this is the response from the external partner. Non-XML is the default and the most common setting for B2B transactions. Other options are SOAP, XML and Pass Thru.

Partner E-mail Addresses: This field is optional and houses the e-mail addresses for a partner that is using e-mail or AS1 for exchanging B2B Documents.

B2B Partner Profile AS Settings Tab

The AS Settings tab contains fields to house information needed to support AS1, AS2 and AS3 data flows. The fields displayed in the AS Settings tab are different depending on whether the profile is internal or external. This tab is optional;

if AS protocols are not used, this tab can remain unconfigured. A brief description of each field for both partner types is provided in this section. Figure 2-5 shows the AS Settings tab of a sample internal partner profile and Figure 2-6 shows the AS Settings tab of a sample external partner profile.

Figure 2-5 AS Settings Tab – Internal Partner Profile.

Name: This field is carried over from the main tab and you do not need to edit it in this tab.

Inbound Security: This section contains three fields that are used for security of inbound files destined for the internal partner.

Require Signature: This field is used when you want to require the inbound files to be signed. The default is set to unchecked.

Require Encryption: This field is used when you want to require the inbound files to be encrypted. The default is set to unchecked.

Inbound Decryption Identification Credentials: This field is used to hold the credentials needed to decrypt inbound files. Credentials consist of an X.509 key and certificate. When you click on the + sign you can create a decryption object and import the key and certificate into the object. External Partners encrypt files with the public certificate you provide them and your internal profile will use the private key to decrypt the files.

Outbound Security: This section contains four fields that are used for security of outbound files destined for the external partner.

Sign Outbound Messages: This field is used when you want to apply a signature to the files that are sent to the external partner. The default is set to unchecked. When checked the Signing Digest Algorithm field is displayed.

Signing Identification Credentials: This field is used to hold the credentials needed to sign outbound files. Credentials consist of an X.509 key and certificate. When you click on the + sign you can create a signature identification object and import the key and certificate into the object. Internal Partners sign outbound files with their private key and the external partner will use the public certificate you provide them to verify the signature.

Signing Digest Algorithm: This field is used to denote which algorithm to use for hashing outbound files during signing; sha1 is the default and most commonly used, other options are md5, sha256, sha384 and sha512.

Signing S/MIME Version: This field denotes which version of S/MIME to use when signing outbound files. V3.1 is the default; V3.2 is the other option.

Advanced Settings: This section contains two fields that are used for advanced features related to the AS specification.

Override AS Identifier: This field is used to assign a different ID to the AS(1,2,3)-From and AS(1,2,3)-To header in the messages rather than the ID extracted from the payload. The default is blank which will retain the ID as extracted. This setting is typically used when exchanging data with VANs as the AS ID's are typically those of the VAN and not the final recipient.

Preserve Filename: This field is used to support the AS2 Filename Preservation specification.   When checked the Content-Disposition header of an inbound AS2 message is exposed and the receiving partner can retrieve the original file name that is contained in the header using processing policy.

NOTE—Processing Policy and Services

A good developerWorks article on how to use AS2 Filename Preservation is available at the following URL:
http://www.ibm.com/developerworks/websphere/library/te charticles/1411_kinard/1411_kinard.html

Figure 2-6 represents a sample external partner AS Settings screen; it is very similar to the internal partner AS Settings screen with the exception of not having an Outbound Security section and the Inbound Security section is slightly different. Only the differences will be described below; all other fields have the same meaning as described for the internal partner profile.

Configure B2B Partner Profile

| Main | **AS Settings** | sbMS Settings | Destinations | Contacts |

B2B Partner Profile

Apply Cancel   Help

Name   AcmeInc_Partner   *

Inbound Security
Inbound Signature Validation Credentials   AcmePartner_ValCred ▼ + ...

MDN SSL Proxy Profile   AcmeIncSSL ▼ + ...

Advanced Settings
Override AS Identifier   AcmeIncAS2

Allow Duplicate AS Inbound Message   never ▼

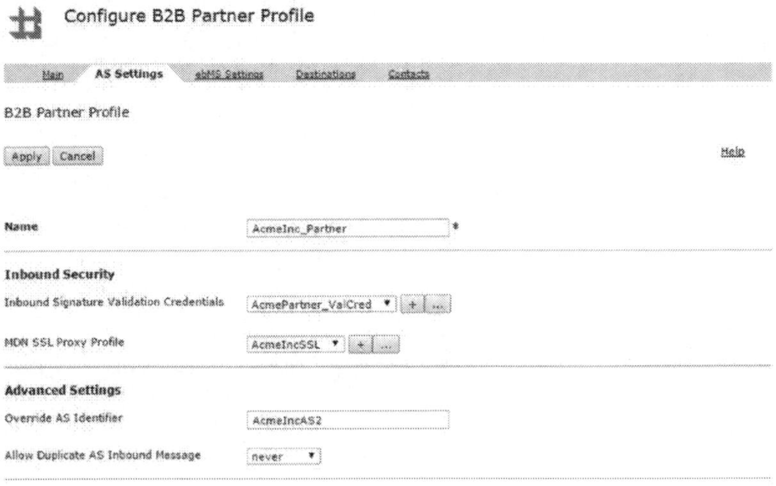

Figure 2-6 AS Settings Tab – External Partner Profile.

Inbound Security: This section contains two fields that are used for security of inbound files coming from the external partner and connection security of the response/MDN that is returned to the external partner.

Inbound Signature Validation Credentials: This field is used to hold the credentials needed to verify the signature of inbound files coming from the external partner. Credentials consist of an X.509 public certificate. When you click on the + sign you can create a signature validation object and import the certificate into the object.

MDN SSL Proxy Profile: This field is used to hold the SSL proxy profile needed to establish an SSL connection to the partner when sending the MDN back to them. SSL Proxy Profiles are described in more detail in Volume 1 of this book series.

B2B Partner Profile ebMS Settings Tab

The ebMS Settings tab contains fields to house information needed to minimally support the ebMS V2.0 standard. This tab is only used when the B2B Gateway is not Collaboration Protocol Agreement (CPA) enabled and when you want to use ebMS to only transfer files. If you want to use ebXML to integrate processes between partners you will need to enable CPA's at the B2B Gateway to support downstream business process. An ebMS V2.0 scenario that provides details about CPA and non-CPA gateways is presented later in this B2B book.

The fields displayed in the ebMS Settings tab are different depending on whether the profile is internal or external. This tab is optional; if ebMS V2.0 is not used or if the B2B Gateway is CPA enabled, this tab can remain unconfigured. A brief description of each field for both partner types is provided in this section; many are similar to the AS Settings fields but have additional options to support ebXML. Figure 2-7 shows the ebMS Settings tab of a sample internal partner profile and Figure 2-8 shows the ebMS Settings tab of a sample external partner profile.

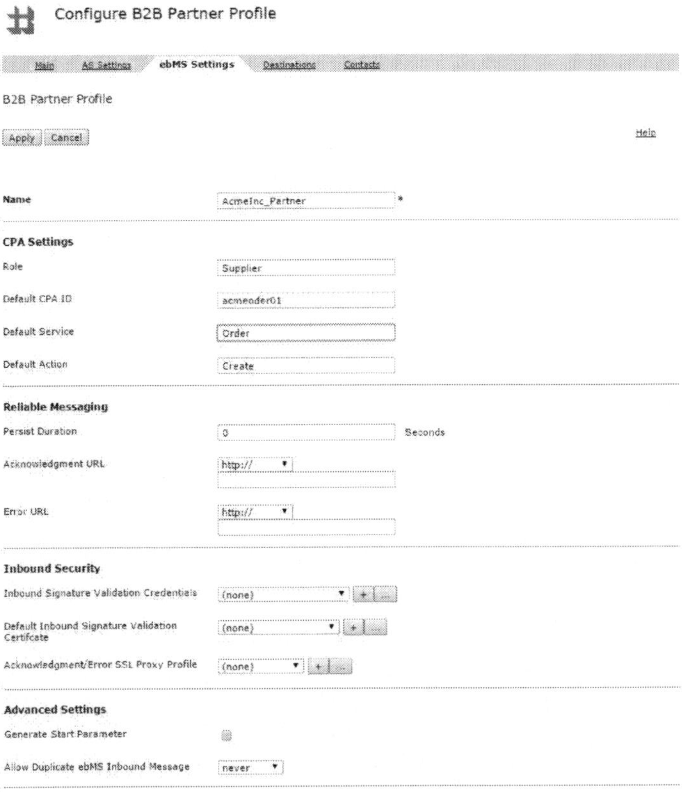

Figure 2-7 ebMS Settings Tab – Internal Partner Profile.

Name: This field is carried over from the main tab and you do not need to edit it in this tab.

CPA Settings: This section contains one field that is used for setting the minimum CPA requirement for inbound ebMS messages.

Role: Specifies the name of authorized role of the Internal Partner which represents the From party element in the ebXML message. E.g. Buyer, Supplier, Initiator, Consumer, etc.

Inbound Security: This section contains three fields that are used for security of inbound files destined for the internal partner.

Require Signature: This field is used when you want to require the inbound files to be signed, if they are not signed the AS file will be rejected. The default is set to unchecked.

Require Encryption: This field is used when you want to require the inbound files to be encrypted, if they are not encrypted the AS file will be rejected. The default is set to unchecked.

Inbound Decryption Identification Credentials: This field is used to hold the credentials needed to decrypt inbound files. Credentials consist of an X.509 key and certificate. When you click on the + sign you can create a decryption object and import the key and certificate into the object. External Partners encrypt files with the public certificate you provide them and your internal profile will use your private key to decrypt the files.

Outbound Security: This section contains four fields that are used for security of outbound files destined for the external partner.

Sign Outbound Messages: This field is used when you want to apply a signature to the files that are sent to the external partner. The default is set to unchecked. When checked three additional fields associated with signing are displayed.

Signing Identification Credentials: This field is used to hold the credentials needed to sign outbound files. Credentials consist of an X.509 key and certificate. When you click on the + sign you can create a signature identification object and import the key and certificate into the object. Internal Partners sign outbound files with their private key and the external partner will use the public certificate you provide them to verify the signature.

Signing Digest Algorithm: This field is used to denote which algorithm to use for hashing outbound files during signing. Sha1 is the default and most commonly used; other options are sha256, sha512, ripemd160, sha224, sha384 and md5.

Signature Algorithm: This field sets the algorithm used to sign the outbound files that are sent by the internal partner. The default is dsa-sha1 and is the most commonly used algorithm; other options are rsa-sha1, rsa-sha256, rsa-sha512, rsa-sha384, rsa-ripemd160, rsa-ripemd160 2010 and rsa-md5.

Signature Canonicalization Method: This field is used to set the algorithm used to canonicalize the SOAP

Enveloped XML and exclude comments before signing outbound ebMS messages. The default is c14n, which is recommended by the ebMS specification; other options are exc-c14n, c14n-comments and exc-c14n-comments.

Advanced Settings: This section contains one field that is used for advanced features related to the ebMS specification.

Generate Start Parameter: Indicates whether to generate a start parameter for the ebMS message. The start parameter identifies the root part of the ebMS message. This setting is disabled by default. The Start Parameter is option in the ebMS specification; however it is commonly used to trigger downstream business process.

Figure 2-8 represents a sample external partner ebMS Settings screen. This screen differs from the Internal Partner ebMS Settings screen in that it provides additional CPA settings that are used when packaging outbound messages and it adds a section for Reliable Messaging. Additionally, the Internal Security section uses signing credentials instead of decryption credentials.

Figure 2-8 ebMS Settings Tab – External Partner Profile.

Name: This field is carried over from the main tab and you do not need to edit it in this tab.

CPA Settings Section: This section contains four fields that are used for setting the minimum CPA requirements needed to build valid outbound ebMS messages.

Role: Specifies the name of authorized role of the External Partner which represents the To party element in the ebXML message. E.g. Buyer, Supplier, Initiator, Consumer, etc.

Default CPA ID: Sets the CPA ID to be packaged in the outbound ebMS message header. If the CPA ID is set in the Destination it overrides this value.

Default Service: Sets the Service to be packaged in the outbound ebMS message header. If the Service is set in the Destination it overrides this value.

Default Action: Sets the Action to be packaged in the outbound ebMS message header. If the Action is set in the Destination it overrides this value.

Reliable Messaging Section

Persist Duration: The time, which can be obtained from a CPA, indicates to the receiving partner the minimum length of time the message should be kept in persistent storage. When receiving inbound messages, the Persist Duration is used to compute the expiry time using the formula: Time to Persist = Persist Duration + Current Time. When a message is not expired, it is not eligible to be archived; Default to 0 (zero) to expire the received document at the time the document is received.

Acknowledgment URL: When an asynchronous reply is requested by the inbound ebMS document, this field is required to determine where to send the acknowledgment. Though optional, it is recommended to set the URL.

Error URL: If an error occurs, this field is used as the error reporting location to send the error message which contains the error code and description of the error. The Error URL should not be empty if the Acknowledgment URL is specified.

Inbound Security Section: This section contains three fields that are used for security of inbound files destined for the internal partner.

Inbound Signature Validation Credentials: This field sets the validation credentials needed to verify the signature on an Acknowledgment or inbound ebMS message from this external partner. For ebMS messages, the DataPower appliance supports only X.509 Data and Key Name signature methods.

Default Inbound Signature Validation Certificate: Set the default validation certificate to verify the signature of an inbound ebMS message or an acknowledgment. The default signature validation certificate is used if either the KeyInfo element is missing or the signature method is unsupported.

Acknowledgment/Error SSL Proxy Profile: Sets the SSL proxy profile to establish an SSL-enabled, secured connection to external partners who request an asynchronous reply (the response can be an Acknowledgment or an Error Message) sent to HTTPS addresses. To specify an SSL proxy profile for specific URLs, configure a user agent for the XML manager associated with the gateway.

Advanced Settings Section: This section contains two fields that are used for advanced features related to the ebMS specification.

Generate Start Parameter: Indicates whether to generate a start parameter for the ebMS message. The start parameter identifies the root part of the ebMS message. This setting is disabled by default. The Start Parameter is optional in the ebMS specification; however, it is commonly used to trigger downstream business process.

Allow Duplicate ebMS Inbound Message: Controls when to allow and reprocess duplicate ebMS inbound messages. Note that this option does not apply to the MDN or ACK.

B2B Partner Profile Destinations Tab

The Destinations tab is a mandatory tab that contains destinations to be used for this partner profile. Destinations contain the transport protocol and location where to transfer files. A partner profile can have an unlimited number of destinations, however only one destination is used by default. The default destination is the one at the top of the destination list and the default can be changed by moving the destination to the top using the arrows on the right side of the list. Destinations can also be selected dynamically using a stylesheet in a processing policy.

Having multiple destinations provides the flexibility for the user to dynamically pick a destination using a processing policy. For instance, let's say you want all of your EDI files to go to a MQ queue that is integrated to Sterling B2B Integrator, all of your XML files to go to a MQ queue that is integrated to IBM Integration Broker and all of your binary files of to go to a FTP location inside the trusted zone. In this case you would have two MQ destinations and one FTP destination. Internal destinations are typically locations inside your network where external destinations are typically partner connections over the Internet.

Figure 2-9 is an example of the Destination List view.

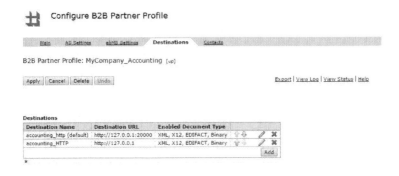

Figure 2-9 B2B Partner Profile Destinations Tab – List View.

Figure 2-10 represents a detailed view of an AS2 Destination and lists all of the destination options available when you click on the Destination URL drop down. Each destination has different fields depending on which transport protocol you choose. This section does not go into detail for each and every protocol; many of the common protocols will be described in detail in the scenarios demonstrated in other chapters of this book.

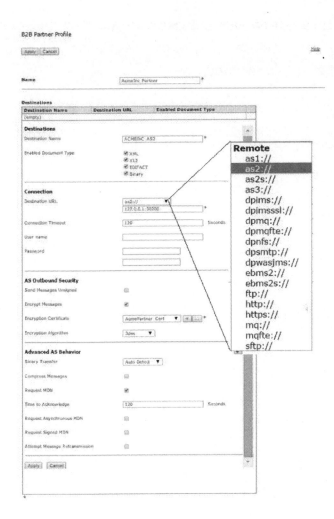

Figure 2-10 B2B Partner Profile - AS2 Destination & Protocol List.

B2B Partner Profile Contacts Tab

The Contacts tab is an optional tab containing fields that provide you with information about whom to contact for this partner when issues arise when transferring files between your gateway and the partner's gateway. This tab is not meant to be used as a robust contact management solution, but rather give you the convenience of quickly identifying the responsible parties for this connection.

Figure 2-11 is an example of the Contact screen.

Figure 2-11 B2B Partner Profile - Contact View.

B2B Gateway Service

B2B Gateway Services are essentially, individual instances of a B2B hub and there is no limit to how many can be configured in the B2B Module. The B2B Gateway Service configuration object contains all of the information needed to process the secure exchange of files between partners and it provides a mechanism to automatically archive and purge data to ensure the system never runs out of storage space. Profiles are associated with the B2B Gateway Service and can also be shared between B2B Gateway Services that reside in the same domain. This comes in handy when you have multiple company divisions or lines of business that each need their own B2B Gateways, but also need to share partner profiles using a different destination and/or different certificates for transporting files.

The B2B Gateway Service can be created using the B2B Gateway Service icon on the Control Panel screen or by clicking on the link in the left navigation menu for Services→B2B Services→B2B Gateway Service (Figure 2-12).

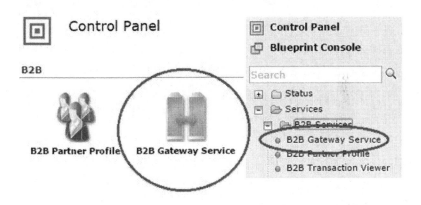

Figure 2-12 Launch B2B Gateway Service Configuration.

When you click on the B2B Gateway Service icon or link you will be presented with either a blank list (if you have not yet configured any B2B Gateways) or a list of the B2B Gateways you have already configured. Figure 2-13 is an example of a list that contains a configured B2B Gateway Service.

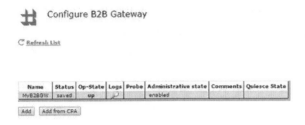

Figure 2-13 B2B Gateway Service - List View.

When you click on the Add button to create a B2B Gateway Service you are presented with a detailed B2B Gateway configuration screen which contains several tabs with fields that hold the specific information about the B2B Gateway you are configuring. There is also the option to add a gateway if it doesn't already exist, using an ebXML V2.0 CPA, however, the details related to a CPA enabled gateway are described in detail in chapter 6 of this book and will not be covered in this section. The information that follows describes each tab and field in the B2B Gateway Service in detail.

B2B Gateway Main Tab

The Main tab contains several fields that can be populated with information about the B2B Gateway Service; a brief description of each field is provided in this section. Figure 2-14 shows the Main tab of a sample B2B Gateway Service.

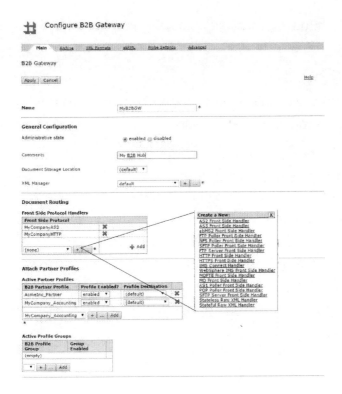

Figure 2-14 B2B Gateway Service – Main Tab & FSPH List.

Name: This field is a mandatory field that contains a unique name for this B2B Gateway. It is recommended to use descriptive names such as your company name and line of business. E.g. AcmeInc_AccountingDept.

General Configuration Section: This section contains four fields that contain specific information used to control B2B Gateway behavior.

Administrative State: This field is a mandatory field and is used to enable or disable this B2B Gateway. You may wish to temporarily disable a gateway if you have the back-end down for maintenance. This enables you to disable the gateway without affecting other B2B Gateways you may have configured.

Comments: This field is an optional field and is used to give a descriptive comment about this B2B Gateway Service.

Document Storage Location: This drop-down field is used to determine where you want the B2B off-the-wire payloads to be stored. The default location is on the AES Encrypted portion of the local hard drive. Optionally, you can configure a NFS mount point that will also show up in the drop down list. These off-the-wire payloads are used for legal non-repudiation and internally to support automated and manual file resends. The Document Storage Location must be available or the B2B Gateway will not be enabled; it will show down. Additionally, B2B Persistence must be enabled to allow for persistence of metadata.

XML Manager: This field is used to manage the B2B Gateway Service. The XML manager contains the reference to a user agent. The user agent defines the default settings for how the service connects to external services.

Document Routing Section: This section contains a configuration list used to house the configured Front-Side Protocol Handlers (FSPH) to be used for getting files into the service. FSPH's can be either a listener or a poller and are created using the + (Plus) button and edited using the ... button to the right of the drop down in the Front Side Protocol box. This section does not go into detail for each and every front side protocol; many of the common front side protocols will be described in detail in the scenarios demonstrated in other chapters of this book.

Attach Partner Profiles Section: This section contains two lists that are used to house individual active partner profiles and active partner profile groups.

Active Partner Profiles: This box lists the Partner profiles you want to associate with the B2B Gateway. At the B2B Gateway level you can enable/disable the B2B Partner from using this B2B Gateway and also select which Destination the B2B Gateway should use. You can create B2B Partner Profiles from within the B2B Gateway screen by clicking on the + (plus) button or edit them by clicking on the ... button. If you already created your profiles using the B2B Partner Profile icon or menu item, then they will be displayed in the drop-down for selection. At a minimum, one internal and one external profile must be associated to the B2B Gateway Service.

Active Profile Groups: This box lists profile groups you want to associate with the B2B Gateway. Profile Groups are simply a logical grouping of profiles to provide an easier mechanism of identifying which profiles belong to a single large organization. E.g. IBM has many divisions, you may decide to represent IBM as the group and then list each profile for each line of business within the group; this way all you have to do is associate the IBM group with the B2B Gateway. Profile groups can be created and edited from inside the B2B Gateway by clicking on the + (Plus) button or ... button to the right of the Profile Group drop down or it can be started from the Objects→B2B Configuration→B2B Partner Profile Group left navigation menu.

B2B Gateway Archive Tab

The Archive tab is mandatory and it is used to make sure the files and metadata persisted by B2B Gateway Service do not fill up the local hard drive. There are two different archive modes each screen is slightly different depending on which mode you select. Figure 2-15 shows the Archive and Purge Mode and figure 2-16 shows the Purge Only mode.

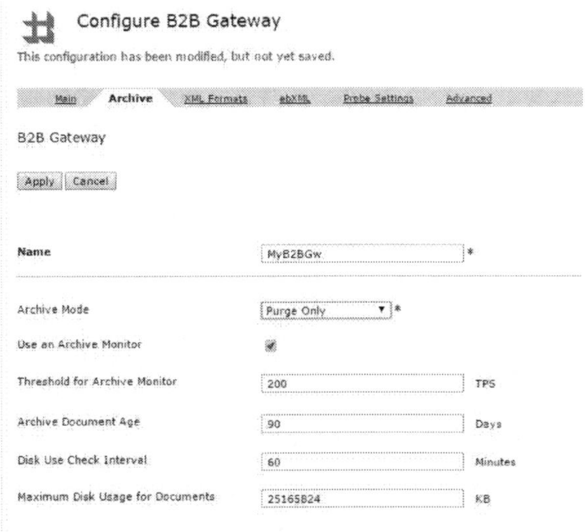

Figure 2-15 B2B Gateway Service – Archive and Purge Mode.

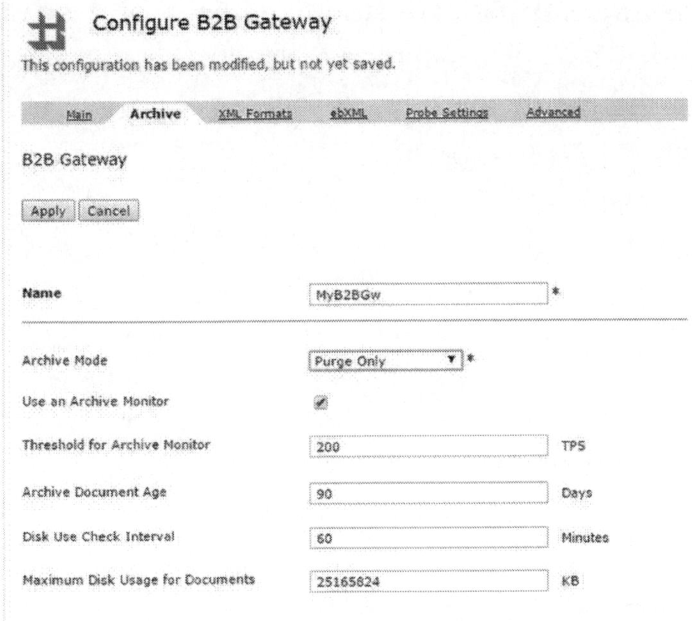

Figure 2-16 B2B Gateway Service – Purge Only Mode.

Name: This field is carried over from the main tab and you do not need to edit it in this tab.

Archive Mode: This mandatory drop down box is used to change the mode from the default which is Archive and Purge to Purge Only. The Archive and Purge mode will write all of the metadata and payloads into a XML file and then GZIP the file and store it off device in the location specified in the Archive Directory URL field. Only transactions older than the Archive Document Age setting will be archived and removed. The Purge Only mode simply deletes all metadata and files only retaining the number of documents specified in the Archive Document Age field.

Use an Archive Monitor & Threshold for Archive Monitor: These fields indicate whether to use an Archive Monitor to limit the message injection rate to prevent archive problems in a critical situation like performance testing or on a heavily loaded device. When checked you can specify the threshold in the Threshold for Archive Monitor field which specifies the maximum number of transaction to allow per second during an archive task. When the maximum number is reached, the service queues incoming transactions for later processing. If the queue is full, the service rejects incoming transactions and generates a log message. Use any value between 10 and 10000 transactions per second (TPS). The default value is 200 TPS.

Archive Directory URL: This mandatory field is only displayed when using the "Archive and Purge" mode and is used to specify the URL location where you want the file to be archived. This location is typically inside the trusted zone. Use the fully qualified name of the directory. The supported off-device protocol schemes are: HTTP (http://) and HTTPS (https://), NFS (dpnfs://), FTP and FTPS (ftp://), and SFTP (sftp://). To store locally in a RAID volume, specify a subdirectory in the configured Hard Disk Array; for example, local:///ondisk. The message archive is in binary. When archiving to an FTP (or FTPS) destination, ensure that the FTP policies in the associated XML manager enable "Image (Binary) Data" for data transfer.

Archive Filename Template: This mandatory field is only displayed when using the "Archive and Purge" mode and is used to specify the base file name for archive files; the current timestamp will be appended to the base file name.

Archive Minimum Size: This field is only displayed when using the "Archive and Purge" mode and specifies the minimum size of the document store before triggering the archive operation. The default is 1024 KB. This field is helpful to prevent archiving when the document store does not have enough meaningful data to justify an archive. Most users set this to between 10 MB and 50 MB.

Archive Document Age: This field is used to specify the maximum duration to retain processed documents. When this value is exceeded the system will automatically archive or purge processed documents that are older than the value of this field. Use any value of 1 to 3650 days. The default is 90 days. If you are processing large volumes of documents (millions per day) and would like to improve the viewer performance you may choose to retain less data on the appliance. Users with high volumes typically only retain data for 7 days on the device and Archive data for longer retention periods.

Archive Minimum Documents: This field is only displayed when using the "Archive and Purge" mode and is used to specify the minimum number of documents to retain in the document store at the end of an automatic archive operation. The minimum is 1. The default is 100.

Disk Use Check Interval: This field is used to set time interval for checking the document age. If any documents exceed the Archive Document Age they are archived or purged. Use any value between 1 and 1440. The default is 60 minutes.

Minimum Disk Usage for Documents: Specifies the maximum storage size for documents. When storage exceeds this value, documents are archived or purged. The default is 25165824 KB.

Documents to Back Up: This field is only displayed when using the "Archive and Purge" mode and is used to specify which type of B2B messages to back up. If nothing is checked, no AS or ebMS off-the-wire packaged files will be archived, however, the content file is always archived regardless of which transport protocol is used.

B2B Gateway XML Formats Tab

The XML Formats tab is an optional tab and is only used if you are trading XML documents that contain partner IDs in the content. This tab allows you to list the XML formats that you expect the B2B gateway to consume from back-side systems or from partners. When configured, the B2B Gateway will extract the partner IDs from the XPaths provided in the XML Format object. Figure 2-17 shows an example view of the XML Formats list screen.

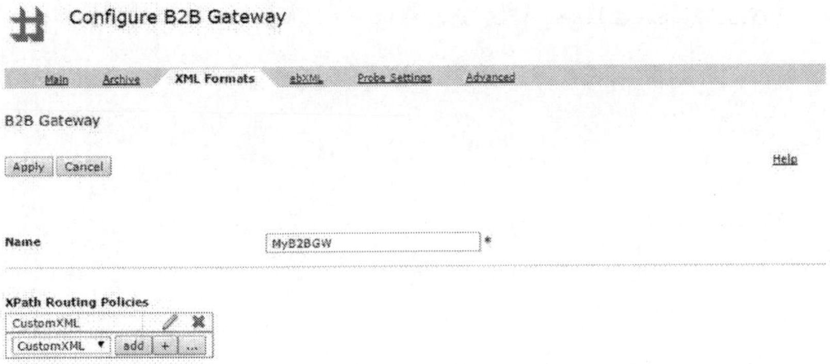

Figure 2-17 – B2B Gateway Service – XML Formats tab list view.

Name: In the list view above, this field is carried over from the main tab and you do not need to edit it in this tab.

XPath Routing Policies: This box holds all of the XPath Policies created to find partner IDs inside of an XML B2B document. To add an XPath Routing Policy to the list click on the + (plus) button or to edit an existing policy click on the ... button. Both buttons are to the right of the policy drop down field.

Figure 2-18 is an example of a configured XPath Routing Policy.

Configure B2B XPath Routing Policy

Main

B2B XPath Routing Policy

Apply Cancel   Help

Name	CustomXML	*
Administrative state	◉ enabled ○ disabled	
Comments	XML PO Format	
Sender XPath	/OrderFile/FileHeader/Sender/Cont [XPath Tool]	*
Receiver XPath	/OrderFile/FileHeader/Receiver/Col [XPath Tool]	*
Document ID XPath	/OrderFile/Order/Header/PO_No [XPath Tool]	
Transaction Timestamp XPath	/OrderFile/Order/Header/PO_Date [XPath Tool]	

Figure 2-18 B2B Gateway Service – XML Format tab detail view.

Name: This field is a mandatory field that contains a unique name for this XPath Policy. It is recommended to use descriptive names such as PartnerXMLPO.

Administrative State: This field is a mandatory field and is used to enable or disable this XPath Policy.

Comments: This field is an optional field and is used to give a descriptive comment about this XPath Policy.

Sender XPath: This field is a mandatory field and is used to hold the XPath that represents where the sending party's business ID is located within the XML.

Receiver XPath: This field is a mandatory field and is used to hold the XPath that represents where the receiving party's business ID is located within the XML.

Document ID XPath: This field is an optional field and is used to hold the XPath that represents where the Document ID is located within the XML.

Transaction Timestamp XPath: This field is an optional field and is used to hold the XPath that represents where the Transaction Timestamp is located within the XML.

NOTE—DataPower XPath Tool

Use the DataPower XPath tool; it is an easy way to find the correct XPath in your XML file. The tool allows you to upload a sample of the XML file to DataPower and then all you need to do is click on the element to be used in the XPath.

B2B Gateway ebXML Tab

The ebXML Formats tab is an optional tab and is only used if you have imported or created an ebXML CPA for this B2B Gateway. If the B2B Gateway is CPA enabled this tab can be used to access the CPAs and partner collaborations, allowing you to fine tune them after import. The B2B Module has full support for the ebXML Collaboration-Protocol Profile and Agreement (CPPA) V2.0 specification which allows you to use a standards based partner profile and profile agreement mechanism to fully integrate your systems with your partner's systems using ebXML. When a B2B Gateway is CPA enabled the ebMS Settings tab in the partner profile can no longer be used; any configuration that is stored in the partner profile ebMS settings tab will be ignored. Each of the fields in the

CPA list box holds many nested fields of configuration information related to the ebXML CPA configuration; those detail screens will not be displayed in this section because they will be covered in great detail in chapter 6 of this book.

Each field in this tab, CPA ID, Service, Internal Partner Profile, and External Partner Profile must be specified to allow the B2B Gateway Service to identify the received ebMS message or route the ebMS message to be sent. Figure 2-19 shows an example view of the ebXML screen.

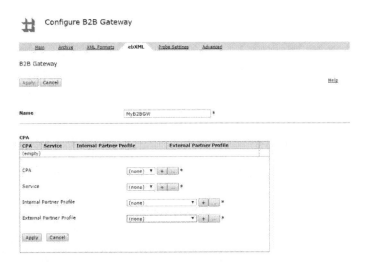

Figure 2-19 B2B Gateway Service - ebXML tab.

CPA: This field is used to specify the CPA to attach to the B2B Gateway.

Service: This field is used to specify the service to attach to the CPA. A service is either a business collaboration service for exchanging business messages, or a Message Service

Handler (MSH) signal service for exchanging MSH signals, including Acknowledgment, Error, Status Request, Status Response, Ping, and Pong. The value of a MSH signal service is "urn:oasis:names:tc:ebxml-msg:service"; A value other than this one represents a business collaboration service.

Internal Partner Profile: This field is used to specify the name of the internal partner profile to attach the CPA.

External Partner Profile: This field is used to specify the name of the external partner profile to attach the CPA.

B2B Gateway Probe Settings Tab

The Probe Settings tab is used to select the diagnostic mode for processing policies. When enabled, you can view details about the state of variables and contexts for a captured transaction in the probe. The default value is Off. The other options are On, which will contain the number of transactions defined in the Transaction History field and Unbounded, which enables the probe to contain 250 transactions (equivalent to specifying 250 in the Transaction History field).

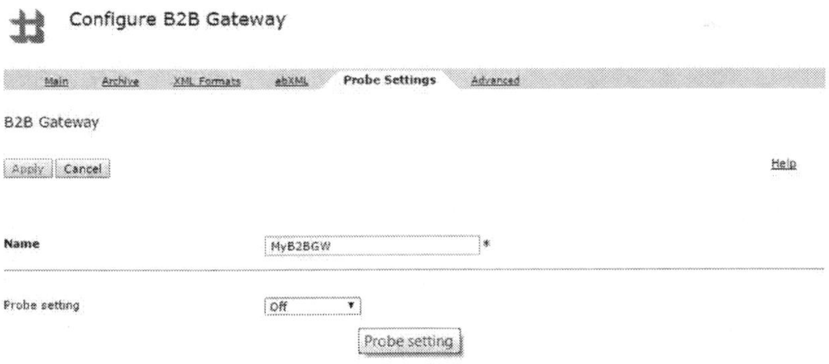

Figure 2-20 B2B Gateway Service - Probe Settings tab.

WARNING—Don't Use the Probe in Production!

Transaction diagnostic mode using the probe is not intended for use in a production environment. Transaction diagnostic mode consumes significant resources that can slow down transaction processing.

B2B Gateway Advanced Tab

The Advanced tab contains several fields that cannot be categorized under other tabs; fields in this tab set the service priority, set defaults for B2B messaging protocols, provides routing capabilities for binary flows, enables tight MQ File Transfer Edition transaction integration and provides a timeout for all front side handlers.

Figure 2-21 B2B Gateway Service – Advanced tab.

Name: This field is carried over from the main tab and you do not need to edit it in this tab.

Service Priority: This field is used to set the service scheduling priority. When system resources are in high demand, "high" priority services will be favored over lower priority services. The default is Normal; other options are High and Low.

Default As1 MDN Return E-mail: This field is used to set the default e-mail address to send an AS1 asynchronous MDN. An AS1 MDN Redirection E-mail address in the partner destination overrides this value.

AS1 MDN SMTP Server Connection: This field is used to set the SMTP server connection to use for sending the MDN response to the specified e-mail address.

Default AS2 MDN Return URL: This field is used to set the default URL to send an asynchronous MDN. It is commonly used for configurations that require the use of a reverse proxy for inbound traffic. An AS2 MDN Redirection URL in the partner destination overrides this value.

Default AS3 MDN Return URL: This field is used to set the default URL to send an asynchronous MDN. It is commonly used for configurations that require the use of a reverse proxy for inbound traffic. An AS3 MDN Redirection URL in the partner destination overrides this value.

Document Routing Preprocessor: This field is used to specify the location of the XSL style sheet to run against each transaction that cannot be natively parsed for sender and receiver IDs. This style sheet examines information from transport headers and other non-content sources to select relevant trading partners. The default file is b2b-routing.xsl; by default, this file will do nothing and binary messages will fail for lack of partner ID information.

SQL Data Source: This is the SQL Data Source object that is associated with current B2B gateway; it points to the database which stores the MQ MFT transfer metadata that is stored in the MQ MFT instance that DataPower is integrated with. MQ MFT transfer metadata can be retrieved by clicking the integration ID from B2B viewer as long as MQ MFT logger is enabled and this SQL data source object is configured correctly. It is recommended that all transactions within one B2B gateway that utilize the MQFTE front side handler or MQFTE URL opener should use the same database as MQ MFT logger backend database because only one SQL data source object can be associated per B2B gateway.

Front Side Timeout: This field controls the amount of time a front side client connection can be idle before the connection is canceled within a transaction. For a B2B outbound transaction, a front-side connection means the connection between an internal back-end application and a B2B gateway. For aB2B inbound transaction, a front-side connection means the connection between an external partner and a B2B gateway

B2B Transaction Viewer

The B2B Transaction Viewer is an at a glance view of the state of any transactions that flow through the B2B Gateway. The columns displayed depend on which filter has been selected;

Show All, Show AS only or Show ebMS only. Under each filtered view you have the ability to modify the query to further filter the data and display only those transactions you want to see. Using DataPower's Role Based Management feature, you also have the capability to allow business partners to directly access the B2B Transaction Viewer and restrict them to only their transactions.

Figure 2-22 shows the Modify Query screen. This box allows you to search the B2B metadata for specific messages based on specific IDs, specific partners processed in a specific B2B Gateway during a specific time period. Like the viewer itself the Modify Query screen also allow you to filer on "All" transactions, only "Success" transactions or only "Failure" transactions.

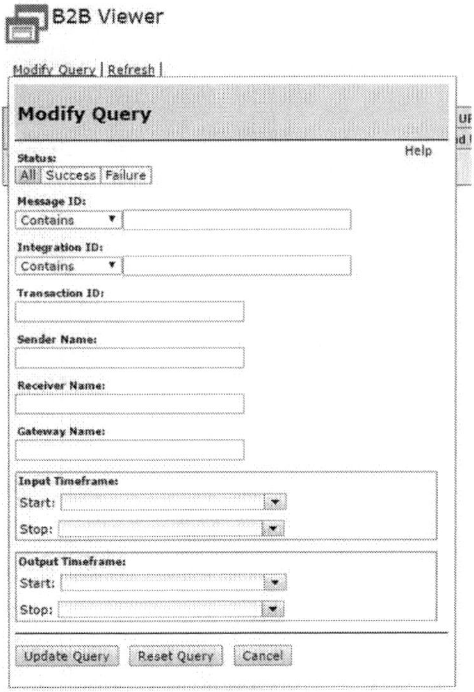

Figure 2-22 B2B Viewer – Modify Query.

Figure 2-23 shows the B2B Viewer columns when using the Show All filter.

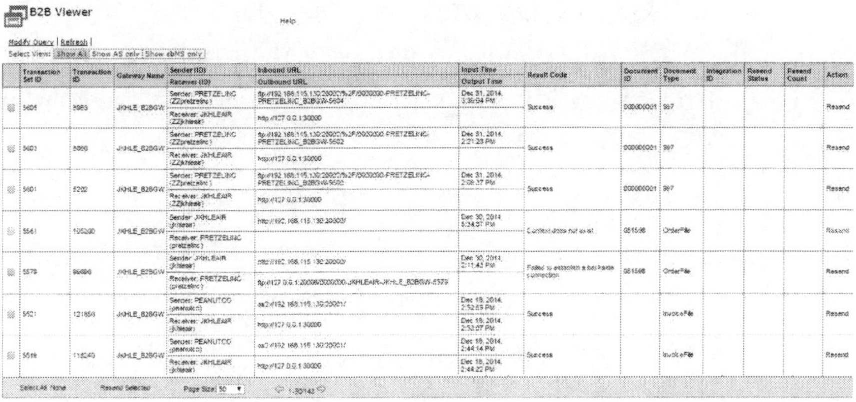

Figure 2-23 B2B Viewer – Show All view.

Transaction Set ID: This column shows a gateway-generated identifier for the transaction in the B2B Metadata store.   The value in this column is a hot link that allows you to view the off-the-wire inbound or outbound transaction, the unencrypted content, the MDN/Ack and the off-the-wire response.

Transaction ID: This column shows the gateway-generated identifier for each event in the transaction.   This value correlates directly to the event IDs in the log files.

Gateway Name: This column shows the name of the B2B Gateway that processed the transaction.

Sender (ID) / Receiver (ID): This column shows on top, the Sender Name and ID of the originator of the transaction and on bottom it holds the Receiver Name and ID of the party that consumed the message.

Inbound URL / Outbound URL: This column shows on top, the URL on which the gateway received the message and on bottom, it holds the URL to which the message was sent.

Input Time / Output Time: This column shows on top, the time stamp of when the gateway received the message, on bottom, the time stamp of when the gateway sent the message.

Result Code: This column shows the status result of the transaction sent or received in the gateway.

Document ID: This column shows the ID of the document. With EDI it is the Control ID of the document, if XML, it is the value that is assigned to the Document ID XPath setting of the XML format defined in the B2B Gateway XML Formats tab. If Binary this field is blank.

Document Type: This column shows information from the document describing the document type. For EDI, this would be the Transaction Set Type, e.g. 810, 850, 997, etc. For XML this would be the value of the root tag, e.g. Order, Invoice, Advanced Ship Notice, etc. For Binary this column is blank.

Integration ID: This column shows the MQ MFT (aka: MQ FTE) integration ID. It is used to link/correlate the transaction in the B2B Viewer to the transaction in the MQ MFT DB Logger. This value in the column is a hot link that will display the status of the transaction as seen in the MQ MFT database.

NOTE—Integration ID Column

The Integration ID column will be empty if MQ FTE handlers are not used in the B2B Gateway. It is possible to programmatically populate the "var://service/mqfte-integ-id" variable with any value you wish. This comes in handy when you have no intention of using MQ FTE and you need to show correlation to other downstream systems like MQ or custom applications. When sending a file you can capture a value sent in HTTP or MQ headers and set the variable. When receiving a file, you can pass an ID based on content or headers in the received message.

Resend Status: This column shows the status of the latest resend action whether it is automatic (function of AS and ebMS protocols) or manual.

Resend Count: This column shows the number of resends that occurred for the transaction.

Action: This column shows a link for manually resending the files from the viewer.

Figure 2-24 shows the B2B Viewer columns when using the Show AS only filter. Only the columns that differ from the Show All filter will be defined below.

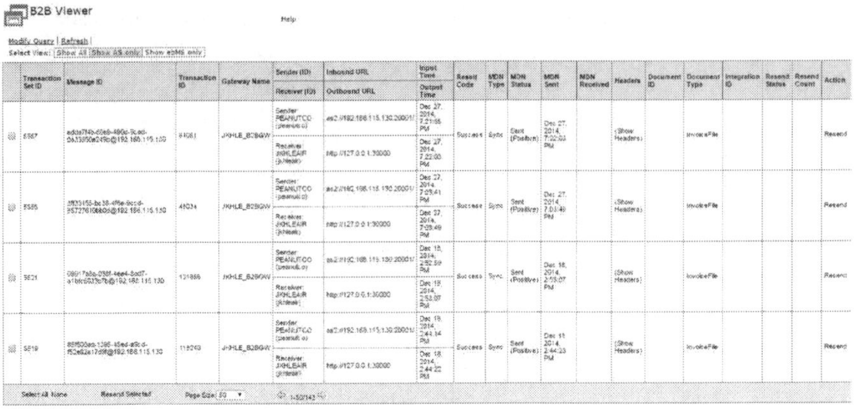

Figure 2-24 B2B Viewer – Show AS only filter.

Message ID: This column shows the AS Message ID for AS1, AS2 and AS3 messages.

MDN Type: This column shows the type of MDN that was either requested or consumed by the B2B Gateway when using AS protocols. The type is either Sync or Async. A row with no value means no MDN was requested or the transaction is not an AS message.

MDN Status: This column shows the status of the MDN. Statuses vary depending on whether the AS message is inbound or outbound.

Inbound messages can result in the following statuses:

Processing - The B2B Gateway received the message and is building the MDN.

Sent (Positive) - The MDN was sent and the Disposition header ends with; "processed".

Sent (Negative) - The MDN was sent and the Disposition header ends with anything other than; "processed".

Not Requested - The inbound AS Message did not request a MDN to be returned to the sender.

Failed - The MDN transmission or the final retransmission failed.

NOTE—MDN Acknowledgements

MDN's are gateway level acknowledgements and are not dependent on back-side processing success or failure, nor are they passed or received from the back-side. You can think of MDN's as similar to an email return receipt.

Outbound messages can result in the following statuses:

Processing - The B2B Gateway received the message and is building the MDN.

Waiting - The B2B Gateway is waiting for an asynchronous MDN which was requested when the AS message was sent to the trading partner.

Received (Positive) - The MDN was received and the Disposition header ends with; "processed".

Received (Negative) - The MDN was received and the Disposition header ends with anything other than; "processed".

Failed - The MDN cannot be processed.

For rows that contain the receipt of an asynchronous MDN, the status can be:

Positive - Same as Received (Positive).

Negative - Same as Received (Negative).

MDN Sent: This column shows the time the MDN was sent to the trading partner.

MDN Received: This column shows the time the MDN was received from the trading partner.

Headers: When you hover over the value in this cell the collection of message headers for the AS message is displayed.

Figure 2-25 shows the B2B Viewer columns when using the Show ebMS only filter. Only the columns that differ from the Show All filter and Show AS2 only filter will be defined below.

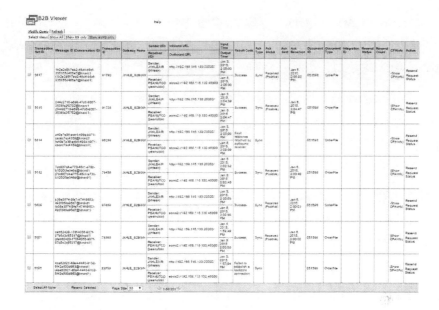

Figure 2-25 B2B Viewer – Show ebMS only filter.

Message ID (Conversation ID): This column shows the ebMS Message ID and Conversation ID.

Ack Type: This column shows the type of Ack that was either requested or consumed by the B2B Gateway when using the ebMS protocol. The type is either Sync or Async. This cell is also contains error information received with using ebMS Acks.

Ack Status: This column shows the status of the acknowledgment message. Statuses vary depending on whether the ebMS message is inbound or outbound.

Inbound messages can result in the following statuses:

Processing - The B2B Gateway received the message and is building the Ack.

Sent (Positive) - The gateway generated a positive acknowledgment message and successfully delivered it to the sending partner.

Ack Sent Failed - After processing the inbound message, the gateway generated a positive acknowledgment message in response, but failed to deliver the acknowledgment message to the sending partner.

Sent (Negative) - The B2B gateway processed the inbound message with an error and generated a negative acknowledgment MessageError message in response, and successfully delivers it to the sending partner.

Sent MessageError Failed - The B2B gateway processed the inbound message with an error and generated a negative acknowledgment MessageError message in response, but fails when delivering the MessageError message to the sending partner.

Not Requested - The inbound message does not contain an AckRequested element.

Failed - The gateway failed to process the inbound message that requested for acknowledgment.

Outbound messages can result in the following statuses:

Processing - The B2B Gateway received the message and is building the Ack.

Waiting - The B2B Gateway is waiting for an asynchronous acknowledgment.

Received (Positive) - The B2B Gateway received a positive acknowledgment message from the receiving partner.

Received (Negative) - The B2B Gateway received a negative acknowledgment MessageError from the receiving partner.

Failed - The acknowledgment or the error message cannot be processed.

For rows that contain the receipt of an asynchronous acknowledgment, the status can be:

Positive - Same as Received (Positive).

Negative - Same as Received (Negative).

Ack Sent: This column shows the time when the acknowledgment or error message is sent to the trading partner.

Ack Received: This column shows the time when the acknowledgment or error message is received from the trading partner.

CPAInfo: When you hover over the value in this cell the CPA-implied values and related transaction information of the message is displayed.

Additional B2B Objects

There are additional items in the B2B Module that can be executed or configured to support B2B data flows and configuration; some of these items act differently depending on whether they are executed in the default domain or other domains. This section describes each object and the fields within.

Archive B2B Transaction Data

This action can be launched from the left navigation menu by expanding Administration→Miscellaneous→Archive B2B Transaction Data or from the link in the upper right hand corner of the B2B Gateway configuration screen (see figure 2-26).

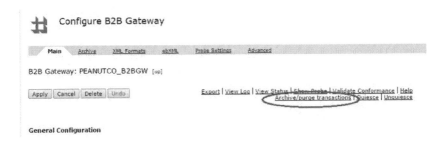

Figure 2-26 Archive/Purge Data – B2B Gateway Configuration Object.

When an archive is launched from within any domain other than the default domain it will cause the archive of all B2B data within that domain. When it is launched from the default domain it will cause the archive of all B2B data in every domain.

When an archive process is launched all data will be archived and/or purged. If archived it will use the information in each B2B Gateway archive tab to create and write the archive file to the appropriate location and with the appropriate filename. After transferring to a permanent archive, the data cannot be imported into the appliance and cannot be viewed through the Transaction Viewer. To view the data you need to use an XML editor/viewer to find the transaction in question inside the archive file.

Figure 2-27 shows the Archive B2B Transaction Data view.

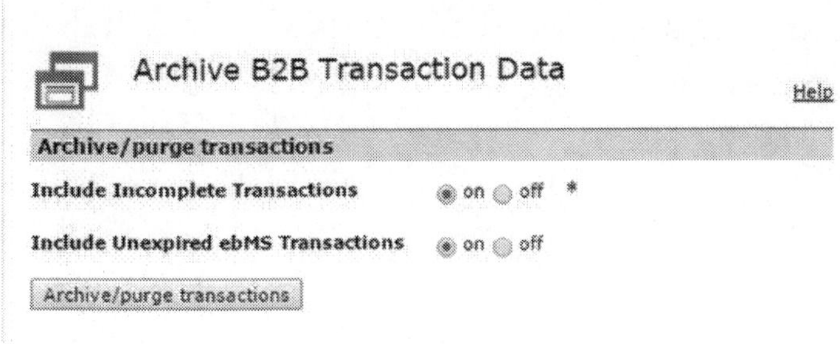

Archive B2B Transaction Data   Help

Archive/purge transactions	
Include Incomplete Transactions	⦿ on ○ off *
Include Unexpired ebMS Transactions	⦿ on ○ off

Archive/purge transactions

Figure 2-27 Archive B2B Transaction Data.

Include Incomplete Transactions: This field indicates whether to archive all transactions or only complete transactions. If the value is on, archive all transactions. If the value is off, archive only transactions that are complete (not in process).

Include Unexpired ebMS Transactions: This field indicates whether to archive data for all ebMS transactions. If the value is on, archive all ebMS transactions, including expired and unexpired ones. If the value is off, archive only ebMS transactions that are older than the TimeToPersist value in the ebMS configuration.

B2B Message Archive Status

This status view is available in all domains and displays the statuses of the latest archive action for each B2B Gateway whether triggered at the planned capacity interval which setup in the Archive tab of the B2B Gateways or triggered immediately using the Archive/purge transaction action. To view the status of current operations, select Status→B2B→B2B Archive Status in the left navigation view to display the status screen.

Figure 2-28 shows an example of what the B2B Message Archive status view looks like.

Figure 2-28 B2B Message Archive Status view.

B2B High Availability Status

This status view is available in all domains and displays the status of the Active/Passive B2B Persistence store synchronization between the two participating devices. This status is only available when the B2B Persistence High Availability tab is enabled and configured. Neither the tab nor this status is used when using an Active/Active deployment model. To view the status of current operations, select Status→B2B→B2B High Availability Status in the left navigation view to display the status screen.

Figure 2-29 shows an example of what the B2B High Availability Status view looks like. The values are blank in this example because B2B High Availability is currently disabled;

however, the cell values you can expect to find are defined in this section.

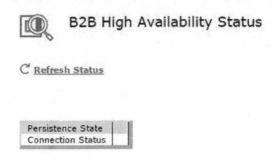

Figure 2-29 B2B High Availability Status view.

Persistence State has the following values:

PRIMARY ACTIVE: The device is the Primary device in the Active/Passive cluster and the connection is not broken.

PRIMARY ALONE: This device is the Primary device in the Active/Passive cluster and the connection is broken.

SECONDARY ACTIVE: The device is the Secondary device in the Active/Passive cluster and the connection is not broken.

SECONDARY ALONE: This device is the Secondary device in the Active/Passive cluster and the connection is broken.

Connection Status has the following values:

CONNECTED: The connection is active. This status is returned from both the primary and secondary servers.

CONNECTING: The primary server is connecting to the secondary server. This status is returned from both the primary and secondary servers.

CATCHUP: The primary server is connected to the secondary server, but the transaction log is not fully copied. This status is returned from both the primary and secondary servers.

BROKEN: The connection is broken. This status is returned from both the primary and secondary servers.

B2B Persistence

This configuration object is only available in the default domain when logged in as an administrator. It is used to configure characteristics about the B2B Metadata store including High Availability (HA). The B2B Gateway Service will not function unless B2B Persistence is enabled. B2B Persistence initializes the database for use with B2B transaction metadata.

B2B Persistence Main Tab

The B2B Persistence Main tab contains four fields used to control how the B2B Persistence store is used. Figure 2-30 shows the B2B Persistence configuration Main screen.

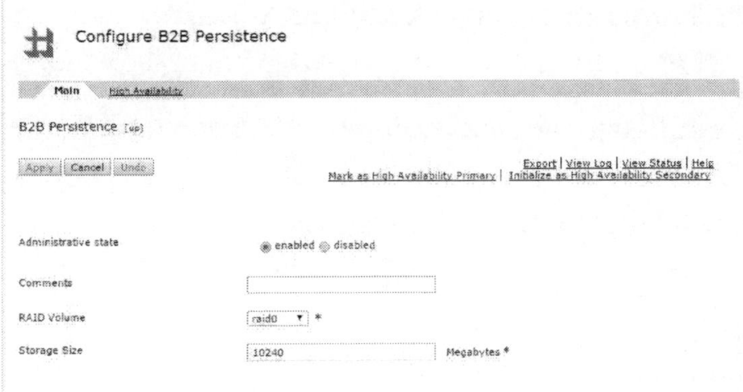

Figure 2-30 Configure B2B Persistence view – Main tab.

Administrative State: This field is a mandatory field and is used to enable or disable B2B Persistence. It is disabled by default when the module is first enabled, due to the need to first initialize the RAID device for B2B. B2B Persistence must be enabled to use B2B Gateway Services.

Comments: This field is an optional field and is used to give a descriptive comment about the B2B Persistence store.

RAID Volume: This is the RAID volume to store B2B Metadata, it is a drop down for future use; it should be RAID0 by default in all current releases.

Storage Size: This field is used to set the maximum size, in megabytes, for the persistent metadata store. By default it is set to 1024 MB. If you plan on having long retention periods on the device or your volumes are very high, it is a good idea to set this to use the maximum allowable space on the internal hard drive which is 65536 MB.

B2B Persistence High Availability Tab

The B2B Persistence High Availability tab contains six fields used to configure the Active/Passive high availability mode for the B2B metadata store. Figure 2-31 shows the B2B Persistence High Availability configuration screen.

Configure B2B Persistence

Main **High Availability**

B2B Persistence [up]

Apply   Cancel   Undo

Export | View Log | View Status | Help
Mark as High Availability Primary | Initialize as High Availability Secondary

High Availability Enabled	⊙ on ○ off *
Replication Listener Address	192.168.1.1	Select Alias	*
Replication Listener Port	1320	*
Replication Remote Hostname	192.168.1.2	*
Replication Remote Port	1320	*
Virtual IP Address	192.168.1.3	*

Figure 2-31 Configure B2B Persistence view – High Availability tab.

High Availability Enabled: This field is used to enable B2B Persistence High Availability. When clicked, additional fields are displayed to support the configuration. Enabling this functionality puts the embedded B2B database in state where it allows one-way synchronization of data from the primary database to the secondary database residing on a remote device.

Replication Listener Address: This field is used to set the hostname or IP address that the persistence store uses to support replication of data between the primary and secondary appliances. Since DataPower appliances have many network adapters it is recommended you isolate an adapter for synchronization between devices.

Replication Listener Port: This field is used to set the TCP port to support replication of data between the primary and secondary appliances. The default is 1320. You can access the Web B2B Viewer Management in the default domain by navigating to Objects→B2B Configuration→Web B2B Viewer Management Service.

Replication Remote Hostname: This field is used to define the hostname or IP address that the other device in the HA Cluster is using for B2B metadata synchronization.

Replication Remote Port: This field is used to define the TCP Port that the other device in the HA Cluster is using for B2B metadata synchronization. The default is 1320.

Virtual IP Address: This field is used to define which Virtual IP Address (VIP) should be used to trigger a failover. Typically, this is the VIP of the external entry point into the device from trading partner. This VIP comes from the Standby Control configuration of the DataPower devices.

Web B2B Viewer Management

This configuration object is only available in the default domain when logged in as an administrator. It is used to enable the B2B Transaction Viewer for access by Partners or by anyone whom does not need access to the configuration GUI. Details on how to configure DataPower using User Access and Role Based Management to limit access to transactions and columns inside the B2B Viewer is available in chapter 3 of this book.

Web B2B Viewer Management Service Main tab

The main tab contains six fields that allow the Web B2B Viewer Management to be used. When enabled it presents only the B2B Transaction viewer; no configuration objects are accessible from this service. Figure 2-32 is an example of the main tab of Web B2B Viewer Management configuration screen.

Figure 2-32 Web B2B Viewer Management Service – Main tab.

Administrative State: This field is a mandatory field and is used to enable or disable the Web B2B Viewer Management Service. It is disabled by default.

Local address: This field is the hostname or IP address to use for this service.

Port Number: This field is the port number for this service to listen on.

Access Control List: This field allows you to create an access list to allow or deny access to the B2B Viewer Management Service based on the IP address of the client.

Comments: This field is an optional field and is used to give a descriptive comment about the Web B2B Viewer Management Service.

Idle Timeout: This field sets the amount of idle time to allow before disconnecting the logged on user. The default is 600 seconds. A setting of 0 (zero) will disable the idle timer.

Web B2B Viewer Management Service Advanced tab

The Advanced tab contains two fields used to modify the SSL proxy setting and User Agent settings of the Web B2B Viewer Management Service. Figure 2-33 is an example of the Advanced tab of the Web B2B Viewer Management configuration screen.

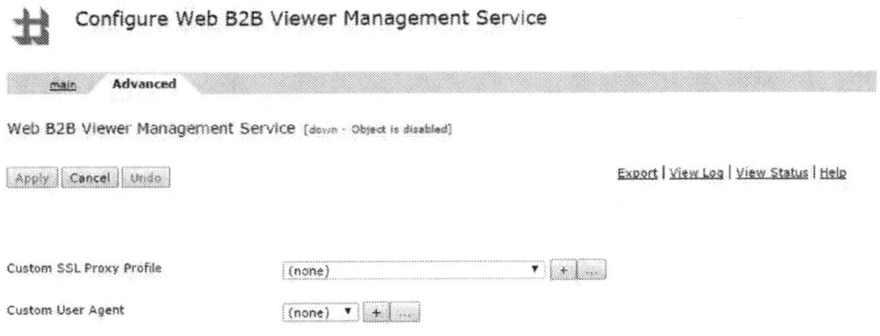

Figure 2-33 Web B2B Viewer Management Service – Advanced tab.

Custom SSL Proxy Profile: Allows users to specify an existing SSL proxy profile or create a new one to be assigned to the Web B2B Management Service instead of the default profile.

Custom User Agent: Allows user to specify an existing User Agent or create a new one to be assigned to the Web B2B Management Service, instead of the default agent.

Summary

In this chapter you learned what key services the B2B Module provides and how to configure the objects that are used within each B2B Service. This chapter goes beyond the DataPower help in that it provides you with examples of why and how you would use many of the objects.

Chapter 3 B2B Trading Partner Transaction Visibility

This chapter presents a detailed description on how you can extend visibility to transactions exchanged to your external partners and how to secure your external users to only be provided visibility to their data and their data alone.

Introduction

In Chapter 2 you were introduced to the B2B Transaction Viewer. This viewer provides visibility to communication sessions that have been conducted between you and your trading partners. All data that flows through a B2B Gateway Service and the respective metadata is rendered in the B2B Transaction Viewer and provides visibility to the status of your transactions.

This viewer can also be extended to your external trading community and their respective user(s). How many times has your customer service department received calls from external partners asking if you had received their files transmitted last night or that morning? How much time do those calls take away from your team? Do you have an easy to use, secure way of rendering visibility to those external partners?

Now you do! DataPower's Role Based Management (RBM) framework lends itself to extending the B2B Transaction Viewer to any user you desire, both internal and external partners. RBM rules can be defined in DataPower to also secure what a user can see, as well as what they can do e.g. read only access, visibility to only their data, visibility to certain B2B Transaction Viewer columns, etc.

Enabling the Web B2B Transaction Viewer Management Service

To limit a user to only see the B2B Transaction Viewer and not navigate a menu of options, you need to turn on the Web B2B Transaction Viewer Management Service. You will have to be logged in as an administrator and in the Default Application Domain to see the Web B2B Service. See Figure 3-1 below.

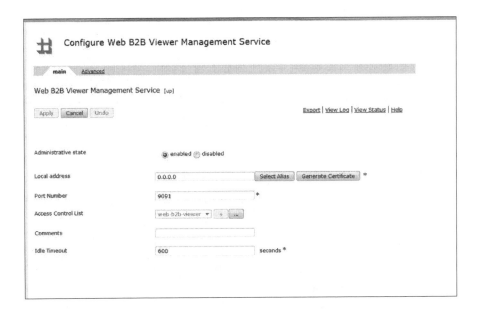

Figure 3-1 Enable Web B2B Transaction Viewer Management Service.

Administrative State: Enable or Disable

Local Address: Specifies which network interface to bind to or default value of all zeros means any interface defined on the appliance.

Port Number: defines the port the Web B2B Management Service listens on.

Access Control List: This Access Control List may be used to allow or deny access to b2bViewer-mgmt based on the IP address of the client.

Idle Timeout: The time, after which an idle session will be invalidated, requiring re-authentication. To disable the idle timer altogether, use a value of 0 (zero).

The URL for the B2B Transaction Viewer is the same as logging on to the devices configuration interface with the port number being the exception. Port 9090 is the default to get to the configuration interface of DataPower Gateway and 9091 is the default to display only the Transaction Viewer. Figure 3-2 shows Travis logging in to the HUB Domain.

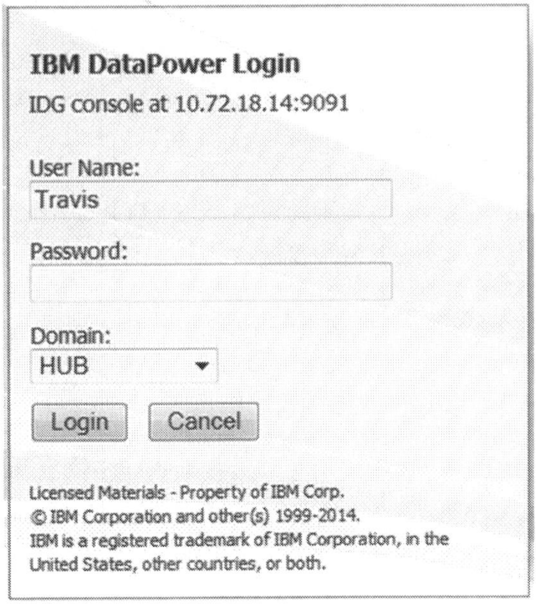

IBM DataPower Login

IDG console at 10.72.18.14:9091

User Name:

Travis

Password:

Domain:

HUB

[Login] [Cancel]

Licensed Materials - Property of IBM Corp.
© IBM Corporation and other(s) 1999-2014.
IBM is a registered trademark of IBM Corporation, in the
United States, other countries, or both.

Figure 3-2 DataPower Login.

Figure 3.3 shows what Travis sees in the B2B Transaction Viewer; note that there are no menu items in the left navigation portion of the screen, effectively limiting Travis to only see his data and have no access to the device configuration after logging on.

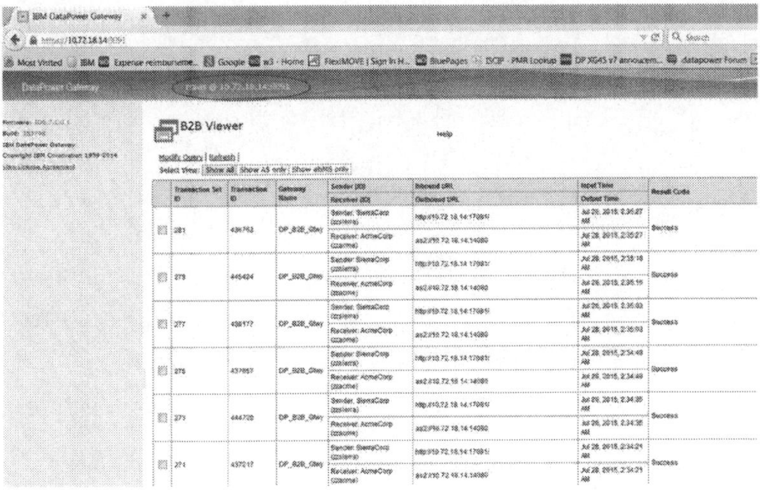

Figure 3-3 B2B Transaction Viewer Partner Visibility.

Configuring Role Based Management

DataPower offers a robust Role Based Management (RBM) framework where you can create user accounts as well as user groups. Within these user groups you can set a variety of rights and privileges.   User accounts are then added to a User Group where they adopt the privileges of that group. An admin can provide or deny access to any object in DataPower including read only and read/write type of access permissions.

A user group represents a collection of users who perform similar duties and require the same level of access to the DataPower appliance. User groups are assigned rights to one or more DataPower resources. When adding these rights to the access profile of the specific user group, each right is known individually as an access policy. A collection of access policies is known as an access profile.

Related trading partner user accounts can be combined into one user group. These individual user accounts are limited to the access profile of the user group account to which they are assigned. For instance, multiple partner IDs from one company can be combined in one group account for access to related transactions.

An admin can also govern which partner transactions an internal or external user can see as well as which columns are visible in the B2B Transaction Viewer. You can also configure the permissions to enable or disable the operations that can be accessed in the Transaction Set ID and action columns. For example, with RBM, you can allow an external user from Trading Partner "X" access directly to the B2B Transaction Viewer and to see only their company's transactions and allow them to resend transactions to themselves.

When using the Web B2B Transaction Viewer Management Service, the user will not be allowed to navigate through menu options, upon successful login; the user is taken directly to the B2B Transaction Viewer. Once there they can be limited to only see records that pertain to that user's company. They would not have access or visibility to other partner's data.

Example of using RBM to Limit Partner Visibility

Ok, let's take a look at how to restrict who has access and what privileges they have in the B2B Transaction Viewer.

To limit access in the B2B Transaction Viewer you need to first configure a user group to define permissions for a set of users; in our example we setup a user group for Beta Corporation. Next you need to setup a user account for a specific user and assign the user to the user group we created; in our example we are using Andy.

Limiting column visibility

Filtering of column data restricts the resultant dataset to specific metadata associated with each transaction. This type of filtering uses the b2b/column-visibility resource of the RBM policy. When defined, the user can view transactional data for the explicitly defined columns only. The policy can contain one or many columns that can be exposed for viewing. The policy string has the format that is shown below, where each column added to the policy string will be viewable in the Transaction Viewer.

<ip>/<domain>/b2b/column-visibility?Access=r&Columns=<column1>+<column2

>+...+<columnN>

If you want to allow read only access to all columns, set the access policy to the following:

<ip>/<domain>/b2b/column-visibility?Access=r

Limiting Partner Visibility

Filtering of partner-sensitive data (rows) restricts the result dataset to specific transactions associated with previously configured user accounts. This type of filtering uses the b2b/partner-visibility resource of the RBM policy. When a Partner-visibility policy string is defined for a user account; the user can view transactional data for the explicitly defined partners only. Each policy string can contain only one user account entry. Therefore, to explicitly allow a user to view data for specific partners, add a policy string for each account.

The policy string has the format that is shown below:

<ip>/<domain>/b2b/partner-visibility?Access=r&Partner=<partner-name>

The administrator can add one or more partner visibility access policies to a user group. The RBM B2B logic will look for these policy strings and filter the resultant data sets returned to users.

Allowing the use of column operations

Limiting the access to various operations controls whether the user can perform the specific B2B Transaction Viewer actions that are in the Transaction Set ID and Action columns. Unless explicitly defined, the user cannot perform the resend or get document actions.

To enable the Resend operation, use the PCRE syntax below:

/*/*/b2b/resend-transaction?Access=x

To enable the Get Documents operation, use the PCRE syntax below:

/*/*/b2b/get-document?Access=x

Dataset Fields

Dataset fields map to the columns and data displayed in the B2B Transaction Viewer so they can be used in our PCRE policy strings to control access to the data. The Table 3-1 defines the mappings.

B2B Transaction Viewer Label	Dataset Field
Transaction Set ID	TransactionSetID InputDoc OutputDoc ContentDoc MDNBodyDoc
Transaction ID	TransactionID
Message ID	MessageID
Gateway Name	GatewayName
Sender Name (ID)/ Receiver Name (ID)	SenderName SenderID ReceiverName ReceiverID
Inbound URL/ Outbound URL	InboundURL OutboundURL
Input Time/Output Time	InputTime OutputTime
Result Code	ResultCode
MDN Type	MDNType
MDN Status	MDNStatus
MDN Sent	MDNSent
MDN Received	MDNReceived
Headers	Headers
Document ID	DocumentID
Document Type	DocumentType
Integration ID	IntegrationID
Resend Status	ResendStatus
Resend Count	ResendCount
Action	Action

Table 3-1 B2B Transaction Viewers Dataset Labels.

Figure 3-4 illustrates a user account called Andy and how this user is tied to a user group called ACME.

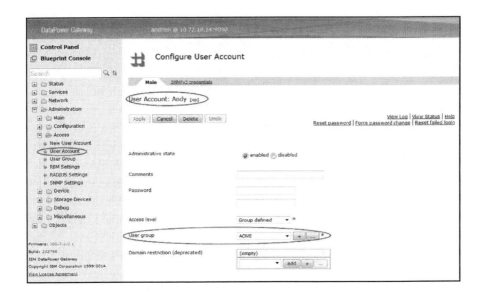

Figure 3-4 Configure User Account.

By clicking on the plus button next to the User group, you can create a group and define the access rules using Pearl Compatible Regular Expression (PCRE). Figure 3-5 shows how we created a group called ACME and limited Andy to see only what we want him to see.

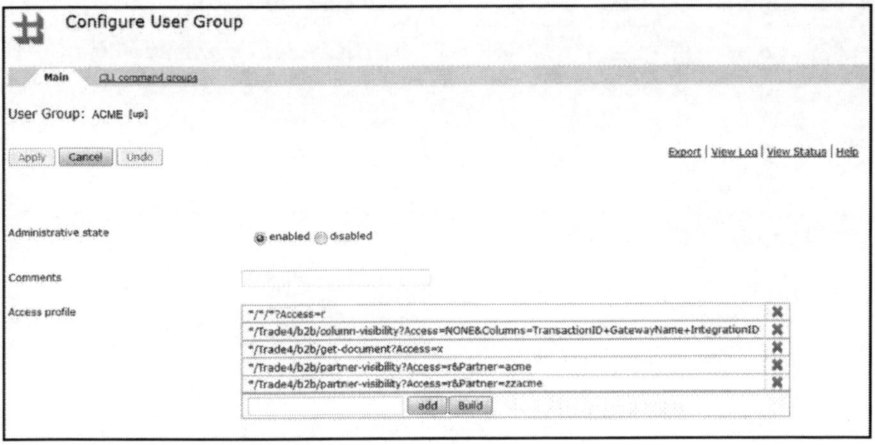

Figure 3-5 Configure ACME User Group.

Each PCRE statement in this group has a specific function as described in Table 3-2.

PCRE Statement	Definition
//b2b/partner-visibility?Access=NONE	Removes all access to all of the partner information in the viewer across all domains.
/Trade4/?Access=r	Gives access to only information in the Trade4 domain.
*/Trade4/b2b/column-visibility?Access=NONE&Columns=TransactionID+GatewayName+IntegrationID	Removes the listed columns from the B2B Transaction Viewer.
*/Trade4/b2b/partner-visibility?Access=r&Partner=acme	Only displays transactions in the B2B Transaction Viewer that belong to the partner with the associated business ID's.
*/Trade4/b2b/partner-visibility?Access=r&Partner=zacme	

Table 3-2 PCRE Statements and definitions.

Figure 3-6 shows the Administrator's view of transactions for this example.

Figure 3-6 – Administrator View of B2B Transactions.

Figure 3-7 shows Andy's view of transactions for this example after the ACME user group is applied.

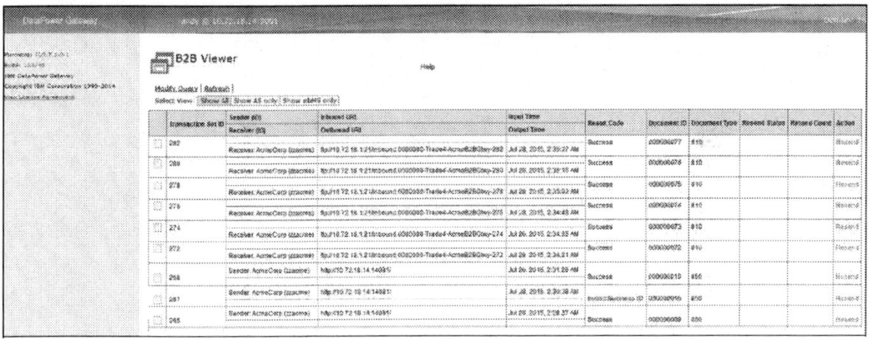

Figure 3-7 Andy's view of the B2B Transaction Viewer.

Summary

In this chapter you learned how to view the transactions that are exchanged between you and your partners. Additionally you learned how the B2B Transaction Viewer not only provides visibility to your company's users but also can be extended to your external partners users as well. Finally, you also learned how using Role Based Management (RBM) you can create Group Profiles, apply rules and append users to the group profile which ultimately limits the columns and records exposed to the user.

Chapter 4 DataPower B2B Messaging Patterns

Messaging Patterns

This chapter describes the B2B messaging patterns that are commonly used with the DataPower B2B Gateway. This chapter describes how each of the services or objects is configured for each B2B Messaging protocol. Each object may be configured slightly different depending on what protocol is being used.

DataPower B2B supports the three most common EDI over the Internet (EDIINT) Applicability Statements (AS); AS1, AS2 and AS3. Each of these statements is described in detail in the Request for Comment (RFC) specifications that define them. A list of RFC's and their Internet links is provided below:

- **AS1 (RFC3335)** - Message exchange is sent using the SMTP Protocol and received using POP3 (email): https://www.ietf.org/rfc/rfc3335.txt

- **AS2 (RFC4130)** - Message exchange is sent using the HTTP or HTTPS (Secured using SSL) protocol: https://www.ietf.org/rfc/rfc4130.txt

- **AS3 (RFC4823)** - Message exchange is sent using FTP or FTPS (Secured using SSL) protocol: https://www.ietf.org/rfc/rfc4823.txt

It is important to note that EDIINT AS patterns are still considered Managed File Transfer (MFT) Patterns. The main difference between this type of MFT and others (FTP, SFTP) is the payloads are wrapped in an S/MIME envelope and each standard provides for encryption and signing of data to provide security and non-repudiation of origin and receipt.

DataPower B2B also supports V2.0 of the E-Business XML Messaging Service (ebMS V2.0). At its simplest form, ebMS can also be considered a Managed File Transfer protocol; it differs from EDIINT protocols by using SOAP messaging and XML security instead of S/MIME security. Additionally, ebMS V2.0 can be extended to allow business process integration between trading partners using a combination of Collaboration Protocol Profiles and Agreements (CPPA) in DataPower B2B and Business Process software in the trusted zone. CPPA's provides a formal agreement for the transfer of files between partners and is used to trigger and tie business processes together. A simple description of the standard and a link is provided below:

- **ebMS V2.0** - Message exchange can be sent using the HTTP(S) or SMTP protocol and is generally described as an extension to the SOAP specification. At this point in time DataPower only supports the use of the HTTP(S) protocol: https://www.oasis-open.org/committees/download.php/272/ebMS_v2_0.pdf

Each of these protocols has different configuration requirements for both the B2B Gateway and B2B Profiles. The following sections will describe each protocol's standard pattern and their DataPower configuration settings.

NOTE—Drummond Interoperability Testing

DataPower B2B participates in Drummond Interoperability testing for AS2 twice a year. This means when using DataPower B2B with trading partners that use another vendor's AS2 software that has also gone through the testing, you are assured the two products will interoperate with each other with little to no issues. The current list of certified product can be found at the following link:

http://drummondgroup.com/b2b-certified-products/certified-products/as2/126-b2b/b2b-products/b2b-certified-products/147-as2-current

---

AS1 Message Exchange Pattern

The Applicability Statement 1 (AS1) specification describes B2B email messages that are exchanged over SMTP and POP3 protocols. AS1 supports extra protocol headers that are not supported by SMTP and POP3 alone. Figure 4-1 depicts an example inbound and outbound AS1 flow.

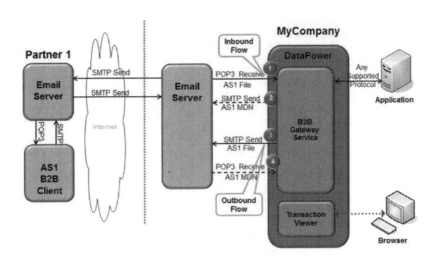

Figure 4-1 AS1 Inbound and Outbound flows.

Inbound AS1 files from an external trading partner are sent to your email server which can reside in the internal network (enterprise) or on the Internet (e.g. Hotmail, Yahoo, Google Mail, etc.). In this picture the email server is in the internal network. Once the file is in a mailbox, DataPower will consume AS1 files over POP3. Outbound AS1 files are consumed from the backside and sent to a partner's email address/server over SMTP. The flow to and from the back side is not described here as it can be any protocol supported by DataPower. A detailed description of the inbound and outbound AS1 flows to and from external partners is described below.

Inbound: The external partner sends an AS1 message to an email address associated with DataPower and the message contains a request to send back a Message Disposition Notification (MDN).

1.   DataPower retrieves the e-mail message from the email server using POP3, verifies the partner identification information and routes the message to the internal partner's destination.

2.   DataPower generates an AS1 MDN and responds back to the client using the email address specified in the AS1 message using a separate connection. All AS1 MDNs are asynchronous and are considered a separate business document by the B2B Gateway representing an independent, but correlated outbound flow.

Outbound: DataPower sends an AS1 message to an external trading partner and requests an AS1 MDN be sent back to a specified email address.

3.   DataPower consumes a file from the back-end and creates an e-mail attachment inside an AS1 message as defined in the External Partner profile. The subject line is then set to the sender and receiver ids.

4.   The partner will, in turn, generate a MDN message and send it back to the sending partner's email address. The B2B Gateway will then correlate the MDN with the originating outbound message and display it in the B2B Viewer.

NOTE—Message Disposition Notification

As with all AS message flows, a Message Disposition Notification (MDN) can optionally be requested; however, it must be sent back to the originating partner if requested. If it is not supplied back to the client, the message exchange is considered to be pending completion, if automated retries are enabled in the partner destination. The transaction is considered failed when not using automated retries or when the maximum retry count has been reached which was configured the partner destination.

Configuring DataPower B2B for AS1

To support this AS1 flow you need a B2B Gateway Service with front side handlers to consume files from AS1 trading partners and from the back-end, you also need at minimum, one internal partner profile and one external partner profile.

The B2B Gateway Service configuration object contains all of the information needed to process and secure the exchange of files between partners. If a B2B Gateway has not already been created, you can create one by clicking on the B2B Gateway object in the Control Panel or by expanding the Services link in the left navigation menu and by clicking on the Add button as seen in Figure 4-2.

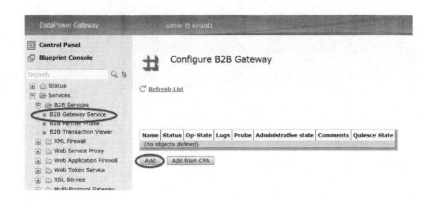

Figure 4-2 Add a B2B Gateway.

There are several tabs in the B2B Gateway; for this example we only need to configure the Main tab, Archive tab and the Advanced tab. In the B2B Gateway Main tab configuration screen you can add the needed AS1 Front Side handler from the drop-down by clicking on the + (plus) sign in the Front Side Protocol Handlers table in the Document Routing section as seen in Figure 4-3.

Configure B2B Gateway

| **Main** | Archive | XML Formats | ebXML | Probe Settings | Advanced |

B2B Gateway

Apply   Cancel   Help

Name   MyB2BGateway   *

General Configuration

Administrative state   ● enabled ○ disabled

Comments

Document Storage Location   (default) ▼

XML Manager   default   ▼   +   ...   *

Document Routing

Front Side Protocol Handlers

Front Side Protocol
(empty)

(none) ▼

Create a New: X
AS2 Front Side Handler
AS3 Front Side Handler
ebMS2 Front Side Handler
FTP Poller Front Side Handler
NFS Poller Front Side Handler
SFTP Poller Front Side Handler
FTP Server Front Side Handler
HTTP Front Side Handler
HTTPS Front Side Handler
IMS Connect Handler
WebSphere JMS Front Side Handler
MQFTE Front Side Handler
MQ Front Side Handler
AS1 Poller Front Side Handler
POP Poller Front Side Handler
SFTP Server Front Side Handler

Attach Par

Active Part

B2B Partn .... le Destination

(empty)

▼   +

Active Pro

B2B Profil

Figure 4-3 Configure B2B Gateway.

The purpose of the AS1 Front Side Protocol Handler is to poll the e-mail account within the mailbox on a mail server for messages. It is specifically designed to expect AS1 messages from external partners. It is programmed to find the partner IDs from the email headers in the message and to process the AS1 message. The AS1 handler uses POP3 to retrieve the messages that contain the transactional information from the external B2B partner.

To configure the AS1 Poller Front Side Handler to retrieve messages you will need the following information:

- The host name or IP address of the POP3 server where your email account resides

- The type of secured connection that will be used to connect to the server (STARTTLS or Implicit SSL) or an unsecured connection

- The listening port (110 or 995 are the most popular)

- The authentication method that will be used to authenticate the account on the POP3 server: Basic authentication or authenticated POP (APOP)

- The username and password of the account that will be accessing the mailbox

An example of a configured AS1 Front Side Protocol Handler is illustrated in Figure 4-4.

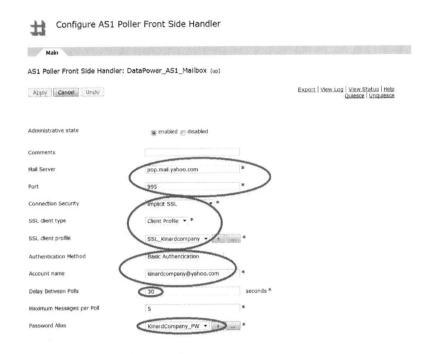

Figure 4-4 As1 Poller Front Side Handler Configuration.

A description of each field configured to support this pattern is provided below; all remaining fields use the defaults and a description of each can be obtained from the GUI interactive help:

- **Mail Server**: This is the host name or IP address for the POP3 Mail Server. This server is typically located in your network, however, it can be a web based service like used in this example. We are testing with Yahoo's mail server.

- **Port**: This is the listening port for the mail server. This is typically 110 or 995 but could be different.

- **Connection Security**: Choose the required level of security to connect to the server. The Yahoo mail server requires Implicit SSL.

- **SSL Client Type**: If using SSL for the connection you can select Proxy Profile (deprecated) or Client Profile. Yahoo mail does require SSL so we set this to Client Profile.

- **SSL Client Profile**: If using SSL this is the object you would store all of the credentials needed to secure connections between the clients and appliance. In our example we created a credential to enable SSL for the client connection to yahoo.com.

- **Authentication Method**: Choose the authentication method that DataPower will use to authenticate to the POP3 Mail Server. For our example we are using Basic Authentication as required by Yahoo.

- **Account Name**: Enter the name of the account used to access the mailbox. In this example we are using an account created in Yahoo mail.

- **Delay Between Polls**: Enter the number or seconds to wait in between polls. If traffic arrives during this delay period, it will not be processed until the delay time expires. The default is 300 seconds. Our example is polling every 30 seconds to make it easier to test. Some email servers will not let you poll that often so a longer polling cycle should be used in production.

- **Password Alias**: This object holds the password for the login account. An Alias is used to allow DataPower to protect the password in logs and configuration files.

When you are done with the AS1 Front Side Protocol Handler configuration and have saved it by clicking on the Apply button, you must also add it to the Front Side Handlers table by clicking Add button.

For our example we also created a HTTP Front Side Protocol Handler to support receiving files from the back-end that are destined for an external partner. The configuration of the HTTP Front Side Protocol Handler is not shown here. The connection from the back-end for outbound files can be any protocol that is supported on DataPower.

NOTE—AS or ebMS Enveloping

When files destined for external partners must be AS or ebMS enveloped, the external profile destination settings dictate how the messages need to be packaged. This packaging step is done in the B2B Gateway Service before sending the file to the external partner. This means files received from the back-side destined for an external partner must not already be AS or ebMS enveloped.

Next, we need to create an External Partner Profile that holds the connectivity information needed to connect to the AS1 Trading Partner. To do this you need to create an External

Partner Profile by clicking on the + (plus) sign in the Active Partner Profiles table in the B2B Gateway Main tab as shown in Figure 4-5.

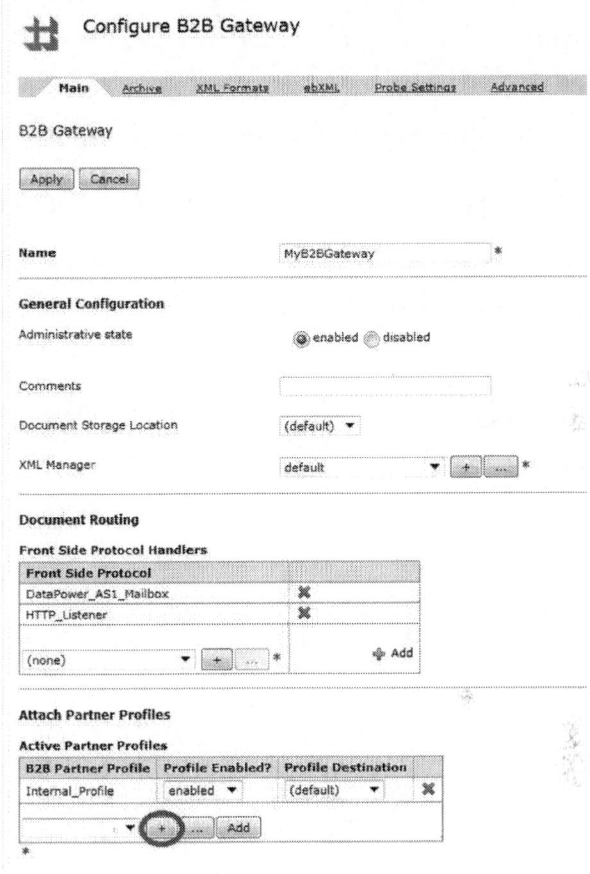

Figure 4-5 Create Profile from a B2B Gateway.

NOTE—Creating Partner Profiles

There are multiple ways to create partner profiles; from inside the B2B Gateway as done in this example or from the Partner Profile Manager from the Control Panel prior to creating the B2B Gateway.

In the External Partner's Main tab we need to provide a Name for the profile, mark it External, provide a business ID and the partner's email address as seen in Figure 4-6.

Figure 4-6 Configure AS1 External Profile – Main Tab.

The next tab in the external profile that we need to configure is the AS Settings tab. This tab holds the security certificates for validating the partner as well as the SSL certificates, if needed, for sending MDNs to the partner and advanced AS settings. In our example, we are using a validation credential to validate the signature applied to this external partner's data. Figure 4-7 illustrates the AS settings tab used in this example pattern.

Figure 4-7 Configure AS1 External Profile – AS Settings Tab.

The final tab we need to configure in the external profile is the Destinations tab. This tab holds the information needed for sending outbound files as AS1 to the trading partner's email inbox. The Destination Name should be unique and descriptive and the Enabled Document Type field should have the document types checked that you want to allow this destination to route. When the Destination URL is set to as1://, the E-mail Address specifies the target e-mail location to send the AS1 messages for this partner. Figure 4-8 illustrates an example of the AS1 Destination configured to support this pattern.

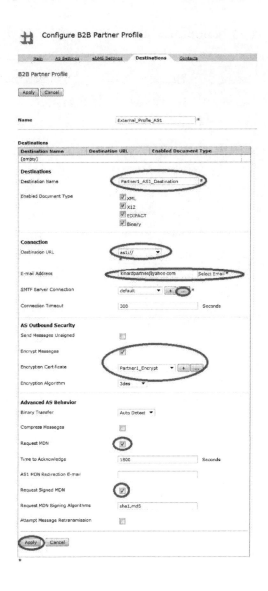

Figure 4-8 Configure AS1 External Profile – Destinations tab.

We also need to be sure an SMTP server is configured for sending outbound email and is available to be used with the destination. The SMTP Server connection setting is the name of the SMTP Server Connection object which contains server connection and credentials information. For our example we are using the default SMTP server. If the default SMTP Server has not yet been configured it can be done by clicking on the ellipses (...) button to the right of the SMTP Server Connection field. The SMTP Server configuration page specifies the Mail Server name, the SSL Profile name, the Mail Server account name and password. The SSL Profile is used to configure the credentials required to establish a secure SSL connection to the SMTP server. The default SMTP Server configuration is illustrated in Figure 4-9.

Figure 4-9 Configure AS1 External Profile – Destination SMTP Server.

When AS1 is selected as the destination protocol for the destination URL, some new fields are made available for configuration. These fields are displayed in the AS Outbound Security and Advanced AS Behavior section of the AS1 Destination screen.

The following additional fields are configurable for an AS1 partner destination:

AS Outbound Security:

- **Send Message Unsigned**: A checkbox that controls whether to override the signing of messages to this destination. Whether to sign the outbound message is part of the configuration of the internal partner AS Settings tab. If this box is enabled in the destination, it never signs messages for this destination.

- **Encrypt Messages**: A checkbox that controls whether to encrypt the body of the outgoing messages. The default is off.

- **Encryption Certificate**: If the Encrypt Messages checkbox is selected, a dropdown is displayed to select the name of the certificate object.

- **Encryption Algorithm**: A dropdown to select the type of encryption that should be performed on outbound AS messages. This is displayed only if the Encrypt Messages checkbox is selected. The default algorithm is 3DES EDE CBC.

Advanced AS Behavior:

- **Binary Transfer**: This dropdown selection controls whether to transfer the message payload in binary mode or ASCII mode. The two options are Auto Detect and Enforce.

- **Compress Messages**: This checkbox controls whether to compress the body of the outbound AS message. The default is off.

- **Compress Before Sign**: This checkbox controls whether to compress the body of outbound AS messages before signing them. The default is off. This allows your business partner to verify the message before it is decompressed.

- **Request MDN**: This checkbox controls whether to request a Message Disposition Notification (MDN) to be returned by the partner for outbound AS messages. The default setting is off.

- **Time to Acknowledge**: This field is used to specify the maximum number of seconds to wait for the MDN acknowledgement before the outgoing message is re-transmitted. Accepted values are integer seconds from 1 to 3600 (1 hour). The default setting is 1800 (30 minutes).

- **AS1 MDN Redirection E-mail**: This field is used to specify an explicit MDN return e-mail address. The partner that receives the AS1 message will send the MDN to the e-mail address specified. If this field is left blank, the MDN acknowledgement of the outgoing AS1 message will be sent to the From address which is the default e-mail address of the sending internal partner.

- **Request Signed MDN**: This checkbox controls whether to request a signed MDN from the external partner in response to an outbound AS message.

- **Attempt Message Retransmission**: This checkbox controls whether to allow the retransmission of one or more messages if the MDN is not received in the specified time.

- **Maximum Retransmissions**: This field is used to specify the maximum number of times to re-transmit the message to the external partner. Enter an integer between 1 and 30. The default value is 3.

After you complete all of the required fields in the Destination tab, you can save the destination by clicking on the Apply button inside the Destinations table and save the profile by clicking on the Apply button in the profile configuration screen. This returns you to the Configure B2B Gateway screen. Be sure the external profile is added to the Active Profiles list by clicking on the Add button inside the table.

Additionally, we created an Internal Partner Profile that represents the internal destination (back-end) of files received from AS1 trading partners. For this example, we are using a profile that sends inbound data to the back-end using HTTP. The example Internal Partner Profile is not pictured here as it is very similar to the creation of the External Partner Profile. The main difference is the email address in the Main tab represents your organization and the AS Settings tab allows for the use of private keys in addition to certificates for both inbound and outbound security. After completion of the Internal Partner Profile, be sure it is added to the Active Profiles list by clicking on the Add button inside the table.

The Archive tab in the Configure B2B Gateway screen also has to be configured to archive metadata and documents off of the device and then purge them, or it must be set to Purge Only. For this example we chose to use Purge Only as seen in Figure 4-10.

Figure 4-10 Configure B2B Gateway – Archive tab.

The final tab that needs to be configured to support the AS1 pattern is the Advanced tab. This tab is used as a catch-all for settings that further enhance the gateway's capabilities. These settings include Service Priority, default values for AS1, AS2 and AS3 MDN Redirection, the SQL Data Source for linking to the IBM MQ FTE DB Logger database and a pointer to the Document Routing Processor for determining sender and receiver IDs for binary data flows. The only field needed in this tab for this AS1 pattern example is to select the AS1 MDN

SMTP Server Connection; for our example we are using Default which we configured in the External Partner Profile Destination.

We are not configuring the Default AS1 MDN Return E-Mail field; we will return the MDN to the senders email address automatically. Figure 4-11 illustrates the B2B Gateway Configuration Advanced tab.

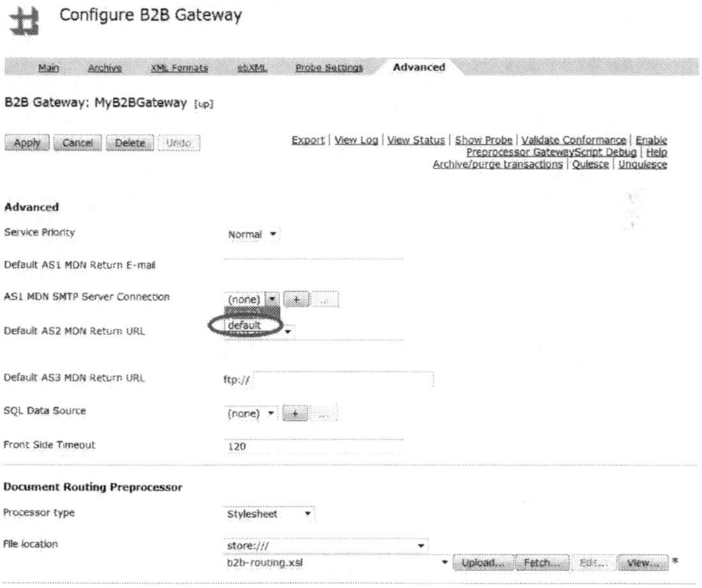

Figure 4-11 Configure B2B Gateway – Advanced tab.

The remaining tabs in the B2B Gateway are not required to support this example. A brief description of each tab is provided below:

- **XML Formats**: If the documents from the back-end are XML documents you can add XML Routing

Policies in the XML Formats tab to tell the gateway where to find the sender and receiver IDs in the XML content using XPATH. For this example, we are not using XML for the outbound flow and thus we did not configure this tab.

- **ebXML**: This tab is only used when the gateway is ebXML CPA enabled. It contains all of the collaborations supported by this B2B Gateway service. We do not need to configure this tab to support this AS2 pattern.

- **Probe Settings**: This tab is only used to enable troubleshooting of the service when a processing policy is used in any of the partner profiles. We are not using the probe for this pattern example. The Probe should be used only for single-transaction testing and never for high-volume test or production scenarios.

The last step is to save the B2B Gateway by clicking on the Apply button in the upper left hand corner of the screen. Also remember to click on Save Configuration in the upper right hand corner of the screen to permanently persist the configuration.

When files are received from the back-end and are destined for an external AS1 trading partner, the files will be wrapped up in an AS1 envelope and sent to the external partner's email inbox. When an MDN is requested it will be sent back to the sender asynchronously. The Asynchronous MDN displays in the B2B Viewer as a separate inbound business document. Figure 4-12 illustrates an example of an

AS1 flow as seen in the B2B Viewer. You can see that transaction 428 is the outbound message, 430 is the returned Asynchronous MDN. Transaction 431 is an outbound message that is waiting for the MDN to be returned.

NOTE—Asynchronous MDNs

In the B2B Viewer, asynchronous MDNs may not be right next to the outbound transactions that they correlate to when high volumes are involved, however, the outbound transaction will always show the status of the MDN response.

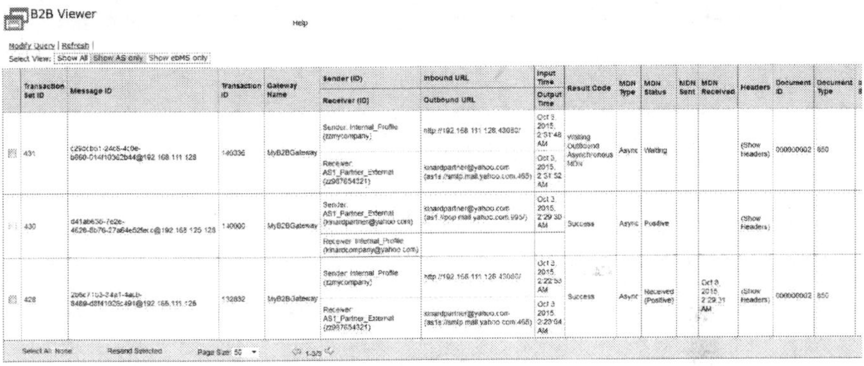

Figure 4-12 B2B Viewer – AS1 Outbound Data Flow.

The AS1 Inbound data flow is not pictured here as transactions look very similar to those pictured above. When receiving inbound AS1 transactions, the viewer will only display the transaction and not the sent MDN. The status of the MDN for the transaction will be Sent (Positive). You will not see the separate asynchronous MDN since the process of sending the MDN happens immediately upon receiving the message.

NOTE—Mail Servers and MessageIDs

When using a web based email service (e.g. Hotmail, Yahoo, Google Mail, etc.) you may find that the mail server will overwrite the MessageID of the incoming AS1 transaction (Google Mail does this), which makes it impossible to correlate MDNs that return to the sender. For this reason IBM advises you use your enterprise email service or an email service that does not change the messageID when sending and receiving AS1 data.

AS2 Message Exchange with Transform

The Applicability Statement 2 (AS2) protocol describes how to exchange structured business data securely over the HTTP protocol. Per the statement, structured business data may be XML, EDI, EDIFACT, or other structured data formats. For more information on AS2 see RFC4130.

Figure 4-13 depicts an example inbound AS2 flow using DataPower B2B.

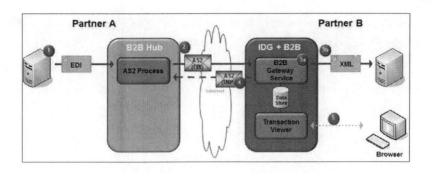

Figure 4-13 AS2 Sample inbound and outbound flow.

To further explain this pattern flow, use the numbers in the above Figure for reference:

1. Partner A sends an EDI file into their B2B Hub.
2. The EDI file is wrapped in an AS2 envelope and sent to Partner B.
3. (a/b) Partner B's DataPower B2B Gateway consumes the AS2 message, processes the AS2 envelope (verify partner, security, decrypt and unpackage the AS2 envelope), transforms the EDI file to XML and sends it to the backend application over any protocol supported by DataPower.
4. After the transaction has been successfully received by the back-end, Partner B's B2B Gateway generates and sends an MDN back to partner A.
5. Optionally, the Admin user can view the state of the transaction in the B2B viewer.

The transformation of messages from EDI to XML is handled by WebSphere Transformation Extender (WTX). The

WTX runtime is embedded in DataPower, however the tools (WTX Design Studio and Industry Packs) to develop file definitions and maps are sold separately and run off device on a workstation or server. The mapping process starts by using a standard drag and drop paradigm to map the input to the output of the transformation. The WTX development tool generates a binary object that is uploaded and then referenced by a binary transform action in a processing rule executed by a partner's specified processing policy object. Volume 3 of this DataPower Handbook, DataPower Development, covers usage of WTX on DataPower.

In addition to providing a mapping function, when there is no pre-existing EDI processing infrastructure, WTX can be used to generate EDI Functional Acknowledgements. DataPower currently supports EDI-X12 and EDIFACT. For example, if a business partner requires both an MDN to acknowledge the receipt of data and the receipt of a valid EDI-X12 document, WTX can generate an EDI-X12 transaction type 997 (FA). The MDN acknowledges that data was received by the B2B Gateway. The 997 (FA) acknowledges that the data was understood to be a valid EDI formatted message. A 997 does not acknowledge the business aspect of the content although it can be extended to included content validation if the need arises and there is an agreement amongst the business partners.

NOTE—WTX on DataPower

DeveloperWorks has a two part, very well written article that describes how to use WTX on DataPower to validate EDI messages and generate FA's. They can be downloaded using the following link:
http://www.ibm.com/developerworks/library/co-edi-websphere-datapower/

TIP—WTX Design Studio for Testing

When building maps to run on DataPower you can integrate WTX Design Studio with DataPower to support a fully integrated testing environment linking Design Studio for map development to DataPower for WTX runtime testing. Detailed instructions are can be found in DataPower's online Knowledge Center at the following link: https://www-304.ibm.com/support/knowledgecenter/SS9H2Y_7.2.0/com.ibm.dp.doc/wtx_mapdevelopmentanddeployment.html

Configuring DataPower B2B for AS2

To support this AS2 flow you need a B2B Gateway Service with front side handlers to consume files from AS2 trading partners and from the back-end, you also need at minimum, one internal partner profile and one external partner profile.

The B2B Gateway Service configuration object contains all of the information needed to process and secure the exchange of files between partners. This section assumes you have already created a B2B Gateway Service as described in the AS1 pattern we created in the first part of this chapter. For this reason we will only show the AS2 specific objects that need to be added to the B2B Gateway to support this pattern.

We will edit the same B2B Gateway we created in the AS1 pattern above. From the B2B Gateway configuration screen you can add the needed AS2 Front Side handler from the drop-down by clicking on the + (plus) sign in the Front Side Protocol Handlers table in the Document Routing section as seen in Figure 4-14.

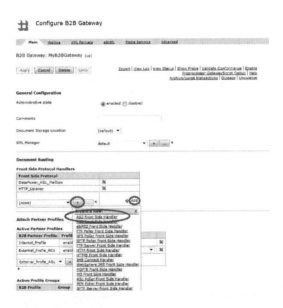

Figure 4-14 Configure B2B Gateway – AS2 Front Side Handler

The As2 Front Side Handler is a HTTP listener that is specifically designed to expect AS2 messages from external partners. It is programmed to find the partner IDs from the

HTTP headers in the message and to process the AS2 messages.

To configure the AS2 Front Side Handler to listen for messages you will need the following information in the Main tab. We do not need to change anything on the Advanced tab:

- The host name or IP you want to listen on. This is typically the IP address or host alias on the DataPower device.
- The listening port number which must be unique for the IP Address you are using.
- SSL Server profile if AS2 transactions are going to be received over HTTPS.
- An AAA Policy if basic Authentication is going to be used.

An example of a configured AS2 Front Side Protocol Handler is illustrated in Figure 4-15. For this example we are not using SSL or basic authentication.

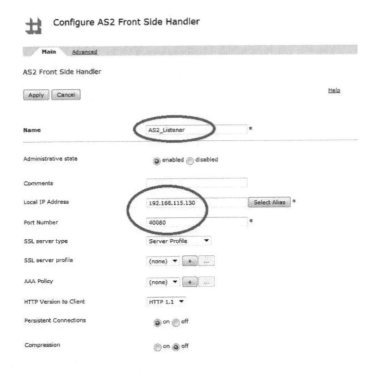

Figure 4-15 B2B Gateway AS2 Front Side Handler

A description of each field configured to support this pattern is provided below; all remaining fields use the defaults and a description of each can be obtained from the GUI interactive help:

- **Name**: This field is a mandatory field that contains a unique name for this protocol handler.

- **Local IP Address**: This is the host name or IP address you want to listen on. This address is one of the IP addresses associated with the device. The default is 0.0.0.0 which represents all IP addresses associated with the device. This is fine for test environments, but it should be a specific address in production.

- **Port Number**: This is the port you want to listen on and is unique to the IP address it is assigned to.

When you are done with the AS2 Front Side Protocol Handler configuration and have saved it by clicking on the Apply button, you must add it to the Front Side Handlers table by clicking on the Add button.

Since we are using the same B2B Gateway service as the above AS1 pattern, the remaining tabs do not need to be changed.

Next, we need to create an External Partner Profile that holds the connectivity information needed to connect to the AS2 Trading Partner. To do this you need to create an External Partner Profile by clicking on the + (plus) sign in the Active Partner Profiles table in the B2B Gateway Main screen or by creating the partner in the B2B Partner Profile Manager prior to adding it to the gateway. For this example we created it from the B2B Gateway.

In the External Partner's Main tab we need to provide a Name for the profile, mark it External and provide a Business ID as seen in Figure 4-16.

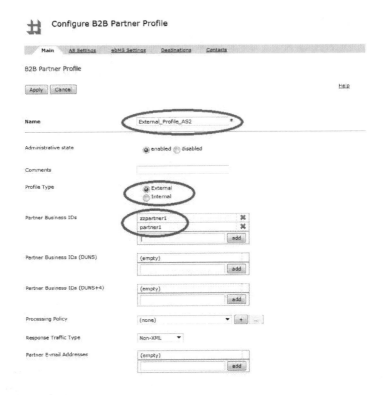

Figure 4-16 Configure AS2 External Profle – Main Tab.

The next tab in the external profile we need to configure is the AS Settings tab. This tab holds the security certificates for validating the partner's signature, as well as the SSL certificates (if needed for sending MDNs to the partner) and advanced AS settings. In our example, we are using a validation credential to validate the signature applied to this external partner's data. Figure 4-17 illustrates the AS settings tab used in this example pattern.

Figure 4-17 Configure AS2 External Profile – AS Settings Tab.

The final tab we need to configure in the external profile is the Destinations tab. This tab holds the information needed for sending outbound files as AS2 messages. To create a new destination, click Add in the Destinations table. The Destination Name should be unique and descriptive and the Enabled Document Type field should have the document types checked that you want to allow this destination to route.

The Destination URL in the Connection section in our example is set to as2:// and the IP address and port number is set to the location to send the AS2 messages. Figure 4-18 illustrates an example of the AS2 Destination configured to support this pattern.

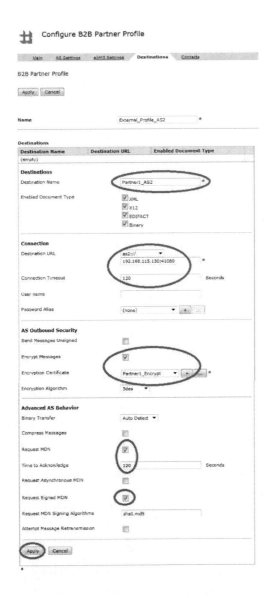

Figure 4-18 Configure AS2 External Profile – Destinations Tab.

When AS2 is selected as the destination protocol in the Connections section for the destination URL, some new fields are made available for configuration. These fields are displayed in the Connection the AS Outbound Security and Advanced AS Behavior section of the AS2 Destination screen.

The following additional fields are configurable for an AS2 partner destination:

Connection:

- **Connection Timeout**: This field specifies the maximum number of seconds to maintain an idle connection. The default is set to 300 seconds, however, if using synchronous MDNs it is recommended to set the value to a smaller number. We are using 120 seconds for this example.

- **User Name**: This optional field is the user name for basic authentication when connecting to the partner's URL if required.

- **Password Alias**: This optional field houses the password alias object for basic authentication when connecting to the partner's URL if required.

AS Outbound Security:

- **Send Message Unsigned**: A checkbox that controls whether to override the signing of messages to this destination. Whether to sign the outbound message is part of the configuration of the internal partner AS Settings tab. If this box is enabled in the destination, it never signs messages for this destination.

- **Encrypt Messages**: A checkbox that controls whether to encrypt the body of the outgoing messages. The default is off.

- **Encryption Certificate**: If the Encrypt Messages checkbox is selected, a dropdown is displayed to select the name of the certificate object.

- **Encryption Algorithm**: a dropdown to select the type of encryption that should be performed on outbound AS messages. This is displayed only if the Encrypt Messages checkbox is selected. The default algorithm is 3DES EDE CBC.

Advanced AS Behavior:

- **Binary Transfer**: This dropdown selection controls whether to transfer the message payload in binary mode or ASCII mode. The two options are Auto Detect and Enforce.

- **Compress Messages**: This checkbox controls whether to compress the body of the outbound AS message. The default is off.

- **Compress Before Sign**: This checkbox controls whether to compress the body of outbound AS messages before signing them. The default is off. This allows your business partner to verify the message before it is decompressed.

- **Request MDN**: This checkbox controls whether to request a Message Disposition Notification (MDN) to be returned by the partner for outbound AS messages. The default setting is off; we have set this to on for this example.

- **Time to Acknowledge**: This field is used to specify the maximum number of seconds to wait for the MDN acknowledgement before the outgoing message is re-transmitted. Accepted values are integer seconds 1 to 3600 (1 hour). The default setting is 1800 (30 minutes). For synchronous MDNs set to a smaller number; we are using 120 seconds for this example.

- **Request Asynchronous MDN**: Controls whether the MDN request for outbound AS2 messages is asynchronous; the default is off. When turned on the below MDN Redirection field is displayed.

- **AS2 MDN Redirection**: This field is used to specify an explicit MDN return URL. The partner that receives the AS2 message will send the MDN to the URL specified. When requesting Asynchronous MDNs, typically the connection must be made to a firewall IP address and this setting allows you to set the return path to the firewall instead of directly to the DataPower IP.

- **Request Signed MDN**: This checkbox controls whether to request a signed MDN from the external partner in response to an outbound AS message.

- **Request MDN Signing Algorithm**: Controls which digest algorithms to ask for when requesting a signed MDN.

- **Attempt Message Retransmission**: This checkbox controls whether to allow the retransmission of one or more messages if the MDN is not received in the specified time. This setting only functions when using Asynchronous MDNs.

- **Maximum Retransmissions**: This field is used to specify the maximum number of times to re-transmit the message to the external partner when the Attempt Message Retransmission is checked. Enter an integer between 1 and 30. The default value is 3.

After you complete all of the required fields in the Destinations tab, you can save the destination by clicking the Apply button inside the Destinations table. Save the profile by clicking on the Apply button in the profile configuration screen. In the Configure B2B Gateway screen, be sure the external profile is added to the Active Profiles list before clicking on the Apply button in the B2B Gateway configuration screen to save the B2B Gateway. Also remember to click Save Configuration in the upper right hand corner of the screen.

The existing Internal Profile associated with the B2B Gateway can be used for this flow since, in our example; it represents your organization for all connections to the back-end.

When files are received from the back-end and are destined for an external AS2 trading partner, the files will be wrapped up in an AS2 envelope and sent to the external partner's URL. When AS2 messages are received from the External AS2 partners the message is unwrapped (verify signature, decrypt, remove AS2 envelope) and the file is sent to the back-end through the internal partner's destination. When using AS2 the partner has the option of requesting MDNs be sent back to them synchronously or asynchronously. The AS2 message headers in the originating message will determine whether the MDN is supposed to be returned synchronously or asynchronously. You also have the option of requesting your MDNs be returned synchronously or asynchronously defined in the external partner's destination.

Figure 4-19 illustrates an example view of an AS2 flow with sync MDN for both inbound and outbound transactions.

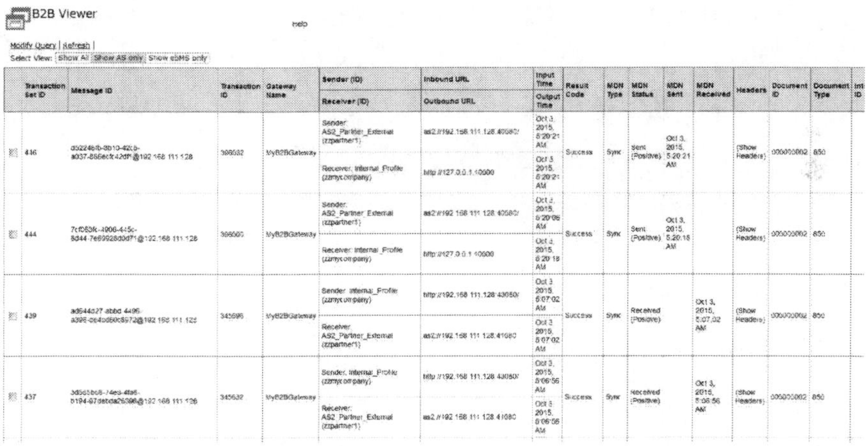

Figure 4-19 B2B Viewer – AS2/EDI Dataflow.

NOTE—AS2 Optional Profiles

AS2 has added some new features over the years that can be optionally used to enhance AS2 patterns. These features are called optional profiles and are listed under AS2 v1.2. DataPower B2B currently supports the Filename Preservation, Multiple Attachments, Filename Preservation for Multiple Attachments, and Secure Hash Algorithm 2 (SHA-2) features of AS2 v1.2; directions on how to configure DataPower B2B to support the AS2 Filename preservation can be found on IBM DeveloperWorks at the following link: http://www.ibm.com/developerworks/websphere/library/techarticles/1411_kinard/1411_kinard.html

---

AS3 File Transfer Patterns

The Applicability Statement 3 (AS3) protocol describes how to use the File Transfer Protocol (FTP) to transport Peer-to-Peer business data securely over the Internet. For more detailed information on AS3, refer to RFC4823.

The AS3 File Transfer Patterns are very similar to the File Transfer Patterns found in Chapter 5. The only real difference is that the AS3 protocol can use the B2B Gateway Service to generate MDNs back to the originator of the message. There are typically two types of AS3 File Transfer Patterns.

- AS3 File Transfer using a DataPower B2B FTP Service
- AS3 File Transfer using a FTP Server Mailbox

Both types of AS3 File Transfer are shown in Figure 4-20.

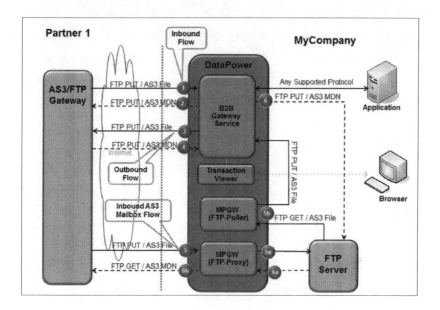

Figure 4-20 AS3 File Transfer Patterns.

AS3 File Transfer using a DataPower B2B FTP Service (Push-Push Pattern)

For this pattern we are only illustrating the front side of the dataflow for both inbound and outbound transactions. The back side connection can be over any protocols that are supported by DataPower. To further explain the DataPower B2B FTP Service pattern flow, use numbers 1 through 4 in Figure 4-20 for reference:

Inbound AS3 Flow: AS3 Messages are received directly into the B2B Gateway over FTP and the partner requests an AS3 MDN be returned. AS3 MDNs are always sent back immediately and the MDN Status is logged with the outbound transaction.

1. The external trading partner establishes an FTP session with DataPower and then executes a PUT action to transmit the AS3 message. The DataPower B2B Gateway Service removes the AS3 envelope and sends the payload to the internal partner's destination using any supported protocol.

2. After the file has successfully been delivered to the back-end, the DataPower B2B Gateway generates an AS3 MDN and establishes a FTP session with the trading partner, a PUT action is then initiated to put the AS3 MDN into the partner's FTP location which was specified in the original AS3 message.

Outbound AS3 Flow: AS3 messages are sent from the DataPower B2B Gateway to an external partner's B2B Gateway over FTP and an AS3 MDN is requested to be returned. AS3 MDNs are always received asynchronously and represent a separate business document in the B2B viewer.

3. When the B2B Gateway receives a file from the back-end that is destined for an AS3 external partner, it tries to parse the file. If it is EDI or XML the sender and receiver IDs are found and the file is routed to the external AS3 partner. If the file cannot be parsed for ID information, a Routing Pre-Processor stylesheet, specified in the B2B Gateway Service configuration, is used to set the sender and receiver IDs. The AS3 message is sent to the

external partner using an FTP PUT action and an AS3 MDN is requested.

4.   The external partner's B2B Gateway generates an AS3 MDN and performs a FTP PUT to send it back to the DataPower Gateway. The AS3 MDN is correlated to the original AS3 message and the transaction is completed.

AS3 File Transfer using an FTP Server Mailbox (Push-Pull Pattern)

Sometimes it is desirable to provide FTP mailboxes (directories on a FTP Server) for trading partners that use custom code or scripting to wrap or unwrap their files in an AS3 envelope. These partners typically do not have a B2B engine to process AS3 data directly. This pattern assumes you want to protect your FTP server by deploying it in the trusted zone and using a DataPower Multi-Protocol Gateway Service to securely proxy data to it. Additionally, DataPower B2B does not provide an AS3 poller, so another Multi-Protocol Gateway Service must be used to poll AS3 files from the internal FTP Server and pass them into a B2B Gateway for AS3 processing. We call this service-chaining and it is very effective and flexible for many different patterns where the use of a B2B Gateway alone does not meet the specific need.

For this pattern we are illustrating only the inbound AS3 message flow. To further explain the DataPower FTP Server Mailbox pattern flow, use numbers 5 through 6 in Figure 4-20 for reference.

Inbound AS3 Mailbox Flow:

5. The trading partner connects to the FTP front-side protocol handler of the Multi-Protocol Gateway (MPGW) FTP Proxy service. The FTP protocol handler has an AAA policy associated with it that performs authentication against a local password file or against an Access Management solution inside the trusted network. Additionally, if there is SSL required, the SSL is terminated at this step.

    a. After authentication and SSL termination (if required), the trading partner performs the PUT action and the message is placed in to the FTP Server's inbox for that partner.

    b. Another MPGW (FTP Poller) is polling the FTP mailbox (inbox) and retrieves the files deposited there. The output for this MPGW is a URL Opener pointing to a HTTP Front Side Handler in the B2B Gateway. The B2B Gateway then processes the inbound message, removes the AS3 envelope and sends the transaction to the internal partner's destination (back-end).

6. The inbound AS3 message requested an MDN. The B2B Gateway generates the MDN and performs a PUT to the trading partner's outbound mailbox (or outbox) on the physical FTP Server.

    a. The trading partner connects to the MPGW FTP Proxy and is authenticated for connection to the internal FTP server.

b.   Once the external partner is authenticated, they perform a FTP GET to retrieve the MDN from the internal physical FTP Server.

NOTE—AS3 Mailbox and FTP Servers

DataPower must use a separate FTP Server when using an AS3 mailbox approach; DataPower cannot hold files in the device for retrieval by external trading partners.

Configuring DataPower B2B Gateway for AS3

To support the B2B Gateway AS3 Service flows (1-4) you need a B2B Gateway Service with front side handlers to consume files from AS3 trading partners and from the back-end, you also need at minimum, one internal partner profile and one external partner profile in the B2B Gateway. To support the AS3 Mailbox flow (5-6) you need two Multi-Protocol Gateway Services with the appropriate front side and backside handlers and the B2B Gateway with profiles that were created for the AS3 B2B Service flows.

We will edit the same B2B Gateway we created in the AS1 pattern we created in the first part of this chapter. We need to use the XML Manager to allow us to provide the authentication credentials needed to support the return path of the partner's MDN. The inbound message will provide the MDN Return URL in the AS3 headers and we must provide our login credentials for that specific URL with a User Agent. From the

B2B Gateway configuration screen you can edit the default XML Manager in the Main tab of the B2B Gateway. This can be done by clicking on the ellipsis (...) to the right of the XML Manager field as seen in Figure 4-21.

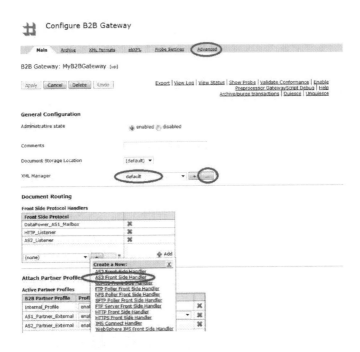

Figure 4-21 Configure B2B Gateway

The XML Manager has many tabs and we only need to configure one field in the Main tab. The name of this object is rather misleading. Over time the XML Manager has evolved to manage much more than just XML flows, but rather all flows that pass through the service. In the Main tab, the XML manager contains the reference to a User Agent. The User Agent defines the default settings for how the service connects to external services. In our case we need to use the User Agent to define a Basic-Auth Policy for the AS3/FTP MDN Return connection and also the FTP Client Policy. Figure 4-22 shows an example of the default XML Manager. To create a User Agent click on the + (plus) sign to the right of the User Agent Configuration field.

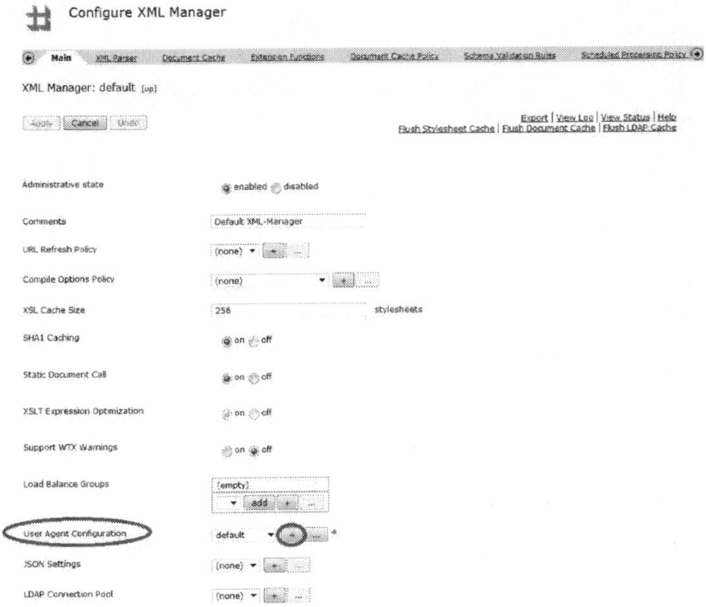

Figure 4-22 Configure XML Manager – Create User Agent.

In the User Agent screen we are only configuring two tabs. Click on the Basic-Auth Policy tab and name the Agent something meaningful, then click on the Add button in the policy table to add a Basic-Auth policy. Figure 4-23 illustrates an example policy that only triggers for a URL match that matches the external partners MDN return path.

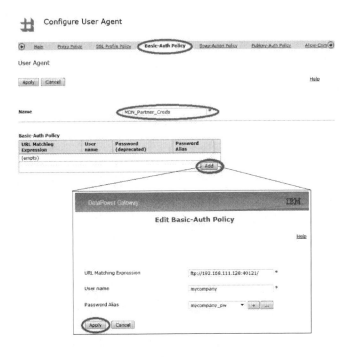

Figure 4-23 B2B Gateway - User Agent Basic-Auth Policy.

After you complete the Basic-Auth Policy, click on the Apply button inside the edit screen to save the policy and return to the Configure User Agent Screen. Next, scroll to the FTP Client Policies tab by clicking on the arrow in the upper right of the tab menu bar and click on the Add button in the policy table to add a FTP Client policy. Figure 4-24 illustrates an example policy that only triggers for a URL match that matches the external partners MDN return path. We will use the default values for all other fields.

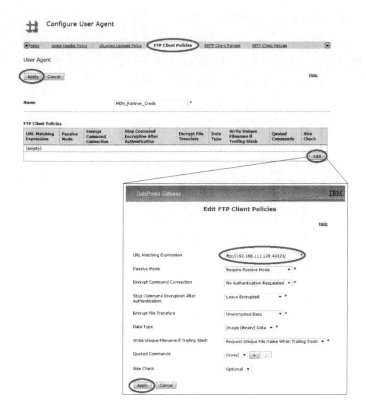

Figure 4-24 B2B Gateway - User Agent FTP Client Policy

After you complete the FTP Client Policy, click on the Apply button inside the edit screen to save the FTP Client Policy and return to the Configure User Agent Screen. Then click on the Apply button in the upper left of the User Agent screen to save the User Agent and return to the XML Manager screen. Finally, click on the Apply button in the XML Manager screen to save the XML Manager and return to the Configure B2B Gateway screen.

From the B2B Gateway configuration screen (Figure 4-21) we need to create the AS3 Front Side handler from the drop-down by clicking on the + (plus) sign in the Front Side Protocol Handlers table in the Document Routing section.

The As3 Front Side Handler is a FTP listener that is specifically designed to expect AS3 messages from external partners. It is programmed to find the partner IDs from the AS3 headers in the message and to process the AS3 messages.

To configure the AS3 Front Side Handler to listen for messages you will need the following information:

- The host name or IP you want to listen on. This is typically IP address or host alias on the DataPower device.
- The listening port number — it must be unique for the IP Address you are using.
- SSL Server profile if AS3 transactions are going to be received over HTTPS.
- A Password AAA Policy for authenticating the AS3 FTP user and password.

An example of a configured AS3 Front Side Protocol Handler is illustrated in Figure 4-25. For this example we are not using SSL.

Figure 4-25 B2B Gateway AS3 Front Side Handler.

A description of each field configured to support this pattern is provided below. All remaining fields use the defaults and a description of each can be obtained from the interactive help in the configuration screen or the user documentation:

- **Name**: This field is a mandatory field that contains a unique name for this protocol handler.

- **Local IP Address**: This is the host name or IP address you want to listen on. This address is one of the IP addresses associated with the device. The Default is 0.0.0.0 which represents all IP addresses associated with the device. This is fine in test but should be a specific address in production.

- **Port Number**: This is the port you want to listen on and is unique to the IP address it is assigned to.

- **Password AAA Policy**: If using Authentication and Authorization this is the object that would store the security policy. For this example we are using an AAA policy and a local AAA file to authenticate the username and password used by the trading partner.

- **Allow Unique File Name (STOU)**: Specify whether the FTP client can use the FTP STOU command. When enabled, the FTP server generates a unique file name for each transferred file.

In this screen we need to create a Password AAA Policy to authenticate inbound AS3 connections. For our AS3 pattern we do not need to configure all of the tabs in the Password AAA Policy so we will jump to the Identity Extraction tab where we selected Processing metadata from the list and chose ftp-username-metadata from the drop down as seen in Figure 4-26.

Figure 4-26 AS3 FSPH – Password AAA Identity Extraction.

Our next step is to configure the Authentication tab where we used the drop down in the Method field and selected Use AAA authentication file. After selecting this option we uploaded the file into the local:/// directory as seen in Figure 4-27.

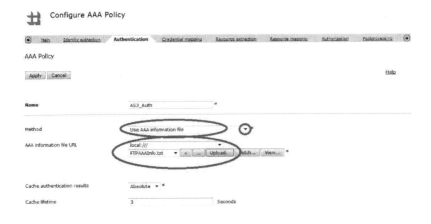

Figure 4-27 AS3 FSPH – Password AAA Authentication.

Listing 4-1 shows the contents of the AAA info file we used for this example.

Listing 4-1 AAA Info File.

```xml
<?xml version="1.0" encoding="UTF-8"?>
<AAAInfo xmlns="http://www.datapower.com/AAAInfo">
  <FormatVersion>1</FormatVersion>
  <Authenticate>
    <Username>mycompany</Username>
    <Password>mycompany</Password>
    <OutputCredential>mycompany</OutputCredential>
  </Authenticate>
  <Authenticate>
    <Username>partner2</Username>
    <Password>partner2</Password>
    <OutputCredential>partner2</OutputCredential>
  </Authenticate>
</AAAInfo>
```

The final tab in the Password AAA Policy for us to configure is the Resource extraction tab. Again, we selected Processing metadata and used the drop down to choose ftp-username-metadata as seen in Figure 4-28.

Figure 4-28 AS3 FSPH – Password AAA Resource Extraction.

After completing the Password AAA Policy you must click on the Apply button in the upper left corner to save the policy into the AS3 Front Side Handler.

When you are done with the AS3 Front Side Protocol Handler configuration and have saved it by clicking on the Apply button, you must add it to the Front Side Handlers table by clicking on the Add button.

Next, we need to create an External Partner Profile that holds the connectivity information needed to connect to the AS3 Trading Partner. To do this you need to create an External Partner Profile by clicking on the + (plus) sign in the Active Partner Profiles table in the B2B Gateway Main screen or by creating the partner in the B2B Partner Profile Manager prior to adding it to the gateway. For this example we created it from the B2B Gateway.

In the external Partner's Main tab we need to provide a Name for the profile; mark it External and provide a business ID as seen in Figure 4-29.

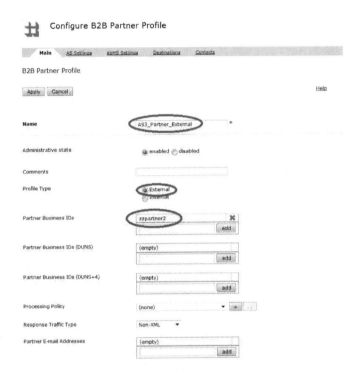

Figure 4-29 Configure AS3 External Profile – Main Tab.

The next tab in the external profile that we need to configure is the AS Settings tab. This tab holds the security certificates for validating the partner's signature as well as the SSL certificates (if needed) for sending MDNs to the partner and advanced AS settings. In our example, we are using a validation credential to validate the signature applied to this external partner's data. Figure 4-30 illustrates the AS settings tab used in this example pattern.

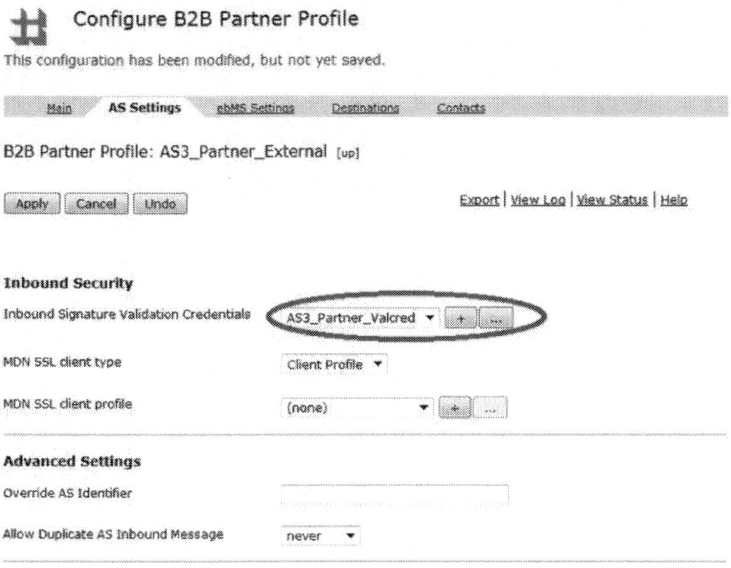

Figure 4-30 Configure AS3 External Profile – AS Settings Tab.

The final tab we need to configure in the external profile is the Destinations tab. This tab holds the information needed for sending outbound files as AS3 messages. To create a new destination, click on the Add button in the Destinations table. The Destination Name should be unique and descriptive and the Enabled Document Type field should have the document types checked that you want to allow this destination to route.

The Destination URL in the Connection section in our example is set to as3:// and the IP address and port number is set to the location to send the AS3 messages. We are not using

SSL for this example pattern. Figure 4-31 illustrates an example of the AS3 Destination configured to support this pattern.

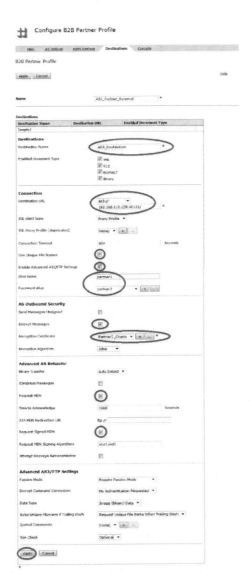

Figure 4-31 Configure AS3 External Profile – Destinations Tab

When AS3 is selected as the destination protocol in the Connections section for the destination URL, some new fields are made available for configuration. These fields are displayed in the Connection the AS Outbound Security, Advanced AS Behavior and Advanced AS3/FTP Settings section of the AS3 Destination screen.

The following additional fields are configurable for an AS3 partner destination:

Connection:

- **SSL Client Type**: As this is a DataPower initiated transaction, the SSL Client type should be set to Client Profile.

- **SSL Client Profile**: This is the SSL Client Profile that will contain the appropriate crypto profiles to establish the SSL connection to the partner's destination.

- **Connection Timeout**: This field specifies the maximum number of seconds to maintain an idle connection. The default is set to 300 seconds. However, if using synchronous MDNs it is recommended to set the value to a smaller number. We are using 120 seconds for this example.

- **Use Unique File Names**: This checkbox specifies whether to enable the generation of unique file names when the message is PUT to the destination directory. If you omit a file name in the destination URL, DataPower will generate a unique name for the outbound file. If you include a file name in the destination URL, DataPower will append the unique file name to the specified file name.

- **Enable Advanced AS3/FTP Settings**: This checkbox will enable additional settings at the bottom of the destination settings page.

- **User Name**: This optional field is the user name for basic authentication when connecting to the partner's URL if required.

- **Password Alias**: This optional field houses the password alias object for basic authentication when connecting to the partner's URL if required.

AS Outbound Security:

- **Send Message Unsigned**: A checkbox that controls whether to override the signing of messages to this destination. Whether to sign the outbound message is part of the configuration of the internal partner AS Settings tab. If this box is enabled in the destination, it never signs messages for this destination.

- **Encrypt Messages**: A checkbox that controls whether to encrypt the body of the outgoing messages. The default is off.

- **Encryption Certificate**: If the Encrypt Messages checkbox is selected, a dropdown is displayed to select the name of the certificate object.

- **Encryption Algorithm**: a dropdown to select the type of encryption that should be performed on outbound AS messages. This is displayed only if the

Encrypt Messages checkbox is selected. The default algorithm is 3DES EDE CBC.

Advanced AS Behavior:

- **Binary Transfer**: This dropdown selection controls whether to transfer the message payload in binary mode or ASCII mode. The two options are Auto Detect and Enforce.

- **Compress Messages**: This checkbox controls whether to compress the body of the outbound AS message. The default is off.

- **Compress Before Sign**: This checkbox controls whether to compress the body of outbound AS messages before signing them. The default is off. This allows your business partner to verify the message before it is decompressed.

- **Request MDN**: This checkbox controls whether to request a Message Disposition Notification (MDN) to be returned by the partner for outbound AS messages. The default setting is off; we have set this to on for this example.

- **Time to Acknowledge**: This field is used to specify the maximum number of seconds to wait for the MDN acknowledgement before the outgoing message is re-transmitted. Accepted values are integer seconds 1 to 3600 (1 hour). The default setting is 1800 (30 minutes). For synchronous MDNs set to a smaller number. We are using 120 seconds for this example.

- **AS3 MDN Redirection**: This field is used to specify an explicit MDN return URL. The partner that receives the AS3 message will send the MDN to the URL specified. When requesting AS3 MDNs, typically the connection must be made to a firewall IP address and this setting allows you to set the return path to the firewall instead of directly to the DataPower IP.

- **Request Signed MDN**: This checkbox controls whether to request a signed MDN from the external partner in response to an outbound AS message.

- **Request MDN Signing Algorithm**: Controls which digest algorithms to ask for when requesting a signed MDN.

- **Attempt Message Retransmission**: This checkbox controls whether to allow the retransmission of one or more messages if the MDN is not received in the specified time. This setting only functions when using Asynchronous MDNs.

- **Maximum Retransmissions**: This field is used to specify the maximum number of times to re-transmit the message to the external partner when the Attempt Message Retransmission is checked. Enter an integer between 1 and 30. The default value is 3.

Advanced AS3/FTP Settings:

- **Passive Mode**: FTP Passive mode differs from Active mode in that in Passive mode, the client initiates all of the connection requests after the initial connection request. The possible options in the drop-down box are: Require Passive Mode, Passive Mode not requested or Require passive mode.

- **Encrypt Command Connection**:   FTP uses a separate command channel to convey commands from the client to the server. The possible options in the drop-down box are: Not Authentication Requested, Request Transport Layer Security (TLS) Authentication or Require TLS Authentication.

- **Data Type**: This drop-down selects the type of data that is being transmitted. The selections available from the drop-down box are: Image (binary) Data or ASCII Data.

- **Write Unique Filename if Trailing Slash**: Overrides the Write Unique Filename if Trailing Slash setting in the FTP client policy for the user agent that the B2B gateway uses. If overriding, indicate how to use sever-generated unique file names when the URL being written to ends in a slash.

- **Quoted Commands**: This field is used to create or select an FTP Quoted Commands object. Quoted commands are used during the FTP session to specify certain properties of the outbound file. A typical use would be to use SITE commands, such as

SITE RECFM = FB for the MVS domain on a z/OS system. The commands in the list cannot be data-transfer related, such as STOU, RETR, PORT, PASV, and so forth.

- **Size Check**: Some FTP Servers support the use of a SIZE command to validate the size of an FTP Transfer. The two options available in the drop-down box are: Optional and Disabled. Optional will continue with the validation of the size of the message. Disabled will not check the size of the file after transfer.

After you complete all of the required fields in the Destinations tab, you can save the destination by clicking on the Apply button inside the Destinations table. Save the profile by clicking on the Apply button in the Profile configuration screen. In the Configure B2B Gateway screen be sure the external profile is added to the Active Profiles list by clicking on the Add button.

The final tab we need to configure in the B2B Gateway is the Advanced tab. In this tab we set the Default AS3 MDN Return URL to the URL we want our MDNs to be returned to. This URL matches the AS3 Front Side Handler we created in the Main tab. The Return MDN URL would be the external firewall address and port if that firewall is providing Network Address Translation (NAT) and Port Address Translation (PAT) for the DataPower IP Address. Figure 4-32 illustrates an example B2B Gateway Advanced tab configuration to support this AS3 pattern.

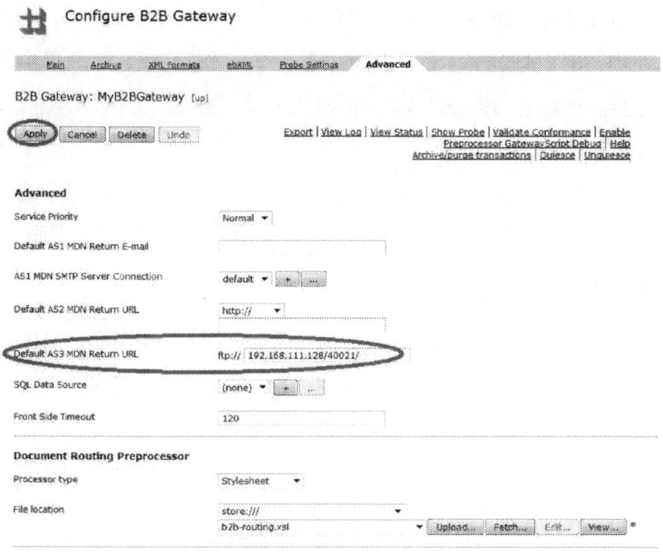

Figure 4-32 Configure B2B Gateway Advanced tab – AS3 MDN.

After completing the Advanced tab, click on the Apply button in the B2B Gateway configuration screen to save the B2B Gateway. Also remember to click on Save Configuration in the upper right hand corner of the screen.

The existing Internal Profile associated with the B2B Gateway can be used for this flow since, in our example; it represents your organization for all connections to the back-end.

Configuring DataPower Multi-Protocol Gateways for AS3 Mailbox

Supporting the AS3 Mailbox flow requires the use of one Multi-Protocol Gateway Service to proxy FTP connections into the internal FTP server and a second Multi-Protocol Gateway to PUT and GET files to and from the appropriate directories located on the internal FTP Server. Instructions for both FTP patterns are available in the FTP section of Chapter 5. Please refer to FTP pattern number 3 for details on configuring a Multi-Protocol Gateway Transparent FTP proxy and FTP pattern number 4 for configuring a FTP PUT/GET flow using a Multi-Protocol Gateway.

When files are received from the back-end and are destined for an external AS3 trading partner, the files will be wrapped up in an AS3 envelope and sent to the external partner's URL. When AS3 messages are received from the External AS3 partners the message is unwrapped (verify signature, decrypt, remove AS3 envelope) and the file is sent to the back-end through the internal partner's destination.

Figure 4-33 illustrates an example view of an AS3 flow for both inbound and outbound transactions. The view will be identical for both of the AS3 patterns discussed in this section. The only exception will be the source and destination for the mailbox pattern which will show the URLs of the Multi-Protocol Gateways used for the mailbox flow. You can see that transaction 489 is the outbound message, 491 is the returned Asynchronous MDN. Transaction 486 is an inbound message that shows the MDN was sent back to the sender asynchronously.

NOTE—B2B Viewer and Asynch MDNs

In the B2B Viewer, asynchronous MDNs may not be right next to the outbound transactions that they correlate to when high volumes are involved. The outbound transaction will always show the status of the MDN response.

Figure 4-33 B2B Viewer – AS3 Outbound/Inbound.

ebMS V2.0 Introduction

To understand the ebXML Messaging Service (ebMS) you first need to understand the basics of the ebXML standard. So let's first look at a brief overview of ebXML V2.0 and then move into how DataPower B2B supports the standard.

What is ebXML V2.0?

OASIS characterizes ebXML (Electronic Business using eXtensible Markup Language), as a modular suite of specifications that enables enterprises of any size and in any geographical location to conduct business over the Internet.

Whereas EDI for years has provided a usable, but expensive way, for companies to exchange information in an automated manner, ebXML now provides a means for companies to integrate their processes much more easily. Based on XML, it provides a methodology for business to determine what information they should exchange and how, as well as a set of specifications to allow automation of the process.

The ebXML V2.0 standard consists of a group of related specifications that are maintained by the United Nations Centre for Trade Facilitation and Electronic Business (UN/CEFACT) and the Organization for the Advancement of Structured Information Standards (OASIS).

Each specification plays a key role in the implementation of ebXML technology. However, all parts are not required for a successful ebXML deployment. Many companies will only use the Messaging Service to securely transport data over the Internet, much in the same way EDIINT is used to securely transfer and repudiate data over a public network. The most common parts of the specification that get implemented are the ebXML Messaging Service (ebMS) and the Collaboration Protocol Profile and Agreement (CPPA). The Business Process used by most companies is typically around existing Business Process for a given implementation; it is not required to use the ebXML Business Process Specification Schema (BPSS). Very few implementations use the optional Registry and Repository for discovery of ebXML content.

Figure 4-34 illustrates the five parts of the ebXML specification.

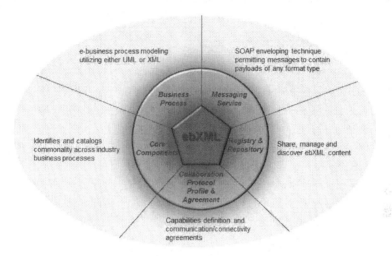

Figure 4-34 ebXML Specification Components.

For the purpose of this B2B Book we are only going to give an overview of the ebMS V2.0 and CPPA V2.0 specifications since these components are the only two specifications that are needed in the Gateway to fully exchange ebXML messages between partners. One important goal of the ebXML project is to use an open message format that can accommodate future extensions. Considering that everything in ebXML rests on the concept of sending messages, the ebMS is surprisingly simple. Each message consists of a number of MIME parts. The first MIME part consists of a SOAP message that provides identification for the message and other information crucial to its processing, and the rest consist of payload parts that carry the documents being transferred.

The general structure and composition of an ebMS V2.0 message is described in Figure 4-35.

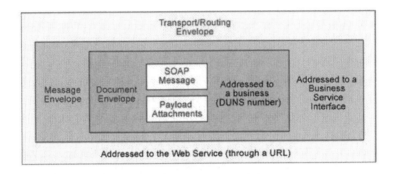

Figure 4-35 ebMS Message Structure

The actual implementation is known as the Message Service Handler (MSH). It starts with a layer on top of the actual application, called the Message Service Interface (MSI). Once requests come through the MSI, the message header is created, including information such as timestamps, digital signatures, and relevant information from the CPA. The delivery module then packs up and prepares the message itself for delivery.

The ebMS specification does not define the business processes or the content of the messages being sent. It only concerns itself with the secure and reliable transmission of the payload. The ebMS Message Service Handler (MSH) sits between the network protocol (SMTP, FTP, HTTP, etc.) and the Business Process at each end. In this way, the MSH is independent of both the transport protocol and the higher level Business Processes. In general, ebMS can be used to transmit any payload over any network connection. However, most implementations only support HTTP(S).

The Collaboration Protocol Agreement (CPA) glues Business Process's Transactions to Delivery Channels, Business Collaborations to ebMS Services, and Business Transaction Activities to Actions for partners to collaborate. A CPA may have multiple Services, where a Service may have a set of Actions. The CPA enumerates technical capability options for transfer, security, reliability, and document envelope details. The CPA is the intersection of two Collaboration Protocol Profiles (CPP); they define the system level agreement for data being exchanged between trading partners. The CPPA supplies (bilateral) metadata values to define features and parameters of MSH configurations. The CPA binds to ebMS. Likewise elements in ebMS messages are counterparts of CPA definitions.

NOTE—OASIS ebXML Resources

Additionally, OASIS maintains many resources for you to get started with ebXML at no cost to you; they include access to all of the specifications, a public forum, sample code and much more at the following URL:
http://www.ebxml.org/ebxml_resources.htm

DataPower B2B ebMS V2.0 Implementation

DataPower B2B supports two separate methods of using ebMS. The first method is simple ebMS enveloping and de-enveloping with no CPA required which allows you to hard code the CPA values in the profile. This method uses ebMS in the same manner as AS protocols (e.g. wrap any file in ebMS and send it to partners and receive ebMS files from partners and send payloads to the back-end). The second method is to use CPAs in the B2B Gateway; this uses collaborations in the gateway in combination with some of the profile information to have more granular control over the ebMS data flow. This type of configuration is more complex but adds the value of being able to support business process that reside on both sides of the relationship through the use of Services and Actions.

DataPower B2B Simple ebMS Pattern

This method gives customers an easy entry point into the world of ebXML by allowing the customer to use the ebMS V2.0 protocol to exchange files without the need for creating and using a CPA. Figure 4-36 illustrates an example of what a simple ebMS flow looks like.

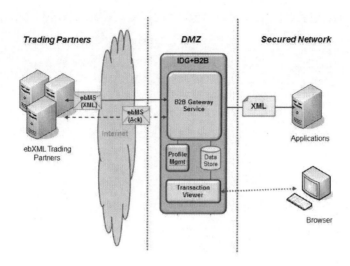

Figure 4-36 Simple ebMS Pattern.

To support this pattern in DataPower B2B you need to have at minimum one internal partner profile, one external partner profile and a B2B Gateway that is not CPA enabled. A CPA enabled B2B Gateway is one that has at least one CPA entry in the ebXML tab. We will explore that pattern later in this chapter. This section assumes the reader already knows how to create partner profiles, B2B Gateways and Front Side Handlers. It will only show how to configure ebXML specific parts of the profiles, B2B Gateway and handlers.

In each partner profile there is an ebMS Settings tab. The tab has different fields depending on whether you are configuring an internal or external profile.

Internal Partner Profile

The internal profile ebMS Settings tab has only a few fields that need to be configured to support this pattern.

- In the CPA Settings section, the Role setting identifies the role that this partner plays when sending or receiving ebXML messages. We are hard coding this value to Supplier but it can be any text string you wish.

- Inbound and Outbound Security sections can be configured to support ebXML message security (signing and encryption).

- In the Advanced Settings section, the Start parameter is used by many customers and identifies the root part of the ebMS message.

- The internal destination can be any supported protocol. However, MQ or HTTP is typically used so a user can pass metadata in headers to downstream systems as needed.

Figure 4-37 illustrates an example of an internal profile ebMS Settings tab.

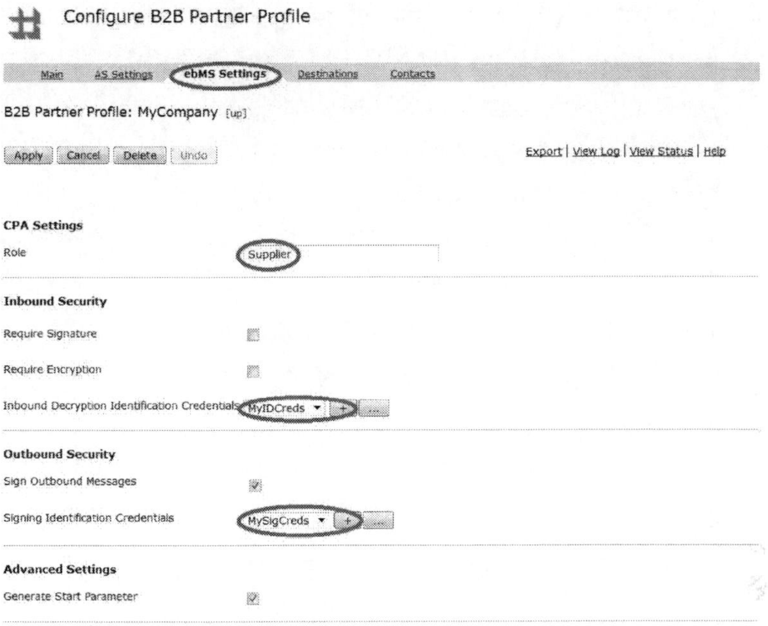

⊞ Configure B2B Partner Profile

| Main | AS Settings | ebMS Settings | Destinations | Contacts |

B2B Partner Profile: MyCompany [up]

| Apply | Cancel | Delete | Undo | Export | View Log | View Status | Help

CPA Settings

Role   (Supplier)

Inbound Security

Require Signature   ☐

Require Encryption   ☐

Inbound Decryption Identification Credentials (MyIDCreds ▼ + ...)

Outbound Security

Sign Outbound Messages   ☑

Signing Identification Credentials   (MySigCreds ▼ + ...)

Advanced Settings

Generate Start Parameter   ☑

Figure 4-37 Internal Profile – ebMS Settings.

External Partner Profile

The external profile ebMS Settings tab has several additional fields that need to be configured to support this pattern. The reason for this is because we are packaging an ebMS V2.0 message that adheres to the ebMS V2.0 specification. This requires many elements to be set in the message and we need to hard code them here to build a valid ebMS V2.0 message. Normally these values are found in the collaboration that is configured by a CPA, when one is used.

- In the CPA Setting section, the Role describes the role this partner plays in the exchange of data with other partners. Do not check the Enable CPA

Bindings box. The Default CPA ID, Default Service and Default Action all are all hard coded to a value of your choice. Keep in mind these values will not be used beyond the creation of the ebXML message. Our goal when not using CPAs is to simply package any file in ebMS and transport it securely over the Internet and then remove the ebMS wrapper and pass the payload to the trusted network. You can think of this pattern as being very similar to the AS2 patterns.

- In the Reliable Messaging section, the Persist Duration indicates to the receiving partner the minimum length of time the message should be kept in persistent storage allowing you to check the status of that message in their gateway up until that time expires. If you are requiring SSL for receiving Acknowledgements, the SSL Client type and profile need to be configured.

- The Inbound Security section is used to support ebXML security (signature validation) with ebMS messages.

- The Advanced Settings section of this screen is used to generate the Start parameter and to allow or disallow duplicate inbound documents from this partner. Figure 4-38 illustrates an example of an external profile ebMS Settings tab.

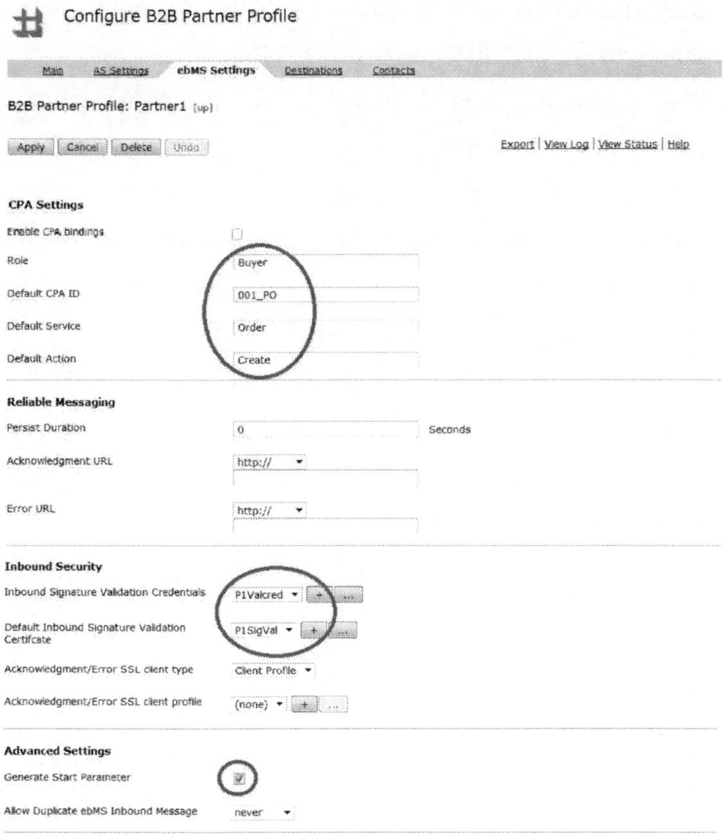

Figure 4-38 External Profile – ebMS Settings.

The destination in the external profile to support this pattern needs to be ebms2:// or ebms2s:// (uses SSL) destination. Any CPA settings in the destination will override the CPA Setting section in the ebMS Setting tab of the profile. This gives you the flexibility of using different CPAID, Services and Actions if the receiving partner wants to use those fields to trigger their downstream processes. To fully make use of multiple destinations you would also need a processing policy in the external profile to dynamically choose which destination to use for a particular situation.

- The Connection section holds the Destination URL provided by the partner, connection time out value, the username and password to be used for basic authentication if required by the partner.

- The Advanced ebMS Settings section holds all the CPA settings for this destination. If this section is configured, it will override the default settings that are done in the ebMS Setting tab for this profile. If you have configured these settings in the ebMS Settings tab you can leave them blank here.

- The ebMS Outbound Security section holds all of the encryption credentials for this partner destination.

- The ebMS Reliable Messaging section holds a lot of information on how build and route the ebMS message. We will not go into detail on each here as the information regarding the detail of each field can be found in Chapter 2.

Figure 4-39 illustrates an example ebMS V2.0 destination for this external partner.

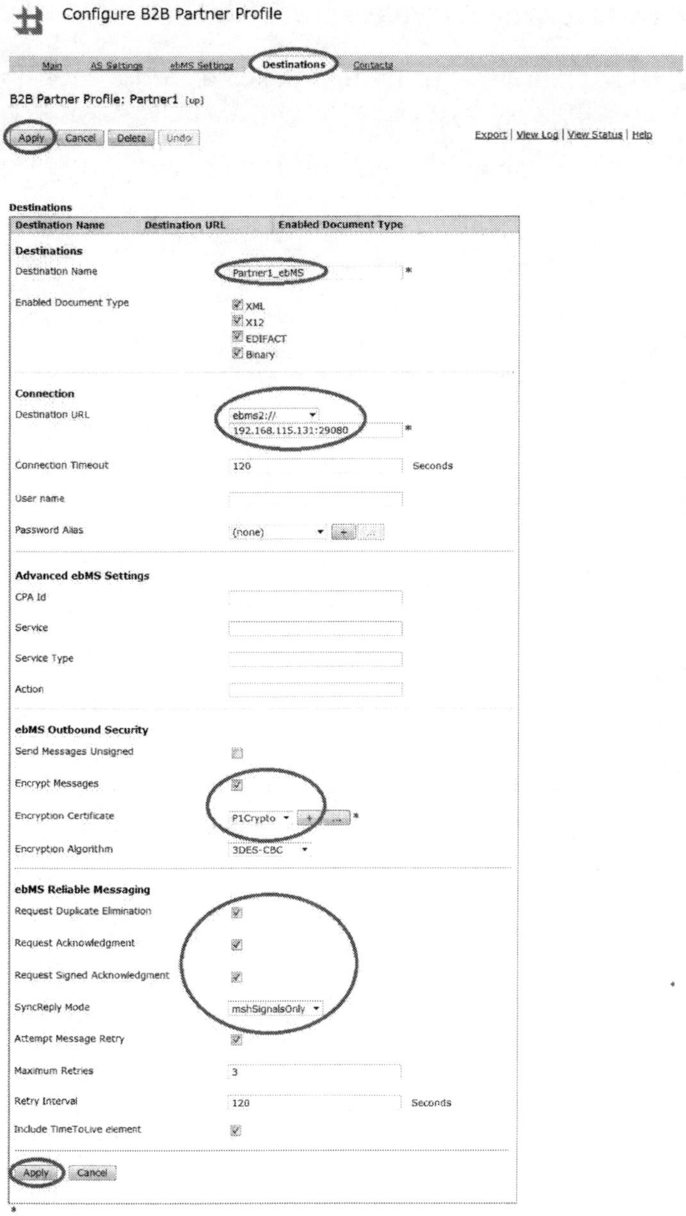

Figure 4-39 External Profile – ebMS Destination.

B2B Gateway Service – No CPA

The B2B Gateway for this pattern must not be CPA enabled. When the Gateway is created you can create it manually by clicking on the Add button as seen in Figure 4-40.

Figure 4-40 Create B2B Gateway – Add.

In the B2B Gateway Service you need an ebMS Front Side Handler to receive ebMS messages from ebXML trading partners. In the Main tab under the Document Routing section in the Front Side Protocol Handlers table, you can click on the plus (+) sign and select the ebMS Front Side Handler from the drop down. This handler is a very simple HTTP listener with logic built in to natively process ebMS messages and since we are not using SSL in this example you can simply set the Handler name, Local IP Address and Port number and take all the remaining defaults. After you complete the handler, you can the Apply button it in the table then click on the Add button to add it to the list of handlers in the B2B Gateway. Figure 4-41 illustrates an example of the ebMS Front Side Handler configuration in the Main tab.

Figure 4-41 B2B Gateway ebMS Front Side Protocol Handler.

We need to add another Front Side Handler to accept files from the back-side that need to be sent to partners over ebMS V2.0. For our example we used a MQ Poller Front Side

Handler to consume files from a MQ backside. This handler is not documented here as it is documented in Chapter 5. Since we are not using CPAs and are hard coding the values needed to support ebMS V2.0, we only need to pick up our files from the queue and do not need to set metadata. For this example we are using XML which makes it easy for the B2B Gateway to extract business IDs from the payload. In the Main tab, after you configure your Front side Handlers you need to add your Internal Profile and the External Profile created to support this ebMS pattern in the Active Partner Profiles table by selecting them from the drop down.

The Archive tab is a mandatory configuration object for the B2B Gateway. Configure it for Archiving and purging B2B transactions or set to Purge only.

Since we are using XML as the payload, the XML Formats tab needs to contain the XML format that we intend to send. In the XML Formats screen click on the + (plus) button in the XPath Routing Policies table to create an XML Format you can use the XPath Tool button to upload a sample XML file and automatically find the XPath just by selecting the element you want to use. Figure 4-42 illustrates an example of the configured an XML Format used for this pattern.

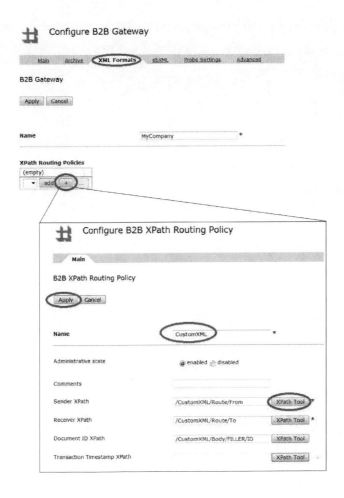

Figure 4-42 B2B Gateway - XML Formats.

After completing the XML Format Routing Policy click on the Apply button to save it and finally click on the Add button to include it in the table.

The ebXML tab in the B2B gateway must have no entries in it for this pattern to work. Figure 4-43 shows what an empty ebXML tab looks like.

Figure 4-43 B2B Gateway ebXML tab – No CPA.

NOTE—ebMS V2.0 Destination

Be sure the B2B Gateway external partner profile has the ebMS V2.0 destination as the default or set the profile in the B2B Gateway to explicitly point to the ebMS V2.0 destination.

When all required B2B Gateway tabs have been completed, click on the Apply button in the upper left of the B2B Gateway Configuration screen to save it. Also click on Save Configuration in the upper left of the console to save the Domain to the persisted configuration.

After properly configuring this pattern you can run files through the B2B Gateway and see the results in the B2B

Transaction Viewer. When you change the filter to show only ebMS transactions you will see all of the columns associated with ebMS transactions. Figure 4-44 illustrates an example of what an inbound ebMS transaction looks like in the B2B Transaction Viewer.

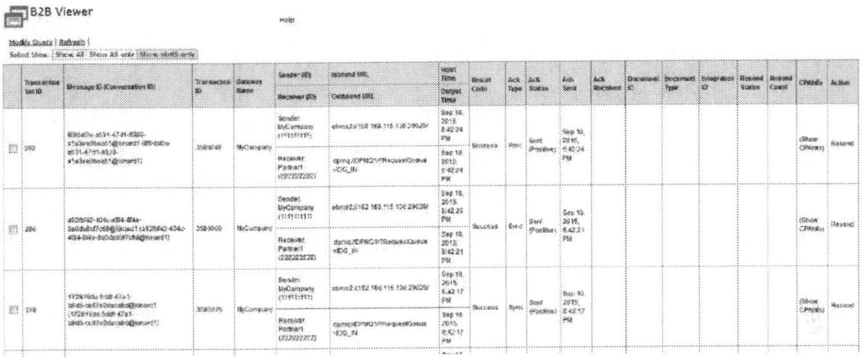

Figure 4-44 – B2B Viewer – ebMS Inbound.

Figure 4-45 illustrates an example of what an outbound ebMS transaction looks like in the B2B Viewer. Additionally, if you hover over the (show headers) entry in the B2B Viewer, you can see the CPA Values we hard coded in this example.

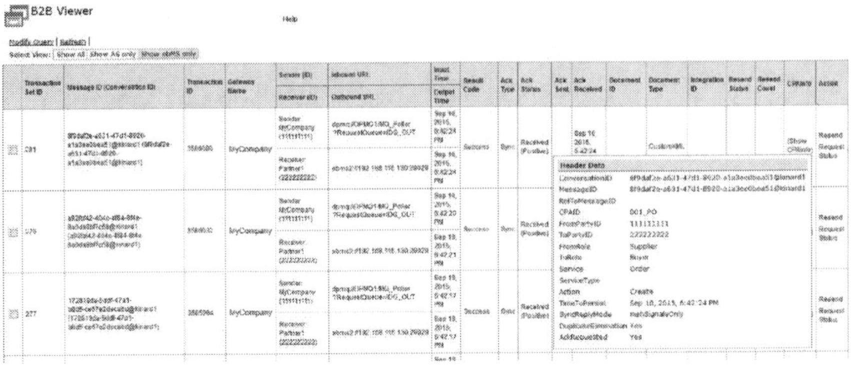

Figure 4-45 B2B Viewer – ebMS Outbound.

DataPower B2B ebMS with CPA Enabled Pattern

When you import one or more Collaboration Protocol Agreements (CPA) into the B2B Gateway that gateway becomes CPA enabled. This means all public partner information, connectivity information; collaboration definitions and security credentials reside in the CPA which is stored in the B2B Gateway. The business IDs, and some optional information in the ebMS Settings tab for each partner are still maintained in each profile to support the collaborations that exist in the B2B Gateway. When a B2B Gateway is CPA enabled it can no longer be used for non-CPA ebMS file transfers. Each ebMS transaction must be associated with a CPA that resides in the B2B Gateway. Figure 4-46 Illustrates an example of what a CPA enabled ebMS flow looks like through DataPower B2B.

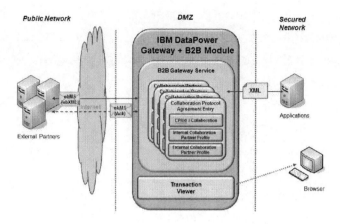

Figure 4-46 CPA Enabled ebMS Pattern.

DataPower only supports portions of the CPPA, Figure 4-47 illustrates the mapping between the CPP/CPA and DataPower B2B Objects.

	CPP/CPA defined features	DataPower B2B Configuration Mapping
Process Specification & Collaborations	The **agreement ID**, the **partner IDs**, the **Service** (for either trading business transaction docs or MSH-level signal such as Ack/Error/Ping...), the **Action**, and the Role of an organization in the context of a service.	• Internal Partner Profile • External Partner Profile • B2B CPA Entries for exchanging either business signal or MSH level signal
Delivery Channels	Defines message-receiving and message-sending characteristics per Service/Action. And enumerates params for transfer, security constraints (non-repudiation, etc.) and mechanism (SSL, encryption with S/MIME and XMLEncryption, and sign with XML-DSIG params), reliability protocols (such as message retry, and duplicate elimination)	• B2B CPA Collaboration(s) • B2B CPA Sender(s) • B2B CPA Receiver(s) • Crypto IdCred / ValCred(s) and Key/Cert(s)
Transport	Defines endpoint for invocation, and the Transport protocols (such as HTTP/SMTP) for the endpoint.	• FSH(s), and SSL Proxy Profile(s)
Other Non-supported	• Document package details in Delivery Channel (how Message Header and MIME parts are packaged, w/ or w/o security, for transmittal over the transport). • CPA doc props such as state and duration of the agreement, and QoS-like parameters	Not imported and not supported by DataPower B2B, if present the information will be ignored.

Figure 4-47 CPP/A Feature to DataPower B2B.

Like the simple ebMS pattern you need to have at minimum one internal partner profile, one external partner profile and a B2B Gateway. The DataPower profiles are used to support optional ebMS settings as well as allow control over whether a particular partner is allowed to do business with you based on business ID. The Internal partner profile needs to have a destination set that connects to the systems inside the trusted network where the payloads are expected arrive for use by downstream systems. CPAs do not contain any information about your internal connections. The CPP's in the CPA only determine what collaborations are allowed to be exchanged between you and external partners and how to secure those collaborations. However, where private keys are required to sign and/or decrypt data, the CPA will show a warning in the import wizard result indicating those certificates were not included and must be added manually.

A CPA enabled B2B Gateway is one that has at least one CPA entry in the ebXML tab. This is accomplished by importing a CPA into an existing B2B Gateway or by using the CPA to create a new Gateway. If the partner profile names represented in the CPA already exist in the DataPower domain and you don't check the box to overwrite existing objects in the import wizard, the CPA will simply use the existing profiles. However, if they do not exist or you choose to overwrite them, DataPower B2B Gateway will create them based on the party information inside the CPA. DataPower does not provide tools for creating the CPAs. These tools are available on the Internet from various sources or the CPAs can be created manually.

DataPower B2B has a CPA Import Wizard that can be triggered when creating a B2B Gateway, Figure 4-48 illustrates the steps the CPA Import Wizard follows.

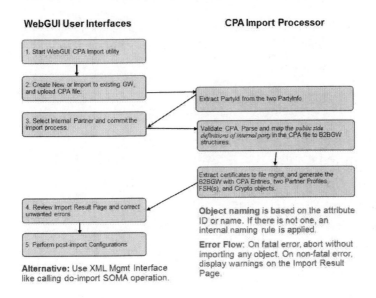

Figure 4-48 DataPower B2B CPA Import Wizard Flow.

To import CPAs into the B2B Gateway click on the B2B Gateway icon on the control panel or from the left navigation menu. In the Configure B2B Gateway screen click on Add from CPA as seen in Figure 4-49.

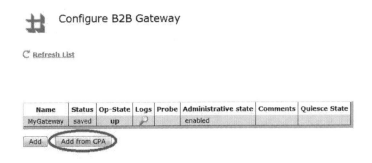

Figure 4-49 B2B Gateway - Add from CPA – Step 1.

If an existing B2B Gateway exists, the import wizard will give you the option of adding the CPA to the existing Gateway or allow the CPA to create a new B2B Gateway. The top half of Figure 4-50 illustrates what the import screen looks like when not checking the box to use an existing B2B Gateway and the bottom half illustrates what it looks like when using an existing B2B Gateway.

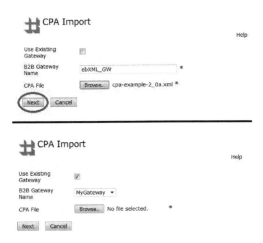

Figure 4-50 CPA Import – Step 2.

After clicking on the Next button you are presented with some options to determine who the internal party is (the CPA has two parties, this step asks which one represents you). Some additional check boxes are available to allow specific object naming and allow overwriting of existing configuration information. Figure 4-51 illustrates an example of this step in the CPA import process.

Figure 4-51 CPA Import – Step 3.

After completing this step, click on the Import button to import the CPA. This will show you the import result and list any errors that need to be addressed in the configuration (scroll down to see all of the results) as seen in Figure 4-52.

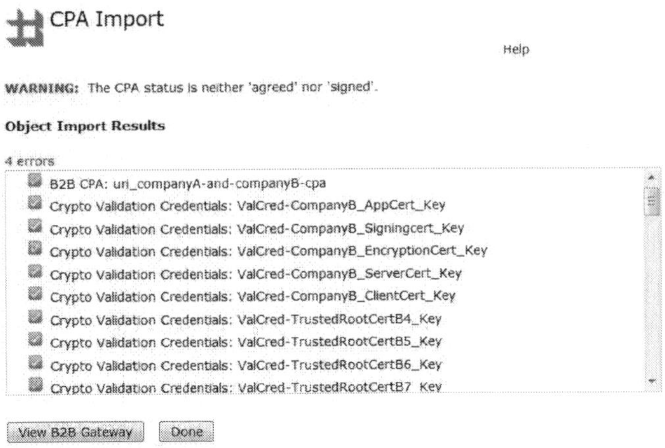

Figure 4-52 CPA Import – Result – Step 4.

Step 5 of the CPA Import process requires some manual configuration as follows:

- Since the import is the public side of the configuration (that is, the external side), you will need to configure the Front Side Handler for accepting message from the back-end systems and need to configure the destinations of internal partners to send message to the back-end systems.

- Since CPAs cannot contain crypto materials of private keys, you need to make sure that the generated Crypto ValCred/IdCred objects are operational by attaching the keys appropriately. This is done by editing the B2B Gateway's ebXML Service in the ebXML tab as seen in Figure 4-53. Follow the red errored objects in the services until you get to where the certificates are needed; upload the certificates and apply each nested object to resolve the error.

Figure 4-53 CPA Enabled B2B Gateway – ebXML tab.

When you have fully configured the B2B Gateway with the appropriate Front Side Handlers to connect to the back-end and have edited your ebXML Services to load the key objects needed for signing and encryption, click Apply in the upper left corner of the Configure B2B Gateway screen. Be sure to also click Save Configuration in the upper right of the console.

Since a majority of the information needed to support an ebXML collaboration between you and your partners is held in the CPAs that are associated with the B2B Gateway, there is not much to be done in the Partner Profile itself to make this pattern work with the exception of adding a destination in the internal partner to point to the back-end where you want the ebXML payloads to be delivered.

If your partner has also imported the same CPA and selected themselves as the internal party you should be able to receive inbound ebMS transactions from them and based on the CPAID, Service and Action, use the appropriate collaboration to pass the payloads to your backend. Your partner should also be able to consume and process ebMS V2.0 messages from you.

Outbound flows, however, must build the ebMS V2.0 message and as a result we need to provide the required information to the ebMS Message Handler (CPA Enabled B2B Gateway). You need to supply the B2B Gateway with the Sender ID, Receiver ID, CPAID, Service and Action so the correct partner profiles and collaborations can be found. This information is typically set in MQ headers, HTTP headers, in the file or using a separate meta-file, etc. by a downstream system before sending the file into DataPower B2B. DataPower must use the routing preprocessor in the B2B Gateway or information in the file to extract the sender and receiver IDs, then a processing policy can be used to extract the CPAID, Service and Action and set the appropriate variables in DataPower to instruct the ebMS Message Handler to use the appropriate collaboration to package and send the outbound file. If these variables are not set, the ebMS Message Handler will use the first CPAID it finds that matches the two parties.

As an alternative to using the binary routing XSL or programmatically sending the information needed to find the CPA to use, you have the option to set the default of which Collaboration to use in the ebMS Settings tab of the External Partner Profile. This feature also allows you to use CPA Bindings by checking the box in the ebMS Settings tab of the External Partner Profile and assigning different Internal

Partner Profiles to define which CPAID, Service and Action to bind to. This simplifies the outbound process by not requiring the ebXML metadata to be passed to the ebMS Message Handler from the back-side and also minimizes the need to use XSLT or GatewayScript to find the appropriate collaboration for outbound flows.

To use CPA Bindings you need to edit the ebMS Settings tab in the External Partner Profile and check the CPA Bindings box. Click the Add button to create a CPA binding entry in the table. You will need to specify an Internal Partner Profile to bind the CPAID, Service and Action. After you complete the configuration, click the Apply button to save the binding entry. You can have as many CPA bindings as you like. Figure 4-54 illustrates an example CPA Binding configuration for an External Profile.

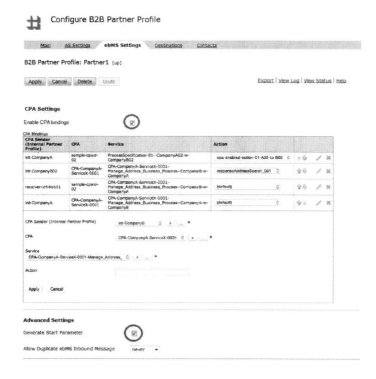

Figure 4-54 – CPA Bindings.

The ebMS Message Handler identifies the CPA sender action with CPA related information in the following order:

1. Process Policy in partner profile: Values set in var://service/b2b-ebms-cpa-id, var://service/b2b-ebms-service, and var://service/b2b-ebmsaction.

2. CPA bindings in partner profile.

3. Default CPA information in partner profile: Default CPA ID, Default Service, Default Action set in ebMS Settings tab.

4.   CPA entries in B2B gateway: First match in the CPA entries.

This means if number 1 is provided, numbers 2 through 4 are ignored, if not then it will look to see if number 2 is enabled and so on. If all options are configured it will use number 1.

NOTE—CPA Bindings in External Partner Profiles

CPA bindings in external partner profiles only apply to ebMS outbound messages and the CPA entry has to be defined in the ebXML settings of the associated B2B Gateway before it can be added to the CPA bindings list.

Transactions in the B2B viewer for this pattern look no different than those in the simple ebMS pattern. For this reason, we are not displaying the viewer for this flow.

Summary

This chapter provided you with a detailed overview of how B2B messaging is used and configured in the DataPower B2B Module. It specifically covers the AS1, AS2, AS3 EDIINT specifications and the ebMS V2.0 specification.

Chapter 5 DataPower B2B File Transfer Patterns

This chapter presents a detailed description of File Transfer patterns that are commonly used with DataPower and the B2B Module. It also shows examples of how each object is configured. Many of the patterns in this chapter do not require the B2B Module; they can also be completed using the Integration Module. This chapter assumes the reader is already familiar with the concepts and configuration of the B2B Gateway Service and the B2B Partner Profiles.

DataPower File Transfer

A common question we often get asked is, "I know DataPower can be used for file transfer, but what about Managed File Transfer?" To answer that question let's first take a look at the definition of Managed File Transfer (MFT). The most common definition amongst most vendors is represented well by Gartner Group at http://www.gartner.com/it-glossary/managed-file-transfer-mft and is as follows:

"Managed file transfer (MFT) is a technology that provides the secure transfer of data in an efficient and a reliable manner. Unlike traditional file transfer tools, such as FTP and scripting, MFT core functionalities include the ability to secure files in transit and at rest, and reporting and auditing of file activity. What also differentiates MFT from other forms of infrastructure and integration technologies is its unique focus on managing the transfer of large file sizes and volume. "

DataPower is first and foremost a security gateway and is used to secure access to systems of record by some of the most security conscious organizations in the world; organizations like financial institutions, government organizations and healthcare organizations. It also provides superior transaction volumes for files of all sizes, provides robust monitoring of file activity and assures delivery of files. These are areas of strength for DataPower and are the most important part of a file transfer. Another area of strength is related to governance and control of a file transfer through the use of policies to define rules that govern how data is transported and/or enriched; this most commonly manifests itself in the form of partner profiles or policies.

For extremely large files, DataPower can use the checkpoint restart feature of FTP when used in Virtual Persistent mode. However, using a Multi-channel Protocol Gateway in streaming mode is a better practice which allows you to take advantage of the checkpoint capabilities of the downstream system which can be FTP, SFTP, MQ MFT or even Sterling File Gateway.

Based on the above definition, you can see that DataPower does support Managed File Transfer. IBM also has other MFT solutions, and each has unique capabilities that when used in conjunction with DataPower provide a much more robust and secure MFT architecture for both internal and external file transfers. For instance, DataPower does not have mail-boxing capabilities, but Sterling does. Using DataPower in the DMZ to front-end Sterling File Gateway in the trusted zone gives you the best of both worlds for file transfer and at the same time you get the additional capabilities offered by DataPower's Multi-channel Gateway, securing other channels like APIs, Mobile, SOA, Web and Cloud. Additionally, when DataPower B2B is used in conjunction with MQ MFT you can assure delivery of the files to the final destination. This will also provide partner's with end-to-end visibility of the state of their file transfer.

DataPower is a multi-channel gateway that can be configured to support a wide variety of file transfer patterns. It supports the most widely used standards-based file transfer protocols as well as IBM's MQ messaging protocol; each can be used for file transfer using partner profiles and the B2B Gateway Service or in the Multi-Protocol Gateway Service for pass-thru B2B data flows.

When using a B2B Gateway Service, the file transfer is fully managed by using profile management, auditing and data security to assure delivery of files between you and your trading partners. The B2B Gateway Module adds popular B2B Messaging protocols like EDIINT AS1, AS2 and AS3 as well as ebMS v2.0 to the list of supported file transfer protocols. The B2B Gateway Service does not stream data and has an upper file size limit of about 2.5 gigabytes when using the latest IDG hardware model at the time of writing this book. When using the IDG Virtual Edition, file size limits are determined by the amount of memory available to the virtual environment.

When using a Multi-Protocol Gateway Service, file transfer is the more traditional fire and forget method. However, it can be managed if the processing policy is used to non-repudiate, audit and secure the payloads. For the purpose of this book we are only using the Multi-Protocol Gateway Service for transferring extremely large files, where streaming can be used. This will allow the transfer of files of unlimited size. We also use the Multi-Protocol Gateway Service as a pre-process to a B2B Gateway Service.

The most common file transfer patterns used with the DataPower B2B Module are described below. Additionally, this section provides screen shots of the objects needed to successfully configure each pattern.

NOTE—DataPower and WTX

All of these patterns can include any-to-any message transformation utilizing the embedded WebSphere Transformation Extender (WTX) runtime which is included in DataPower as part of the Integration or B2B Modules. File definition, called Type Trees and DataPower compiled maps can be created with the WTX Design Studio tool, which is sold separately by IBM. DataPower also includes a well-documented WTX integrated test environment which allows you to create maps and test them on DataPower from within WTX Design Studio.

NOTE—FTP Rename and Delete Access

Some partners refuse to give Rename and Delete access to your user directory on their SFTP server. In this case you cannot use a SFTP Poller Front-side Protocol Handler to retrieve the files. One work around is to use a SFTP client script or a custom developed application to GET the file and then send it into DataPower over a SFTP Server Front-Side Handler or HTTP. This essentially is a custom protocol bridge. Even when using this solution the issue still remains that you cannot delete the file upon a successful transfer and as such it will be picked up every polling cycle. This can be fixed programmatically by tracking each file and omitting them from being picked up a second time.

NOTE—AAA Policy Placement

Unlike a B2B Gateway, when using a Multi-Protocol Gateway the AAA Policy can be put into the Processing policy before the transform action instead of adding it to the Front-Side Protocol Handler. It will work in either one of the two places.

FTP(S) Patterns

The FTP pattern is the most common file transfer pattern in use by DataPower customers and typically represents the starting point for file exchange between two companies. Although FTP usage is still common, we are seeing a trend where companies use it to support legacy connections while at the same time trying to move their partners away from FTP onto a more reliable method of MFT like AS1, AS2, AS3 or ebMS v2.0. In some cases a proprietary file transfer solution like IBM MQ Managed File Transfer, Sterling Connect Enterprise or IBM Aspera may be used. Our example patterns are not using FTP over SSL; however this is an option if you chose to secure the connection.

NOTE—FTPS vs SFTP

FTPS is FTP over SSL and is sometimes confused with SFTP which is FTP over SSH. SFTP is covered later in this chapter.

Figure 5-1 shows five FTP patterns. They include FTP flows used in both the B2B Gateway Service and the Multi-Protocol Gateway Service. Each of these patterns is described in detail in the following sections.

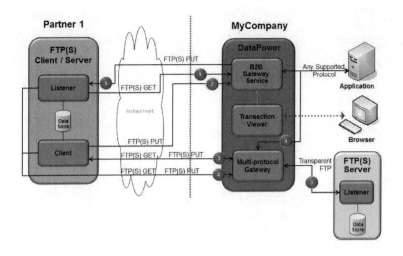

Figure 5-1 FTP(S) DataPower Patterns.

1. Inbound GET from an external FTP Server using a B2B Gateway Service

This pattern requires the B2B Module and is commonly used by customers who want to retrieve files from a partner's FTP server. DataPower uses a FTP poller front-side handler on a configurable polling frequency to retrieve the files. The files are routed to an internal partner destination configured in the internal profile defined by the business ID in the B2B payload or the ID set using the Document Routing Pre-processor in the B2B Gateway Service Advanced tab.

The file location where files are picked up from must be accessible by DataPower with full Read/Write/Delete access rights. DataPower locks the file by changing its name during pick-up. This prevents other DataPower nodes from picking up the same file at the same time.

A FTP Poller Front-side protocol handler can be added to a B2B gateway by creating it in the Document Routing section in the Main tab as seen in Figure 5-2.

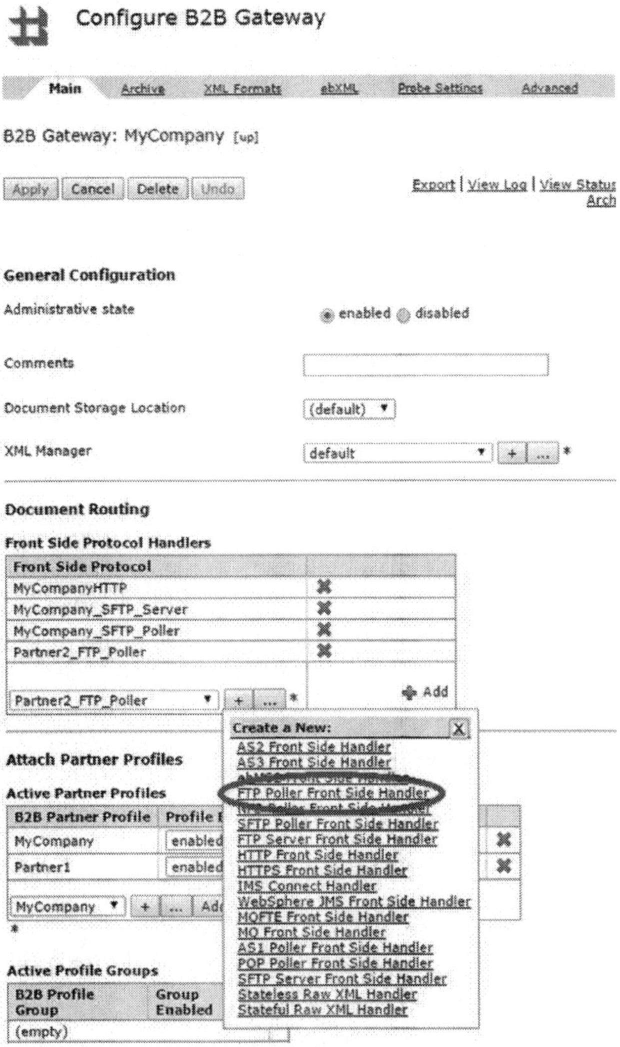

Figure 5-2 Add FTP Poller – B2B Gateway.

The FTP Poller configuration screen in our example as seen in Figure 5-3 has many settings not shown (hidden due to answers checked in those specific fields) that allow you to define patterns for identifying how to rename files after retrieval and how to treat errors if they should happen. To keep it simple we checked the Delete Input File on Success and Delete file on processing error. We are not generating a result file, so by doing this the GUI automatically hides unnecessary fields.

The Target directory is a full FTP path setting where we will poll for files of any type every 5 seconds. This field could contain the connection credentials in the URL string as well, but they are in the clear and may represent a security concern. So, for security purposes, we are letting the XML Manager pass credentials to the FTP server securely. You can create the XML Manager for housing the FTP credentials by clicking on the + (plus) sign to the right of the XML Manager field as seen in Figure 5-3.

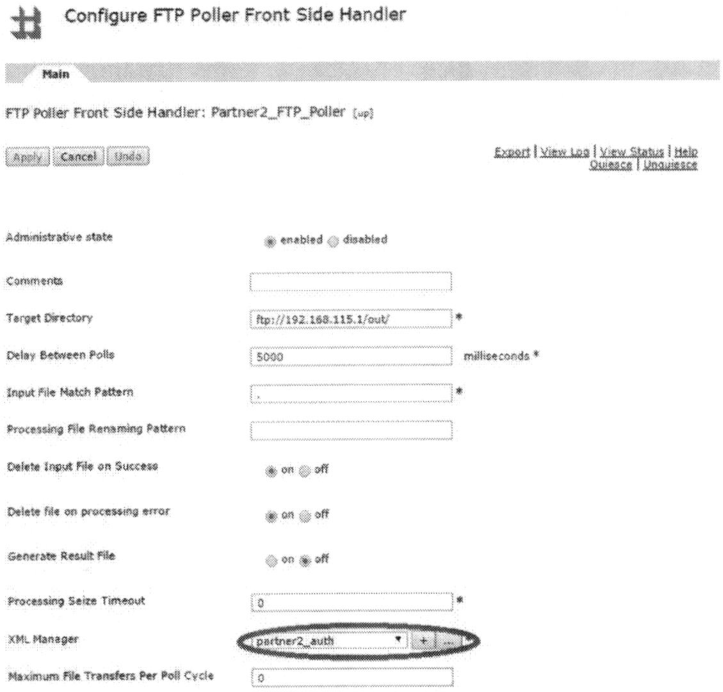

Configure FTP Poller Front Side Handler

Main

FTP Poller Front Side Handler: Partner2_FTP_Poller [up]

Apply Cancel Undo

Export | View Log | View Status | Help
Quiesce | Unquiesce

Administrative state	● enabled ○ disabled
Comments	
Target Directory	ftp://192.168.115.1/out/ *
Delay Between Polls	5000 milliseconds *
Input File Match Pattern	. *
Processing File Renaming Pattern	
Delete Input File on Success	● on ○ off
Delete file on processing error	● on ○ off
Generate Result File	○ on ● off
Processing Seize Timeout	0 *
XML Manager	partner2_auth ▼ + ...
Maximum File Transfers Per Poll Cycle	0

Figure 5-3 Configure FTP Poller – B2B Gateway.

The XML Manager houses many configuration objects to allow granularity when creating and managing a service. We are only going to use the User Agent in the Main tab to set the FTP login credentials for accessing Partner2's FTP server. As seen in Figure 5-4 the User Agent Configuration can be created by clicking on the plus sign to the right of the field in the Configure XML Manager Main tab.

Figure 5-4 Configure XML Manager – User Agent.

Like the XML Manager, the Partner2 User Agent we created has many additional configuration tabs. We are going to only use the tabs related to allowing access to Partner2's FTP server. In Figure 5-5 you can see we created a Basic-Auth Policy that holds the FTP user credentials for the partner's FTP server. If we were doing FTP over SSL we could also create a SSL Proxy Profile policy to hold the SSL credentials and certificates by clicking on and configuring the tab.

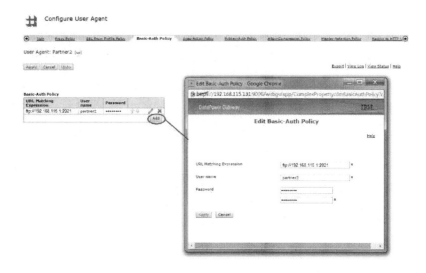

Figure 5-5 Configure User Agent – Basic Auth Policy.

The last step in configuring the User Agent requires us to slide all the way over to the right of the tabs until we reach the FTP Client Policies tab; in that tab we created a FTP Client Policy for all connections using this agent to match on everything and use unique file names as seen in Figure 5-6.

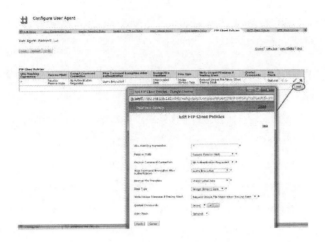

Figure 5-6 User Agent Config – FTP Client Policies.

After applying the changes to the User Agent, XML Manager and FTP Poller, be sure to click on the Add button in the Document Routing section of the B2B Gateway Service Main tab to add the handler to the list.

NOTE—Backside Protocol

The back-side (or destination) does not have to be FTP. It can be any protocol that DataPower supports; DataPower natively bridges between transport protocols. If the file being sent into the B2B Gateway is not able to be parsed by the service, it is considered BINARY. To identify binary data we use a routing pre-processor in the B2B Gateway Advanced tab to identify the sender and receiver IDs to be used for routing the file. Listing 5-1 is an example of a Routing Pre-Processor that uses the filename of the file to identify partners.

Listing 5-1 Document Routing Pre-processor Stylesheet

```
<?xml version="1.0" encoding="UTF-8"?>
<!-- DataPower B2B Document Routing Preprocessor Stylesheet
Licensed Materials - Property of IBM
IBM WebSphere DataPower Appliances
Copyright IBM Corporation 2008,2009. All Rights Reserved.
US Government Users Restricted Rights - Use, duplication or
disclosure
restricted by GSA ADP Schedule Contract with IBM Corp.
-->
<xsl:stylesheet version="1.0"
    xmlns:xsl="http://www.w3.org/1999/XSL/Transform"
    xmlns:dp="http://www.datapower.com/extensions"
    xmlns:str="http://exslt.org/strings"
    extension-element-prefixes="dp">
    <xsl:template match="/">
    <!-- Gather whatever info seems useful here. For instance:-->
```

```
<xsl:variable name="content-type"
    select="dp:variable('var://service/content-type')"/>
<xsl:variable name="protocol"
    select="dp:variable('var://service/protocol')"/>
<xsl:variable name="path"
    select="dp:variable('var://service/URL-in')"/>
<!-- Set the sending and receiving partner ids based on the
filename -->
<xsl:message>protocol = <xsl:value-of select="$protocol" />
</xsl:message>
<xsl:message>path = <xsl:value-of select="$path" />
</xsl:message>
<xsl:variable name="filename" select="substring-after($path,
'%2F/' )" />
<xsl:message>Filename = <xsl:value-of select="$filename" />
</xsl:message>
<xsl:variable name="tok-filename"
select="str:tokenize($filename, '.')"/>
<xsl:message>Tokenized Filename = <xsl:value-of select="$tok-
filename" /> </xsl:message>
<dp:set-variable name="'var://service/b2b-partner-from'"
                        value="$tok_filename[1]"/>
<dp:set-variable name="'var://service/b2b-partner-to'"
                        value="$tok_filename[2]"/>
<xsl:choose>
    <xsl:otherwise>
        <!-- By default, do nothing. This will autodetect the
        message type, but binary messages will fail for lack
        of partner IDs. -->
    </xsl:otherwise>
</xsl:choose>
    </xsl:template>
</xsl:stylesheet>
```

NOTE—Preserving the Original Filename

With this pattern, many customers wish to preserve the original filename of the picked up file. This can be done by adding a processing policy in an internal partner profile that captures the front-side filename and passes it to the back-side. There are many ways you can do this using XSL. Listing 5-2 shows an example XSL that captures the front-side filename, when FTP is used, and sets the FTP URI path which will override the URI in the destination being used.

Listing 5-2 Preserve Original Filename

```
<?xml version="1.0" encoding="utf-8"?>
 <xsl:stylesheet version="1.0"
   xmlns:xsl="http://www.w3.org/1999/XSL/Transform"
   xmlns:dp="http://www.datapower.com/extensions"
   xmlns:func="http://exslt.org/functions"
   xmlns:dpfunc="http://www.datapower.com/extensions/functions"
   xmlns:dpconfig="http://www.datapower.com/param/config"
   xmlns:str="http://exslt.org/strings"
   extension-element-prefixes="dp func dpfunc dpconfig"
   exclude-result-prefixes="dp func dpfunc dpconfig">
   <xsl:template match="/">
 <!--
This stylesheet is used to preserve (propagate) the URI, which
includes the filename,

from an inbound FTP/SFTP transaction when used with the B2B Gateway.
Additionally if

an underscore is found, it will be translated to a '/' to allow for
the selection of a

subdirectory. The URI contains the filename and is extracted from the
routing-url service variable.
```

```
The outbound (destination) protocol(ftp|sftp), userid/password,
hostname and IP address is

configured in the destination tab in the partner profile. If there is
a need to select a different

destination besides the default destination, the stylesheet can be
modified to select an alternatedestination. The B2B Gateway does not
provide access to the contents of the destination URL nor does it
provide a mechanism to change the routing of the destination
protocol/user/password/host/port. -->


<!-- Grab the incoming URL -->
    <xsl:variable name="InboundURI"
select="dp:variable('var://service/routing-url')"/>


<!-- Check to see if there is a %2F (FTP) and set the OutboundURI
variable to the URI portion of the URI -->
    <xsl:variable name="OutboundURI">

     <xsl:if test="contains($InboundURI,'/%2F/')">

        <xsl:copy-of select="substring-after($InboundURI,'/%2F/')"
/>   <!-- FTP Style URL -->

     </xsl:if>

     <xsl:if test="not(contains($InboundURI,'/%2F/'))">

         <xsl:copy-of select="substring-after($InboundURI,'/')"/>
<!-- SFTP Style URL -->

     </xsl:if>

   </xsl:variable>


   <!-- The filename syntax is senderid.receiverid.directory_filename

        so the first two elements are used by the B2B GW so we'll
strip

        them off-->
   <xsl:variable name="URIFolder">

        <xsl:variable name="tok-filename"
select="str:tokenize($OutboundURI, '.')"/>

        <xsl:copy-of select="$tok-filename[3]" />

        </xsl:variable>

   <xsl:message>Tokenized: <xsl:value-of select="$URIFolder" />
</xsl:message>
```

```
<!-- Change the underscore to a / to denote directory -->

   <xsl:variable name="URIFolderName"> <xsl:copy-of
select="translate($URIFolder,'_','/')" /> </xsl:variable>

   <xsl:message>Translated: <xsl:value-of select="$URIFolderName" />
</xsl:message>


   <!-- Set the URI service variable -->

   <dp:set-variable name="'var://service/URI'"
value="$URIFolderName"/>

  </xsl:template>
</xsl:stylesheet>
```

To complete the B2B Gateway Service you also need to have at minimum one internal and one external partner profile associated with it and the Archive tab would need to be configured. If you are sending Binary files, you will also need to create a Routing Pre-Processor in the Advanced tab.

When you connect to the partner's FTP Server and pull files into this service, the files will be routed to the internal profile's destination, which is typically an internal system or application.

Figure 5-7 illustrates an example of the flow as seen in the B2B Transaction Viewer where the receiving partner is MyCompany.

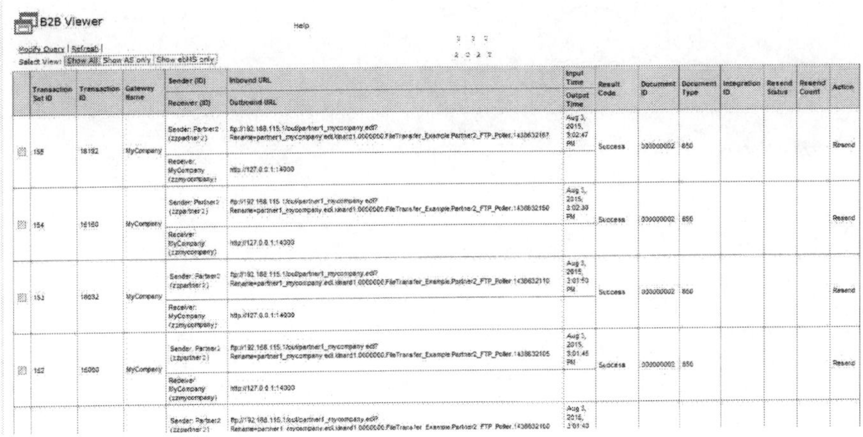

Figure 5-7 B2B Transaction Viewer – Inbound FTP Get.

2. Inbound FTP(S) PUT to a B2B Gateway Service

This pattern requires the B2B Gateway Module and is commonly used by customers who want to allow partners to put files onto the Gateway, which will then be routed to an internal partner destination configured in the internal profile defined by the business ID in the B2B payload or the ID set using the routing pre-processor in the B2B Gateway Service Advanced tab.

This pattern is configured in a B2B Gateway Service. A FTP Server Front-side protocol handler can be added to a B2B Gateway by creating it in the Document Routing section in the Main tab as seen in Figure 5-8.

Configure B2B Gateway

| Main | Archive | XML Formats | ebXML | Probe Settings | Advanced |

B2B Gateway: MyCompany [up]

Apply Cancel Delete Undo

Export | View Log | View Status | Show Probe | Validate Conformance | Help
Archive/purge transactions | Quiesce | Unquiesce

General Configuration

Administrative state   ⦿ enabled ⦾ disabled

Comments

Document Storage Location   (default) ▾

XML Manager   default ▾ + ... *

Document Routing

Front Side Protocol Handlers

Front Side Protocol	
MyCompanyHTTP	✖
MyCompany_SFTP_Server	✖
MyCompany_SFTP_Poller	✖
Partner2_FTP_Poller	✖

(none) ▾ + ... *   ✛ Add

Create a New: ✖
AS2 Front Side Handler
AS3 Front Side Handler
ebMS2 Front Side Handler
FTP Poller Front Side Handler
NFS Poller Front Side Handler
FTP Server Front Side Handler
HTTP Front Side Handler
HTTPS Front Side Handler
IMS Connect Handler
WebSphere JMS Front Side Handler
MQFTE Front Side Handler
MQ Front Side Handler
AS1 Poller Front Side Handler
POP Poller Front Side Handler
SFTP Server Front Side Handler
Stateless Raw XML Handler
Stateful Raw XML Handler

Attach Partner Profiles

Active Partner Profiles

B2B Partner Profile	Profile I		
MyCompany	enable		✖
Partner1	enabled		✖

MyCompany ▾ + ... Ad

Active Profile Groups

B2B Profile Group	Group Enabled
(empty)	

▾ + ... Add

Figure 5-8 Add FTP Server – B2B Gateway.

The Configure FTP Server Front Side Handler screen as seen in Figure 5-9 has two tabs. We are only concerned about the mandatory fields in the Main tab. You must configure the Local IP Address and Port Number fields; this is the address and port you want DataPower to listen on. The file system type is defaulted to Virtual Ephemeral. Virtual Persistent can also be used; Transparent should not be used since a file list cannot be passed from the back-side. We also need to create a Password AAA Policy and Allow Unique Filenames.

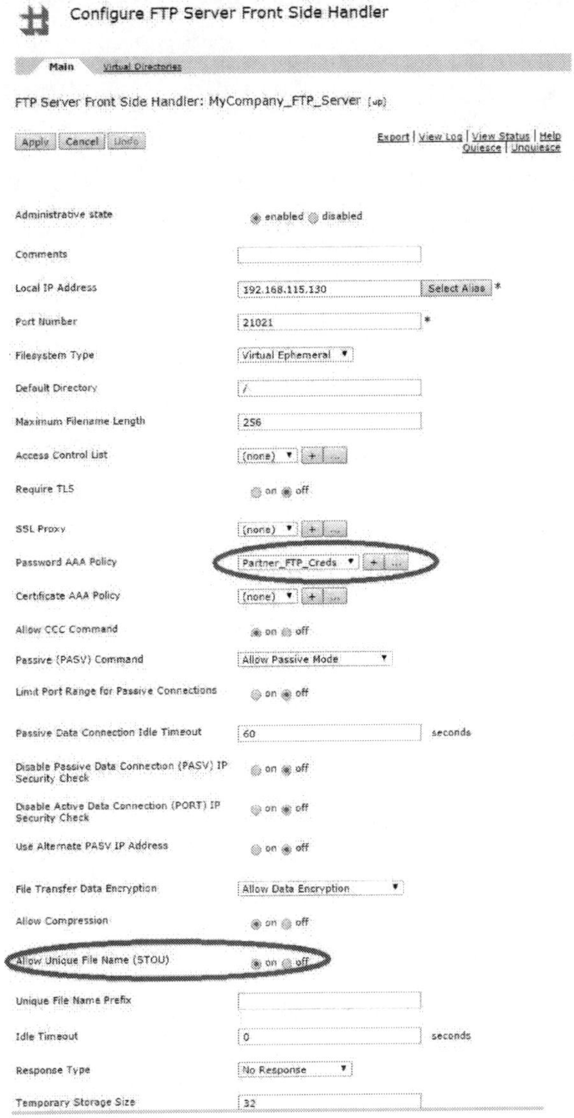

Figure 5-9 Configure FTP Server Front Side Handler.

The Password AAA Policy has many tabs with many configuration objects to provide maximum granularity and flexibility. For our example, the policy is only used to validate the username and password credentials that are received from the trading partners; this can be created by clicking on the plus sign to the right of the AAA Policy field. In the Configure AAA Policy screen we only need to configure the Identity extraction, Authentication and Resource extraction tabs as seen in Figure 5-10. In the Identity extraction screen we selected Processing metadata and in the Processing metadata items drop down field we selected ftp-username-metadata.

Figure 5-10 Configure AAA Policy – Identity extraction.

In the Authentication tab we are using an on-board AAA information file as the userid/password registry for this example you can use any authentication method in the drop down list as seen in Figure 5-11. The on-board AAA file is OK for development purposes, but for production you will likely have a more robust registry, such as IBM Security Identity and Access Manager or some other access management solution. The content of the DataPower AAA information file is shown in Listing 5-3.

Listing 5-3 DataPower AAA Info file example

```
<?xml version="1.0" encoding="UTF-8"?>
<AAAInfo xmlns="http://www.datapower.com/AAAInfo">
  <FormatVersion>1</FormatVersion>
  <Authenticate>
    <Username>partner2</Username>
    <Password>partner2</Password>
    <OutputCredential>partner2</OutputCredential>
  </Authenticate>
  <Authenticate>
    <Username>partner3</Username>
    <Password>partner3</Password>
    <OutputCredential>partner3</OutputCredential>
  </Authenticate>
</AAAInfo>
```

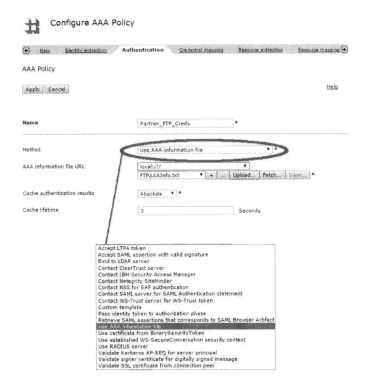

Figure 5-11 Configure AAA Policy – Authentication.

The final tab we configured is the Resource extraction tab where we selected processing metadata and set the metadata items to ftp-username-metadata as seen in Figure 5-12.

Figure 5-12 Configure AAA Policy – Resource extraction.

After applying the changes to the Password AAA Policy and the FTP Server Front-side Handler, be sure to click on the Add button in the Document Routing section of the B2B Gateway Service Main tab to add the handler to the list.

To complete the B2B Gateway Service you also need to have at minimum one internal and one external partner profile associated with it. The Archive tab would need to be configured. If sending Binary files you will need to create a Routing Pre-Processor in the Advanced tab.

When the partners send files into this service, the files will be routed to the internal profile's destination which is typically an internal system or application.

Figure 5-13 illustrates an example of the flow as seen in the B2B Transaction Viewer where the receiving partner is MyCompany.

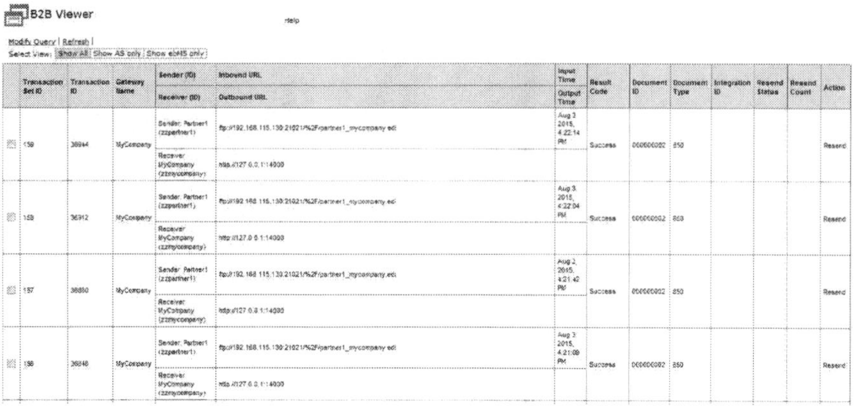

Figure 5-13 B2B Transaction Viewer – Inbound FTP PUT.

3. Transparent FTP(S) PUT/GET with your FTP(S) Server through a Multi-Protocol Gateway Service

This pattern does not require the B2B Module; it can also be accomplished using the Integration Module. This pattern is commonly used by customers who want to allow partners to put files to or get files from their FTP Server sitting inside the protected network. This is typically done when you need to stream extremely large files that are larger than a B2B Gateway Service can handle or when you simply want to proxy FTP connections to your internal FTP servers.

DataPower works well as a transparent proxy to FTP when all you need to do is browse directories and PUT and GET files. If you are using FTP in a fashion where your partners do a lot of renaming of files or making and deleting directories while logged on to your FTP server, then a DataPower transparent proxy cannot be used. When using transparent mode the following FTP commands are supported:

CDUP, CWD, DELE, EPRT, EPSV, FEAT, GET, LIST, MODE, NLST, NOOP, P@SW, PASS, PASV, PORT, PROT, PUT, PWD, QUIT, RETR, STAT, STOR, STOU, STRU, TYPE, USER, XCUP, XCWD, XPWD

This pattern is configured in a Multi-Protocol Gateway Service which can be created by clicking on the Add button in the Multi-Protocol Gateway list view.

The Multi-Protocol Gateway Configuration screen as seen in Figure 5-14 has many tabs and configuration objects. For this example we only need to configure the General tab and add a processing policy.

Figure 5-14 Configure Multi-Protocol Gateway.

We need to set the Type to dynamic-back-ends since we want to use processing policy to propagate the username and password from the front-side of the service to the back-side FTP server. To do this we use a processing policy which is shown in Figure 5-15 and 5-16.

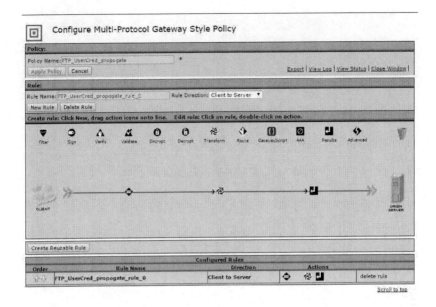

Figure 5-15 Configure Processing Policy.

The transform action being used is executing a small XSL script that captures the username and password from the front-side login and passes them to the back-side by setting the back-side FTP URL. We set the IP Address of the internal FTP Server in a custom parameter in the Advanced tab. An example of the transform action is shown in Figure 5-16.

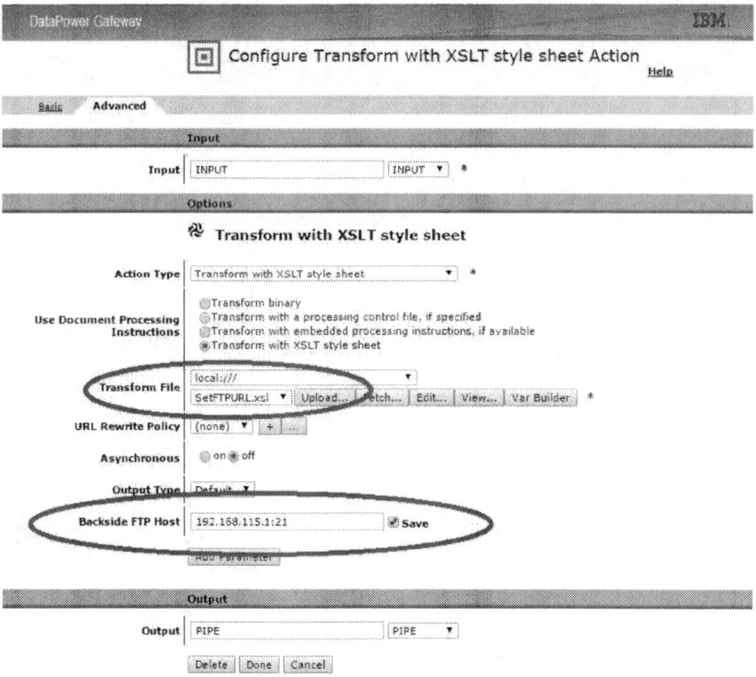

Figure 5-16 – Configure Transform Action.

The content of the example XSL file that passes the user credentials to the back-side is provided in Listing 5-4.

Listing 5-4 Copy front side credentials to back side connection.

```
<?xml version="1.0" encoding="utf-8"?>
 <xsl:stylesheet version="1.0"
  xmlns:xsl="http://www.w3.org/1999/XSL/Transform"
  xmlns:dp="http://www.datapower.com/extensions"
  xmlns:func="http://exslt.org/functions"
  xmlns:dpfunc="http://www.datapower.com/extensions/functions"
  xmlns:dpconfig="http://www.datapower.com/param/config"
```

```
extension-element-prefixes="dp func dpfunc dpconfig"

exclude-result-prefixes="dp func dpfunc dpconfig">


<xsl:param name="dpconfig:backsideFTPHost"
select="'ftp.server.com'"/>

<dp:param name="dpconfig:backsideFTPHost" type="dmString" xmlns="">

  <display>Backside FTP Host</display>

  <default>ftp.server.com</default>

  <description>Backside FTP Host</description>

</dp:param>


<xsl:template match="/">
  <!-- grab the username and password sent by the FTP client to
build the backend FTP URL using them. We encode the username and
password to accommodate for any special characters that may be used
in each -->
  <xsl:variable name="URI"
select="dp:variable('var://service/URI')"/>

  <xsl:variable name="username" select="dp:auth-info('basic-auth-
name')" />

  <xsl:variable name="password" select="dp:auth-info('basic-auth-
password')" />

  <xsl:variable name="encodedusername"
select="dp:encode($username,'url')" />

  <xsl:variable name="encodedpassword"
select="dp:encode($password,'url')" />


  <!-- build the backside URL -->

  <xsl:variable name="URL-out"
select="concat('ftp://',$encodedusername,':',$encodedpassword,'@',$dp
config:backsideFTPHost,$URI)" />


  <!-- set backside FTP URL -->

  <dp:set-variable name="'var://service/routing-url'" value="$URL-
out"/>

  <dp:set-variable name="'var://service/URL-out'" value="$URL-
out"/>

</xsl:template>

</xsl:stylesheet>
```

The FTP Server Front-side protocol handler can be added to a Multi-Protocol Gateway Service by creating it in the Front Side Settings section in the General tab of the service. The FTP Server Front-side Handler is very similar to the one we used for the B2B Gateway in pattern #2 above; the only exception is we set the Filesystem Type to Transparent as seen in Figure 5-17. We also need to create and AAA Policy and for this example we are using the same AAA Info File used previously in this chapter.

If you want to use FTP over SSL (FTPS), you would also create an SSL Proxy in the Front Side Handler.

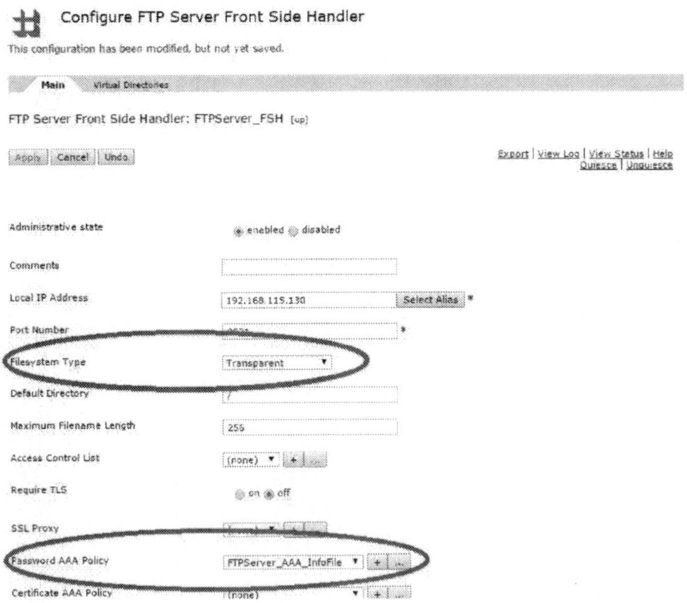

Figure 5-17 Configure FTP Server Front Side Handler.

After applying the Front Side Protocol Handler, we need to finish configuring the Multi-Protocol Gateway by setting the Request and Response type to Non-XML, the Back and Front attachment processing format to Dynamic and the Stream Output to Front and Back to Stream Messages.

When a partner connects to this service over the port assigned to the FTP Server Front Side Handler they will be routed to the internal FTP server and be logged into their home directory. At this point they can send and receive files to/from their home directory.

NOTE—MPGW and B2B Viewer Txn Logging

Since the Multi-Protocol Gateway Service is not linked to the B2B Viewer it will not log any information about the transactions that flow through it.

4. Inbound PUT/GET from an external FTP Solution using a Multi-Protocol Gateway Service

This pattern does not require the B2B Module; it can also be accomplished using the Integration Module. This inbound pattern is commonly used by customers who want to retrieve files from a partner's FTP solution and do not want or need to use profile management or wish to stream the files from the front-side to the back-side due to the excessive size of the file. Additionally, this case comes in handy when you want to use the Multi-Protocol Gateway as a pre-process to a B2B Gateway Service where you can consume a file in a the Multi-Protocol

Gateway, parse the file for information or manipulate the file and then route it to a B2B Gateway or to other locations based on that information.

Figure 5-18 is an example of what a FTP Poller and FTP Server Front side handler using a Multi-Protocol Gateway Service looks like. As you can see, this Multi-Protocol Gateway is very similar to the Multi-Protocol Gateway example in FTP pattern #3. However, in this example we do not need to pass the user credentials to the back-side since we are dedicating this service to a specific partner and we are not using transparent mode on the FTP handlers. We can use any back-side transport protocol we wish to; in this case we are using a static back-side that routes to a HTTP back-end address.

In this example we are also using a processing policy similar to the one explained in FTP pattern #1 that allows us to preserve the original filename to the back-side.

The file location where files are picked up from must be accessible by DataPower with full Read/Write/Delete access rights. DataPower locks the file by changing its name during pick-up. This prevents other DataPower nodes from picking up the same file at the same time.

If you are using SSL to connect to the back-side you would configure the SSL Client Crypto Profile in the Multi-Protocol Gateway Service.

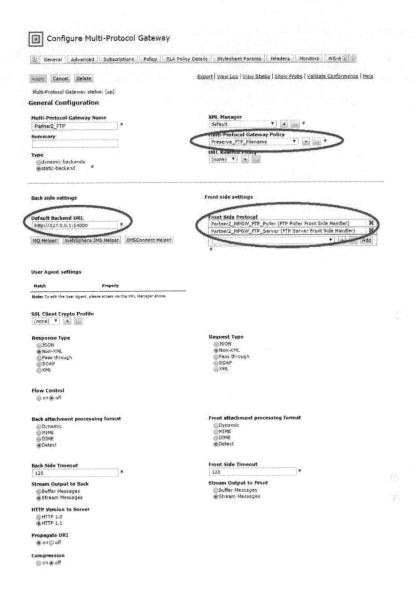

Figure 5-18 Partner2_FTP MPGW configuration.

The example FTP Poller Front Side Handler is shown in Figure 5-19. This poller is identical to the one we used in FTP pattern #1. In this example we are using an XML Manager to set the User Agent object with the Basic Authentication policy needed to connect to the partner's FTP server. This allows us to hide the username and password and not expose them as part of the URL.

If your partner uses SSL for the FTP connection you would also configure the SSL Proxy profile in the User Agent.

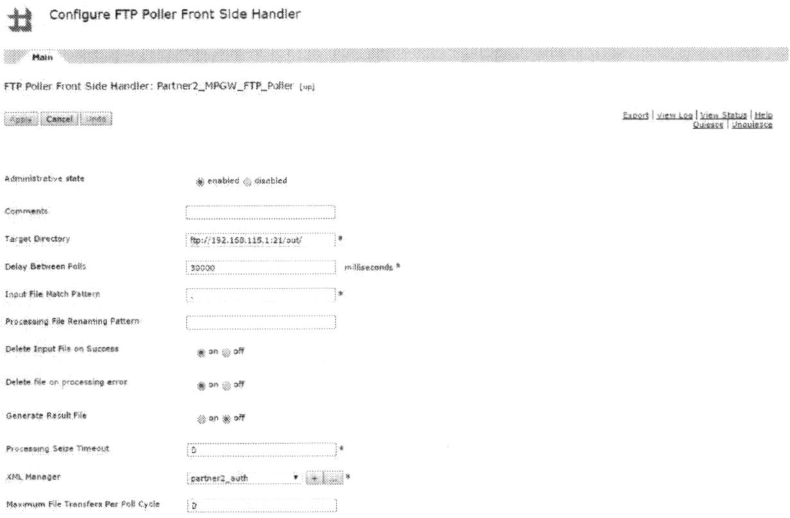

Figure 5-19 Configure FTP Poller Front Side Handler.

The example FTP Server Front Side Handler shown in Figure 5-20 is identical to the one we used in FTP pattern #2. This handler will listen on a unique port and will use a Password AAA Policy needed for connecting to the Multi-Protocol Gateway Service.

When using Virtual Ephemeral and Virtual Persistent Mode in the FTP Server Front Side Handler a broader range of FTP commands are accepted as seen below:

AUTH, CCC, CDUP, CWD, DELE, EPRT, EPSV, FEAT, GET, LIST, MKD, MODE, NLST, NOOP, P@SW, PASS, PASV,PBSZ, PORT, PROT, PUT, PWD, QUIT, REST, RETR, RMD, RNFR, RNTO, SITE, SIZE, STAT, STOR, STOU, STRU,TYPE, USER, XCUP, XCWD, XMKD, XPWD, XRMD

When using the MODE command, MODE S and MODE Z are supported. When using the TYPE command, TYPE A, TYPE A N, TYPE A T, TYPE A C, TYPE I, and TYPE L 8 are supported.

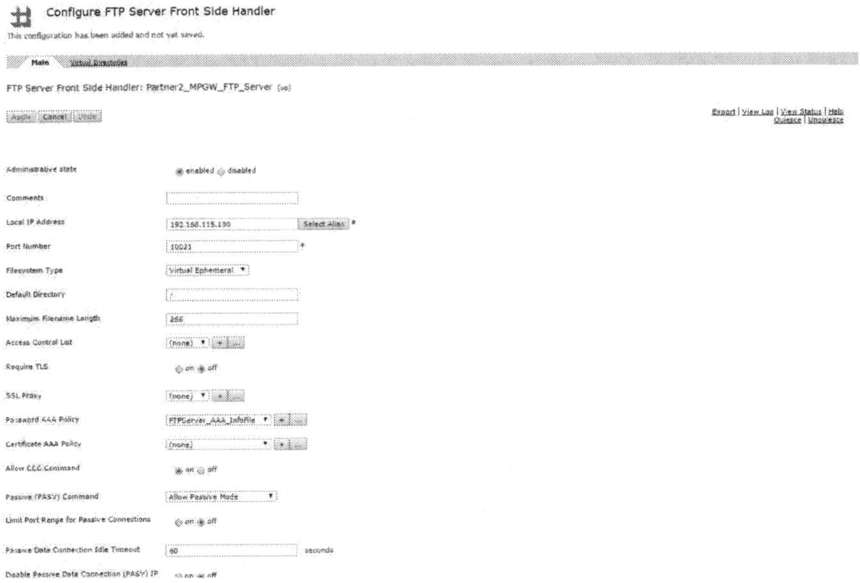

Figure 5-20 Configure FTP Server Front Side Handler.

When a partner connects to this service over the port assigned to the FTP Server Front Side Handler they will be presented with the default directory which is / in our example. They can then PUT files to the DataPower Gateway which will then pass them to the back-end based on the Back side setting in the Multi-Protocol Gateway Service.

The FTP Poller in this service is used to poll the Partner's FTP server and GET files that will then be passed to the back-end based on the Back-side setting in the Multi-Protocol Gateway Service. When the back-side is set to point to a Front Side Handler (typically HTTP) of a B2B Gateway service it acts as a pre-process to the service. A processing policy can be used to dynamically route to multiple B2B Gateway services based on content or header information.

NOTE—Passing MPGW Metadata

Since the Multi-Protocol Gateway Service is not linked to the B2B Viewer it will not log any information about the transactions that flows through it. However, a processing policy can be used to capture some metadata, place it in a small XML file and send the small file into a B2B Gateway where it is consumed and deleted. The entry would then be logged in the B2B viewer and can represent the file received in the Multi-Protocol Gateway Service.

5. Outbound FTP(S) PUT to an external FTP(S) Server through a B2B Gateway Service

This pattern requires the B2B Gateway Module and is used when you need to PUT files to a directory on your partner's FTP server. This pattern could also be accomplished in a Multi-Protocol Gateway Service where the main difference is the outbound flows in a Multi-Protocol Gateway Service do not route based on partner profiles nor does it support B2B Messaging and B2B transaction viewing. Since the two outbound patterns are so closely related we are only showing the example for the B2B Gateway Service.

The file location where files are picked up from must be accessible by DataPower with full Read/Write/Delete access rights. DataPower locks the file by changing its name during pick-up. This prevents other DataPower nodes from picking up the same file at the same time.

Unlike the Multi-Protocol Gateway Service, the output of a B2B Gateway Service is through a partner profile. For files that are destined for a trading partner outside of your network, the profile type used is external. You can access the B2B Partner Profile manager from the GUI in the Control Panel, Left Navigation menu or from inside the B2B Gateway Service Main tab.

Figure 5-21 shows an example of what the external partner profile FTP destination configuration looks like. You will notice the username and password information is entered in the destination instead of requiring a user agent to house the credentials like a Multi-Protocol Gateway Service requires. If

FTP over SSL is required you would also need to create and configure a SSL Proxy Profile.

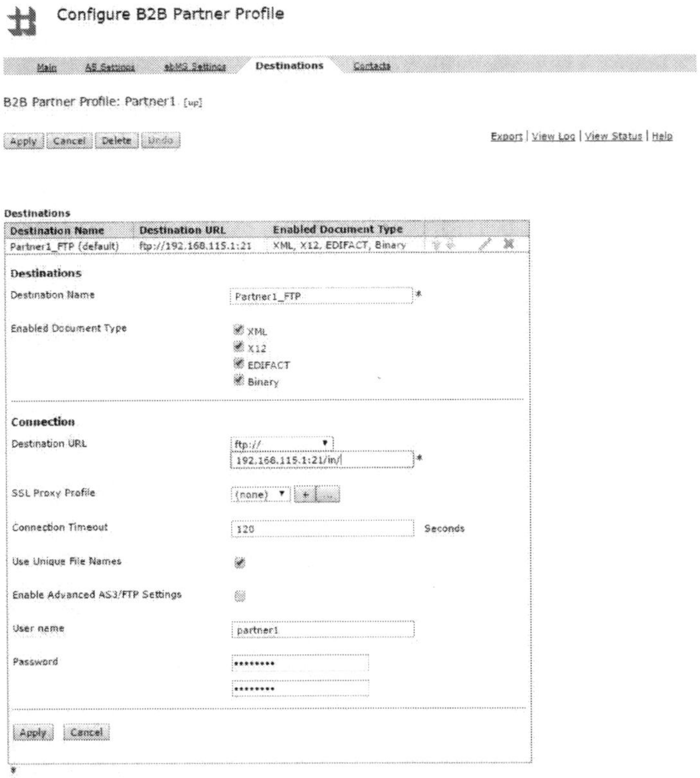

Figure 5-21 B2B Partner Profile FTP Destination.

To save the destination you need to click on the Apply button inside the destination configuration screen and then click on the Apply button again in the profile configuration screen after you have configured all of the required fields for the profile. The Partner Profile must be associated with the B2B Gateway service that will manage sending the file to the destination partner.

When the file is picked up from the back-end location determined to be destined for the external partner; the B2B Gateway Service will use the FTP Destination we configured in the partner profile Destination tab.

Figure 5-22 illustrates an example of this flow as seen in the B2B Transaction Viewer where the receiving partner is Partner1.

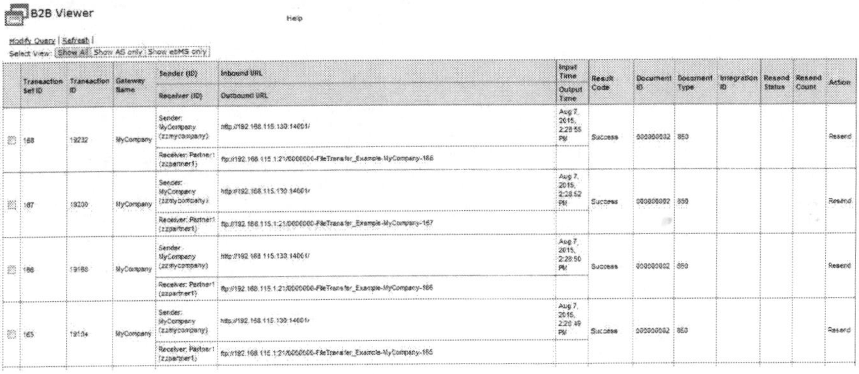

Figure 5-22 B2B Transaction Viewer – Outbound FTP PUT.

SFTP Patterns

Like FTP, the SFTP pattern is a commonly used protocol for exchanging files. DataPower supports this much in the same manner as it supports FTP but allows for partner identification using a username and public/private key pair instead of or in addition to username and password. When using SFTP you place the public key on the server and then connect to the server from a client that already has the private key. If the key pair matches, the system allows access without the need for a password.

Figure 5-23 shows five SFTP patterns; they include SFTP flows used in the B2B Gateway Service as well as the pass-thru SFTP flows used in the Multi-Protocol Gateway Service. Each of these patterns is described in detail in the following sections.

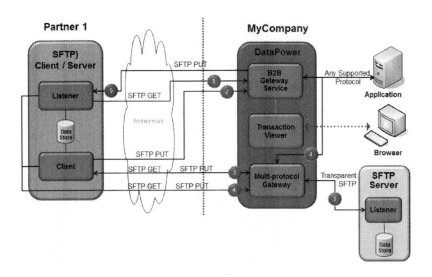

Figure 5-23 SFTP DataPower Patterns.

1. Inbound SFTP GET using a B2B Gateway Service

This pattern requires the B2B Module and is commonly used by customers who want to retrieve files from a partner's SFTP Server. DataPower uses a SFTP poller front-side handler on a configurable polling frequency to retrieve the files. You can think of this poller as a SFTP client. The files are routed to an internal partner destination configured in the internal profile defined by the business ID in the B2B payload or the ID set using the Document Routing Pre-processor in the B2B Gateway Service Advanced tab.

The file location where files are picked up from must be accessible by DataPower with full Read/Write/Delete access rights. DataPower locks the file by changing its name during pick-up. This prevents other DataPower nodes from picking up the same file at the same time.

This pattern requires a B2B Gateway Service. A SFTP Poller Front-side protocol handler can be added to a B2B gateway by creating it in the Document Routing section in the Main tab as seen in Figure 5-24.

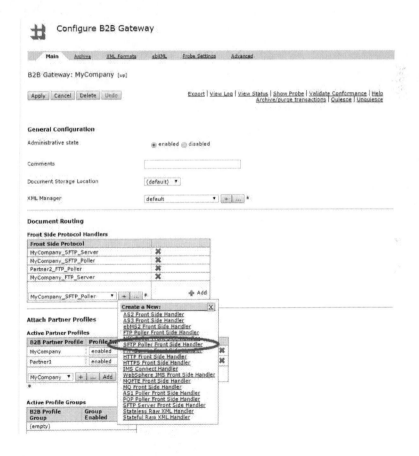

Figure 5-24 Add SFTP Poller – B2B Gateway.

The SFTP Poller configuration screen in our example as shown in Figure 5-25 has many settings not shown that allow you to define patterns for identifying how to rename files after retrieval and how to treat errors if they should happen (these settings are hidden based on which boxes are checked) To keep it simple we checked the Delete Input File on Success and Delete file on processing error and we are not generating a result file, so by doing this the GUI automatically hides unnecessary fields.

The Target directory is a full SFTP path setting where we are polling every five seconds for all types of files. The user credentials for connecting to the Partner's SFTP server are associated to this handler by creating them in the SSH Client Connection field. The SSH Client Connection object can be created by clicking on the plus sign to the right of the field.

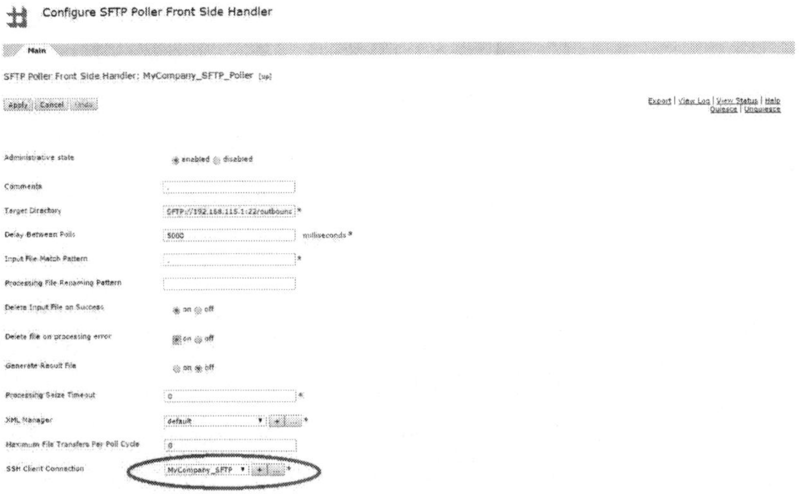

Figure 5-25 Configure SFTP Poller – B2B Gateway.

Figure 5-26 is an example of a configured SSH Client Profile. We are logging on as user mycompany and using Public Key authentication instead of a password. We could optionally include the use of a password or even use password only. We can create a user private key object that contains the key file for this client by clicking on the plus sign to the right of the User Private Key field.

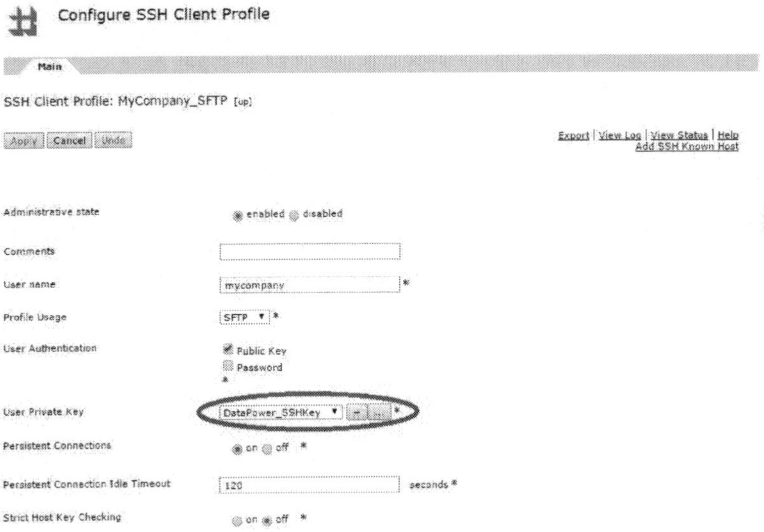

Figure 5-26 Configure SSH Client Profile.

In the Configure Crypto Key configuration screen you can upload a private key file. In the example shown in Figure 5-27 we are using a .pem file format which is the key format most commonly used with DataPower.

Figure 5-27 Configure Crypto Key.

Many servers will not accept the .pem format when uploading the public certificate. In those cases, the certificate will need to be converted into an acceptable format. You can do this from the Configure Crypto Key screen by clicking on the Convert Crypto Key Object link in the upper right hand corner and creating an OpenSSH key using the dialog as seen in Figure 5-28. After the public key file has been saved to DataPower's temporary directory, you can use the File Manager in the Control Panel to navigate to the file and download it to your workstation. You can then provide the public certificate to partners that have SFTP servers you need to connect to.

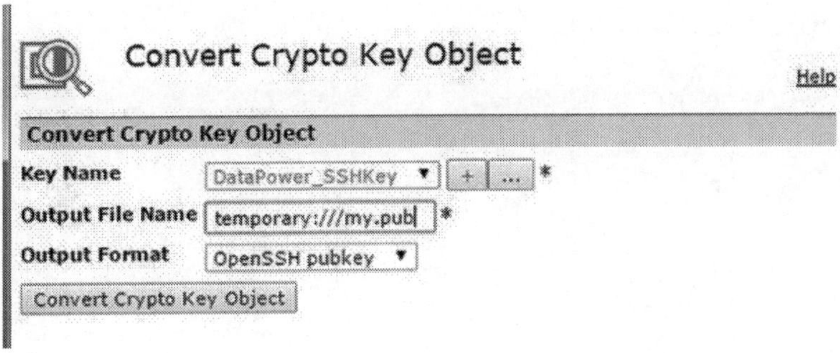

Figure 5-28 Convert Crypto Key Object.

After applying the changes to the crypto key, SSH Client Profile and SFTP Poller Front Side Handler you must also click on Add in the Document Routing section of the B2B Gateway Service before applying the changes to the service.

After adding the SFTP Poller Front Side Handler to the B2B Gateway and applying the changes it will start to poll for files in the specified partner's SFTP server.

Figure 5-29 illustrates an example of the flow as seen in the B2B Transaction Viewer where the receiving partner is MyCompany.

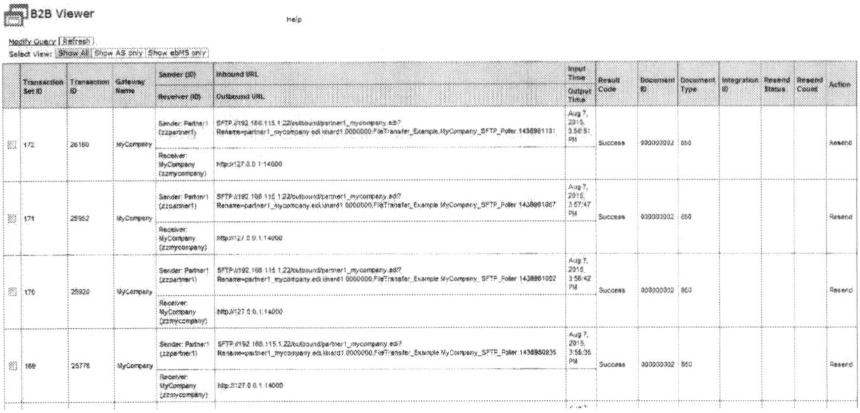

Figure 5-29 B2B Transaction Viewer – Inbound SFTP GET.

NOTE—Protocol Bridging

The internal partner destination does not have to be SFTP. It can be any protocol that DataPower supports. DataPower natively bridges between transport protocols. If SFTP is the Partner Destination you may choose to use a processing policy in the internal profile to preserve the original filename. If the file being sent into the B2B Gateway is not able to be parsed by the service it is considered BINARY. To identify binary data we use a routing pre-processor in the B2B Gateway Advanced tab to identify the sender and receiver IDs to be used for routing the file. Example stylesheets showing a Routing Pre-Processor and filename preservation is provided previously in this chapter.

2. Inbound SFTP PUT to a B2B Gateway Service

This pattern requires the B2B Module and is commonly used by customers who want to allow partners to put files onto the B2B Gateway which will then be routed to an internal partner destination configured in the internal profile defined by the business ID in the B2B payload or the ID set using the routing pre-processor in the B2B Gateway Service Advanced tab.

This pattern requires a B2B Gateway Service. A SFTP Server Front-side protocol handler can be added to a B2B Gateway by creating it in the Document Routing section in the Main tab as seen in Figure 5-30.

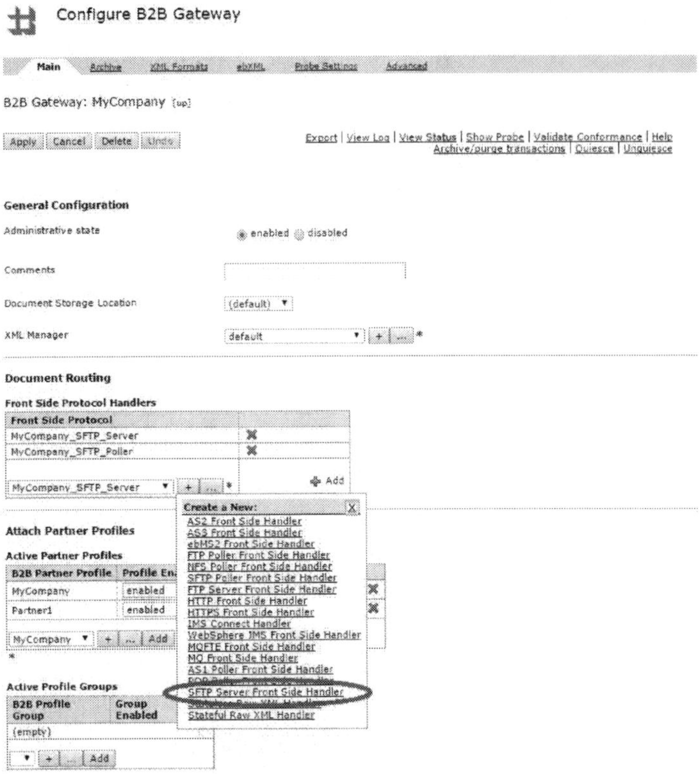

Figure 5-30 Add SFTP Server – B2B Gateway.

The Configure SFTP Server Front Side Handler screen as seen in Figure 5-31 has three tabs. We are only concerned about the mandatory fields in the Main tab. The Allowed Commands tab only applies to Transparent Mode and for this example we are not creating any local virtual directories. You must configure the Local IP Address and Port Number fields; this is the address and port you want DataPower to listen on. The file system type is defaulted to Virtual Ephemeral which is the mode we want to use. We also need to Check the Public Key box and create a Password AAA Policy.

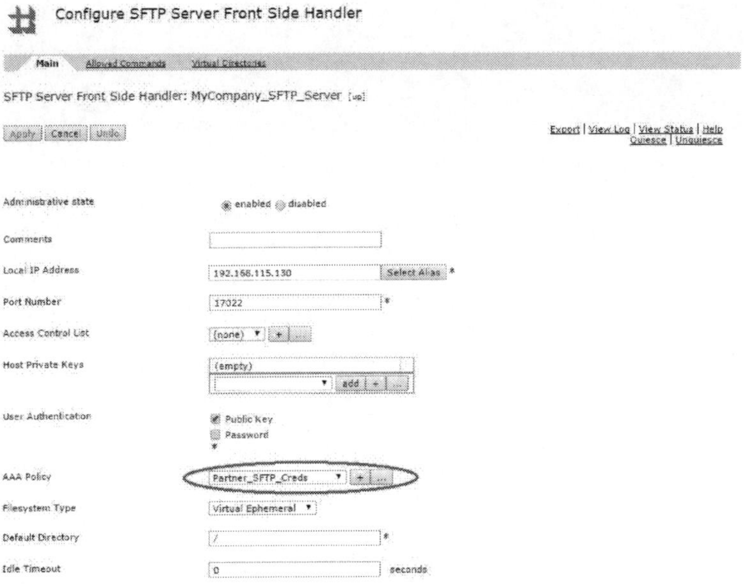

Figure 5-31 Configure SFTP Server Front Side Handler.

The Password AAA Policy has many tabs with many configuration objects to provide maximum granularity and flexibility. For our example, it is only used to validate the username and Client Public Key credentials that are received from the trading partners; this can be created by clicking on the plus sign to the right of the AAA Policy field. In the Configure AAA Policy screen we only need to configure the Identity extraction, Authentication and Resource extraction tabs as seen in Figure 5-32. In the Identity extraction screen we selected Processing metadata and in the Processing metadata items drop down field we selected ssh-password-metadata.

Figure 5-32 Configure AAA Policy – Identity extraction

In the Authentication tab we are using a Custom template
for this example as seen in Figure 5-33.

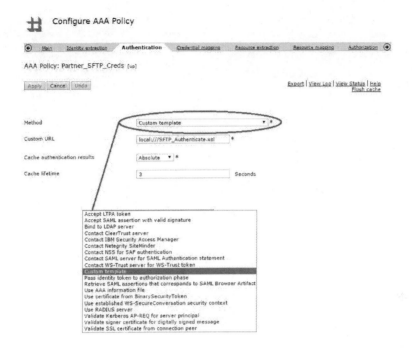

Figure 5-33 Configure AAA Policy – Authentication.

When using a custom stylesheet the pubkey data in the sheet must match the key data from the public certificate of client connecting to the front side handler. The content of the Custom stylesheet named SFTP_Authenticate.xsl is illustrated in Listing 5-5:

Listing 5-5 Verify Public Key Data for SFTP authentication

```
<?xml version="1.0" encoding="UTF-8"?>
    <xsl:stylesheet version="1.0"
xmlns:xsl="http://www.w3.org/1999/XSL/Transform"
        xmlns:dp="http://www.datapower.com/extensions"
```

```xml
        xmlns:dpconfig="http://www.datapower.com/param/config"
        xmlns:dpquery="http://www.datapower.com/param/query"
        xmlns:dpfunc="http://www.datapower.com/extensions/functions"
        extension-element-prefixes="dp
        dpfunc" exclude-result-prefixes="dp dpconfig dpfunc dpquery">
    <xsl:template match="/">
    <!-- Get EI metadata information from datapower, store it to
variables,
log it, and authenticate user/pass or user/pubkey combinations -->
    <xsl:variable name="ssh_user"><xsl:value-of
select="dp:variable('var://context/INPUT/ssh/username')"/></xsl:varia
ble>
    <xsl:variable name="ssh_cert"><xsl:value-of
select="dp:variable('var://context/INPUT/ssh/publickey')"/></xsl:vari
able>
    <xsl:variable name="ssh_pass"><xsl:value-of
select="dp:variable('var://context/INPUT/ssh/password')"/></xsl:varia
ble>
    <xsl:message>The SFTP User is: <xsl:value-of
select="$ssh_user"/></xsl:message>
    <xsl:variable name="output">
      <xsl:choose>
        <xsl:when test="not(string-length($ssh_cert) = 0)">
          <xsl:message>The SFTP Cert is: <xsl:value-of
select="$ssh_cert"/></xsl:message>
          <xsl:call-template name="validatePublicKey">
            <xsl:with-param name="pubkey" select="$ssh_cert"/>
          </xsl:call-template>
        </xsl:when>
      </xsl:choose>
    </xsl:variable>
    <!-- if this is a non-null XML nodeset then the authentication
will PASS -->
    <xsl:copy-of select="$output"/>
  </xsl:template>
<!-- This function performs a simple validation the public key. -->
```

```xsl
<xsl:template name="validatePublicKey">
 <xsl:param name="pubkey"/>
<xsl:choose>
    <xsl:when test="($pubkey = 'ssh-rsa
AAAAB3NzaC1yc2EAAAABJQAAAIEAjLUi5pHySCTcZ956oN1vCHT+8UZPKDry82ie9BBLj
senVIkUOHw7/Oab5GcOb5f7beYX8m5Jo9XWQKOYYz8OLN1mE8OCJRzM4bW6ngySA9AG1u
GeUOij4wH6O8yYfrNGz3OEiyXVnv/zX/amI2v7SAmsrM3qjGfirnURcmo8CFk=')">
<publickey_authenticator
user="partner2">Passed</publickey_authenticator>
    </xsl:when>
    <xsl:otherwise/>
 </xsl:choose>
</xsl:template>
</xsl:stylesheet>
```

The final tab we configured is the Resource extraction tab where we selected Processing metadata and set the metadata items to ssh-password-metadata as seen in Figure 5-34.

Figure 5-34 Configure AAA Policy – Resource extraction.

NOTE—Username/Password vs Client Public Key

If you wish to use username and password instead of username and client public key, you can use the same type of AAA Policy we used for FTP pattern #2 earlier in this chapter.

After applying the changes to the Password AAA Policy and the FTP Server Front-side Handler, be sure to click on the Add button in the Document Routing section of the B2B Gateway Service Main tab to add the handler to the list.

To complete the B2B Gateway Service you also need to have at minimum one internal and one external partner profile associated with it and the Archive tab would need to be configured.

When the partners send files into this service the files will be routed to the internal profile's destination which is typically an internal system or application.

Figure 5-35 illustrates an example of the flow as seen in the B2B Transaction Viewer where the receiving partner is MyCompany.

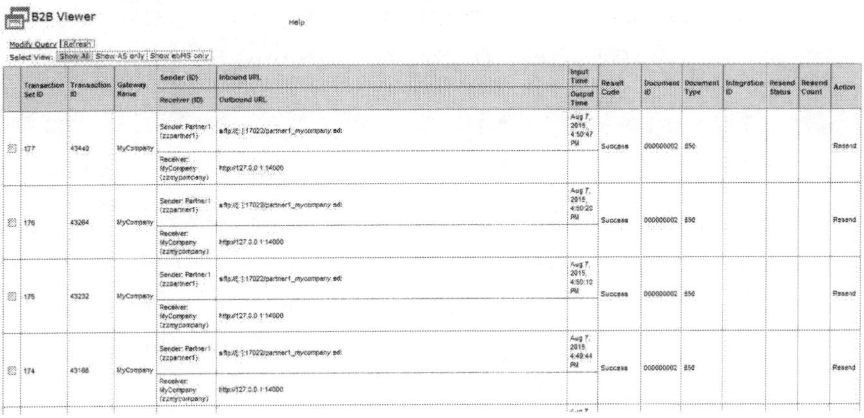

Figure 5-35 B2B Transaction Viewer – Inbound SFTP PUT.

NOTE—Partner Destination Protocol

The Partner Destination does not have to be SFTP. It can be any protocol that DataPower supports. DataPower natively bridges between transport protocols. If SFTP is the Partner Destination you may choose to use a processing policy in the internal profile to preserve the original filename.

If the file being sent into the B2B Gateway is not able to be parsed by the service it is considered BINARY. To identify binary data we use a routing pre-processor in the B2B Gateway Advanced tab to identify the sender and receiver IDs to be used for routing the file. Example stylesheets showing a Routing Pre-Processor and filename preservation is provided previously in this chapter.

3. Transparent SFTP PUT/GET with your SFTP Server through a Multi-Protocol Gateway Service

This pattern does not require the B2B Module; it can also be accomplished using the Integration Module. This pattern is commonly used by customers who want to allow partners to put files to or get files from their SFTP Server sitting inside the protected network. This is typically done when you need to stream extremely large files that are larger than a B2B Gateway Service can handle or when you simply want to proxy SFTP connections to your internal SFTP servers.

DataPower works well as a transparent proxy to SFTP when all you need to do are basic functions like browse directories, rename files, PUT files or GET files.

This pattern is configured in a Multi-Protocol Gateway Service which can be created by clicking on the Add button in the Multi-Protocol Gateway list view.

The Multi-Protocol Gateway Configuration screen as seen in Figure 5-36 has many tabs and configuration objects. For this example we only need to configure the General tab and add a processing policy.

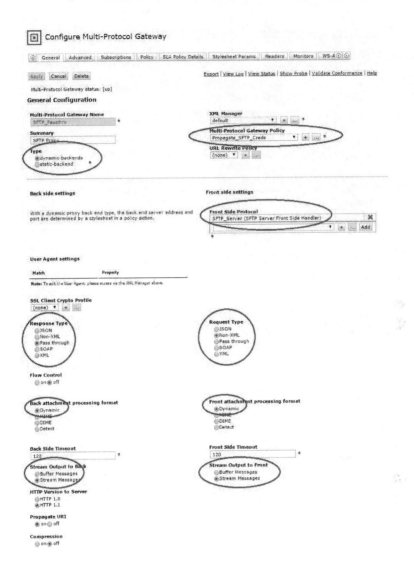

Figure 5-36 Configure Multi-Protocol Gateway.

We need to set the Type to dynamic-back-ends since we want to use processing policy to propagate the username and password from the front-side of the service to the back-side

SFTP server. To do this we use a processing policy which is shown in Figure 5-37.

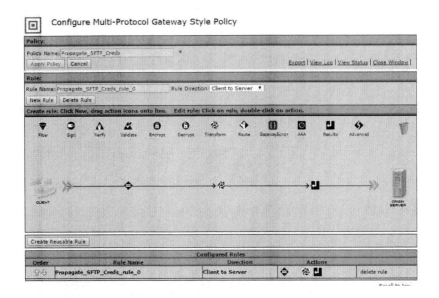

Figure 5-37 Configure Processing Policy.

The transform action being used is executing a small XSL script that captures the username and password from the front-side login and passes them to the back-side by setting the back-side SFTP URL. We set the IP Address of the internal SFTP Server in a custom parameter in the Advanced tab. An example of the transform action is shown in Figure 5-38.

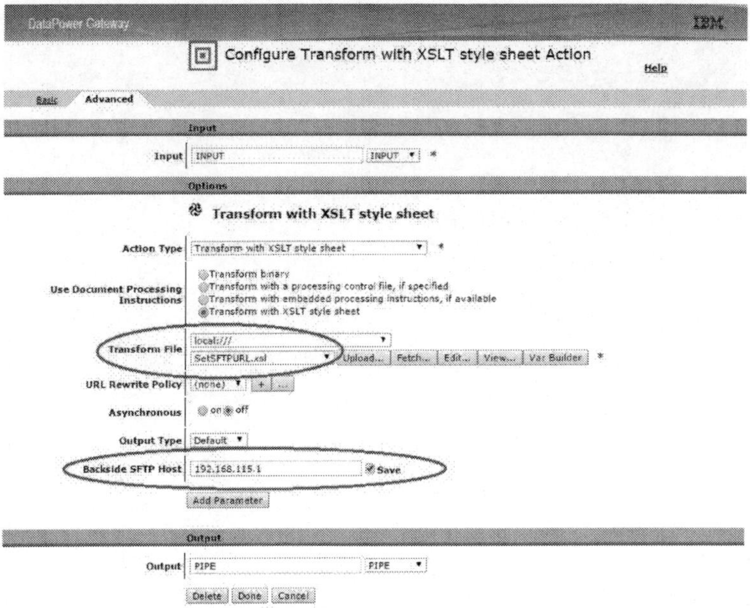

Figure 5-38 – Configure Transform Action.

The content of the example XSL file use to pass the front side credentials to the back side is provided in Listing 5-6.

Listing 5-6 Copy front side credentials to back side connection

```
<?xml version="1.0" encoding="utf-8"?>
 <xsl:stylesheet version="1.0"
  xmlns:xsl="http://www.w3.org/1999/XSL/Transform"
  xmlns:dp="http://www.datapower.com/extensions"
  xmlns:func="http://exslt.org/functions"
  xmlns:dpfunc="http://www.datapower.com/extensions/functions"
  xmlns:dpconfig="http://www.datapower.com/param/config"
  extension-element-prefixes="dp func dpfunc dpconfig"
  exclude-result-prefixes="dp func dpfunc dpconfig">
```

```
<xsl:param name="dpconfig:backsideSFTPHost"
select="'sftp.server.com'"/>

<dp:param name="dpconfig:backsideSFTPHost" type="dmString"
xmlns="">

    <display>Backside SFTP Host</display>

    <default>sftp.server.com</default>

    <description>Backside SFTP Host</description>

</dp:param>

    <xsl:template match="/">

    <!-- grab the username and password sent by the SFTP client to
build the backend FTP URL using them -->

    <xsl:variable name="URI"
select="dp:variable('var://service/URI')"/>

    <xsl:variable name="username" select="dp:auth-info('basic-auth-
name')" />

    <xsl:variable name="password" select="dp:auth-info('basic-auth-
password')" />

    <xsl:variable name="encodedusername"
select="dp:encode($username,'url')" />

    <xsl:variable name="encodedpassword"
select="dp:encode($password,'url')" />

    <!-- build the backside URL -->

    <xsl:variable name="URL-out"
select="concat('sftp://',$encodedusername,':',$encodedpassword,'@',$d
pconfig:backsideSFTPHost,$URI)" />

    <!-- set backside SFTP URL -->

    <dp:set-variable name="'var://service/routing-url'" value="$URL-
out"/>

    <dp:set-variable name="'var://service/URL-out'" value="$URL-
out"/>

  </xsl:template>
</xsl:stylesheet>
```

The SFTP Server Front-side protocol handler can be added to a Multi-Protocol Gateway Service by creating it in the Front Side Settings section in the General tab as seen in Figure 5-36. In the Front Side Handler we set the IP address and Port Number and are using a Transparent Filesystem Type as seen in Figure 5-39. We also need to create and AAA Policy that uses ssh-password-metadata for Identity extraction and Resource extraction and the same AAA Info File for Authentication used previously in this chapter.

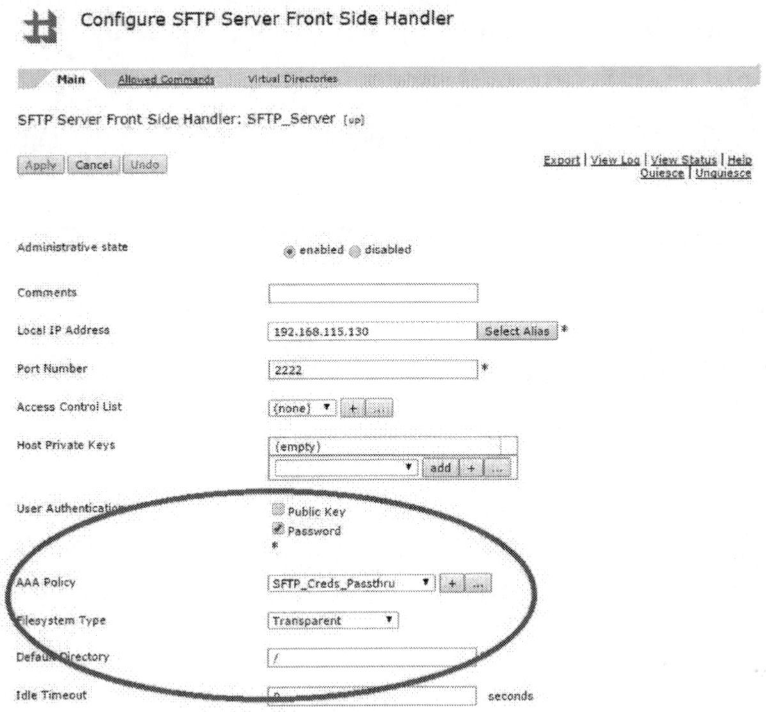

Figure 5-39 Configure SFTP Server Front Side Handler.

After applying the Front Side Protocol Handler we need to finish configuring the Multi-Protocol Gateway by setting the Request type to Non-XML and Response type to Pass-Thru, the Back and Front attachment processing format to Dynamic and the Stream Output to Front and Back to Stream Messages.

When a partner connects to this service over the port assigned to the SFTP Server Front Side Handler they will be routed to the internal SFTP server and be logged into their home directory. At this point they can send and receive files to/from their home directory.

4. Inbound PUT/GET with an external SFTP Solution using a Multi-Protocol Gateway Service

This pattern does not require the B2B Module; it can also be accomplished using the Integration Module. This inbound pattern is commonly used by customers who want to retrieve files from a partner's SFTP Solution and do not want or need to use profile management or wish to stream the files from the front-side to the back-side due to the excessive size of the file. Additionally, this case comes in handy when you want to use the Multi-Protocol Gateway as a pre-process to a B2B Gateway Service where you can consume a file in a the Multi-Protocol Gateway, parse the file for information or manipulate the file and then route it to a B2B Gateway or to other locations based on that information.

Figure 5-40 is an example of what a SFTP Poller and SFTP Server Front side handler using a Multi-Protocol Gateway Service looks like. As you can see this Multi-Protocol Gateway is very similar to the Multi-protocol SFTP Transparent Proxy example in SFTP pattern #3 above. However, in this example we do not need to pass the user credentials to the back-side since we are dedicating this service to a specific partner and we are using Virtual Ephemeral mode on the SFTP Server handler. We can use any back-side transport protocol we wish to. In this case we are using a static back-side that routes to a HTTP back-end address.

For the Poller, the file location where files are picked up from must be accessible by DataPower with full Read/Write/Delete access rights. DataPower locks the file by changing its name during pick-up. This prevents other DataPower nodes from picking up the same file at the same time.

If you are using SSL to connect to the back-side you would configure the SSL Client Crypto Profile in the Multi-Protocol Gateway Service.

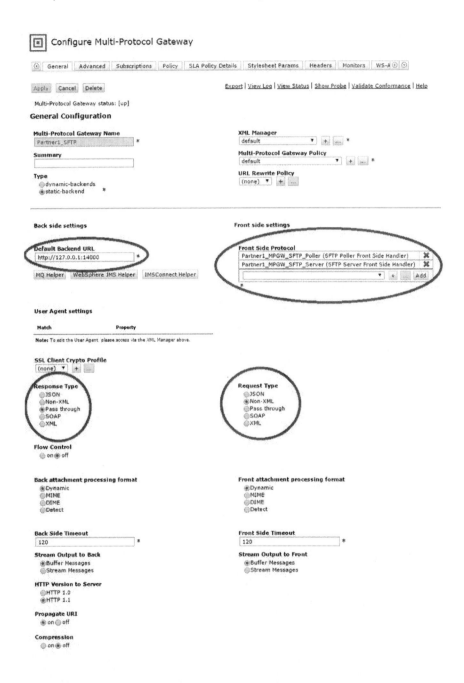

Figure 5-40 Partner1_SFTP MPGW configuration.

The example SFTP Poller Front Side Handler is shown in Figure 5-41. This poller is similar to the one we used in the SFTP pattern #1 above. However, for this example we are using partner1 login credentials instead of mycompany login credentials.

Configure SFTP Poller Front Side Handler

Main

SFTP Poller Front Side Handler: Partner1_MPGW_SFTP_Poller [up]

Apply Cancel Undo   Export | View Log | View Status | Help
                                                              Quiesce | Unquiesce

Administrative state	⦿ enabled ○ disabled
Comments	
Target Directory	SFTP://192.168.115.1:22/outbound *
Delay Between Polls	60000 milliseconds *
Input File Match Pattern	. *
Processing File Renaming Pattern	
Delete Input File on Success	⦿ on ○ off
Delete file on processing error	⦿ on ○ off
Generate Result File	○ on ⦿ off
Processing Seize Timeout	0 *
XML Manager	default ▼ [+] [...] *
Maximum File Transfers Per Poll Cycle	0
SSH Client Connection	Partner1_SSH ▼ [+] [...] *

Figure 5-41 Configure SFTP Poller Front Side Handler.

The example SFTP Server Front Side Handler shown in Figure 5-42 is similar to the one we used in SFTP pattern #2 above. This handler will listen on a unique port and will use a

Password AAA Policy appropriate to connecting to the Multi-Protocol Gateway Service. Additionally, in this example we are using username and password for user authentication instead of public key.

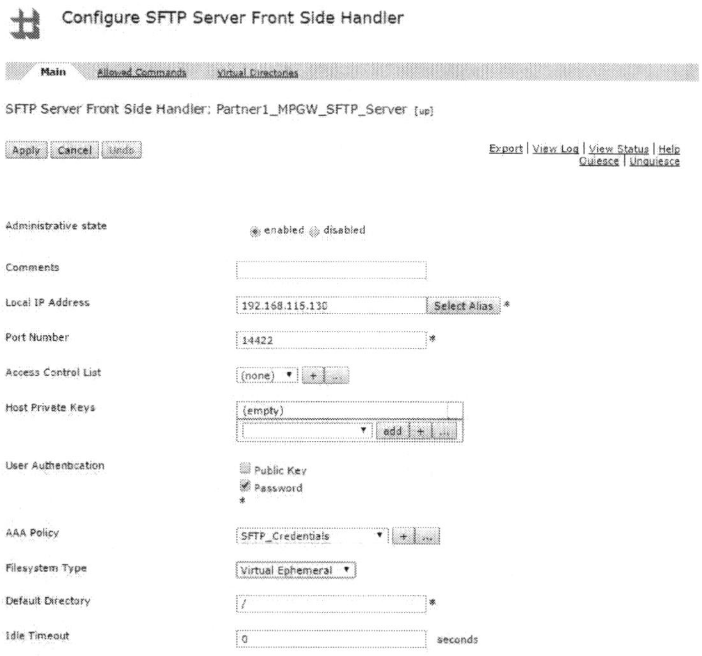

Figure 5-42 Configure SFTP Server Front Side Handler.

After applying the Front Side Protocol Handlers we need to finish configuring the Multi-Protocol Gateway by setting the Request type to Non-XML and Response type to Pass-Thru, the Back and Front attachment processing format to Dynamic and the Stream Output to Front and Back to Buffer Messages.

When a partner connects to this service over the port assigned to the SFTP Server Front Side Handler they will be presented with the default directory which is / in our example. They can then PUT file to the DataPower Gateway which will then pass them to the back-end based on the Back-side setting in the Multi-Protocol Gateway Service.

The SFTP Poller in this service is used to poll the partner's SFTP server and GET files that will then be passed to the back-end based on the back-side setting in the Multi-Protocol Gateway Service.

NOTE—MPGW Processing Policy Metadata

Since the Multi-Protocol Gateway Service is not linked to the B2B Viewer it will not log any information about the transactions that flows through it. However, a processing policy can be used to capture some metadata, place it in a small XML file and send the small file into a B2B Gateway where it is consumed and deleted. The entry would then be logged in the B2B viewer and can represent the file received in the Multi-Protocol Gateway Service.

5. Outbound SFTP PUT to an external SFTP Server through a B2B Gateway Service

This pattern requires the B2B Module and is used when you need to PUT files to a directory on your partner's SFTP server. This pattern could also be accomplished in a Multi-Protocol Gateway Service where the main difference is the outbound flows in a Multi-Protocol Gateway Service do not route based on partner profiles. Since the two outbound patterns are so closely related we are only showing the example for the B2B Gateway Service.

Unlike the Multi-Protocol Gateway Service, the output of a B2B Gateway Service is through a partner profile. For files that are destined for a trading partner outside of your network, the profile type used is external. You can access the B2B Partner Profile manager from the GUI in the Control Panel, Left Navigation menu or from inside the B2B Gateway Service Main tab.

Figure 5-43 shows an example of what the external partner profile SFTP destination configuration looks like. You will notice the credentials we are using to connect to the partner's SFTP server are the same ones we used in SFTP pattern #1 to connect to Partner1's server.

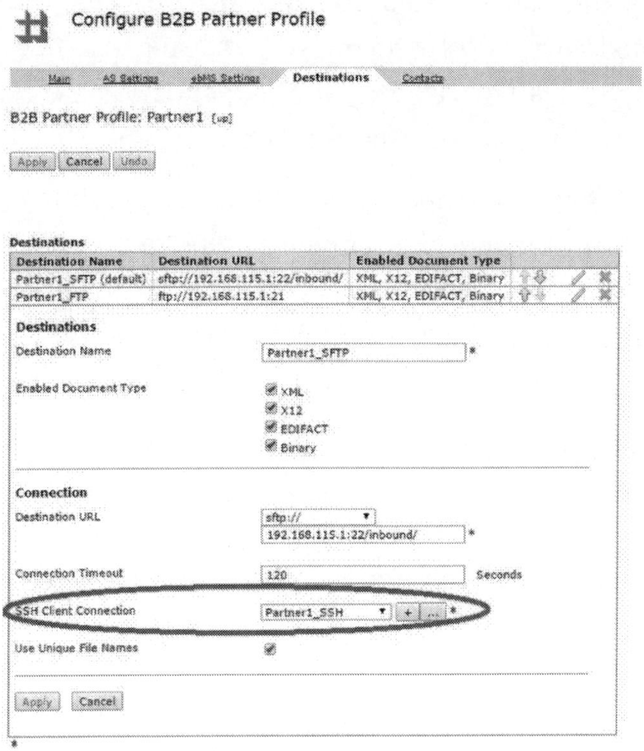

Figure 5-43 B2B Partner Profile SFTP destination.

To save the destination you need to click on the Apply button inside the destination configuration screen and then click on the Apply button again in the profile configuration screen after you have configured all of the required fields for the profile.

If you have multiple destinations configured as we do in the examples provided, you will need to move the SFTP destination to the default location at the top of the Destination list or make sure the B2B Gateway Service has it explicitly selected.

When the file is picked up from the back-end location and determined to be destined for the external partner the B2B Gateway Service will use the SFTP Destination we configured in the partner profile Destination tab.

Figure 5-44 illustrates an example of this flow as seen in the B2B Transaction Viewer where the receiving partner is Partner1.

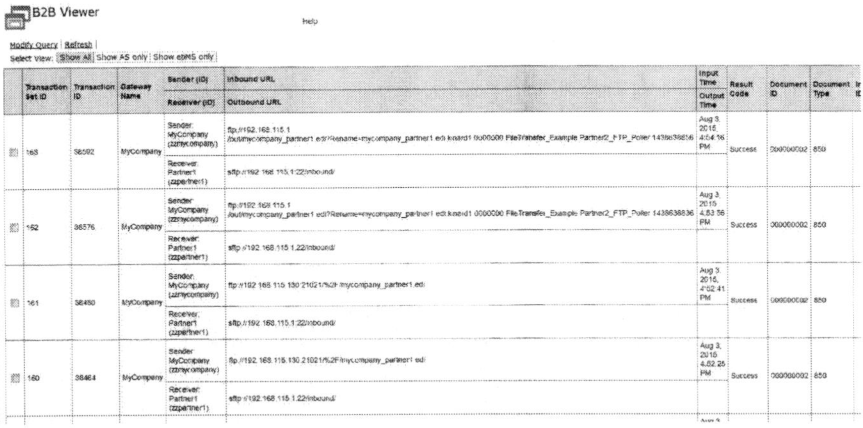

Figure 5-44 B2B Transaction Viewer – Outbound SFTP PUT.

POP3/SMTP Patterns

The email pattern is a commonly used protocol for exchanging files for small trading partners who cannot or will not invest in a packaged Managed File Transfer solution or when you want a simplified mail-boxing solution for your partners. DataPower supports this pattern by providing POP3 and SMTP protocol handlers that can be used on both the front-side and back-side. These handlers are supported in both the B2B Gateway Service and the Multi-Protocol Gateway Service.

Figure 5-45 shows two email patterns; they include inbound and outbound email flows used in the B2B Gateway Service.

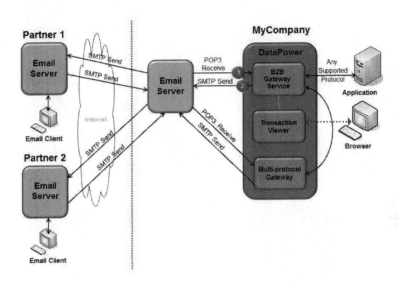

Figure 5-45 POP3/SMTP DataPower Patterns.

1. Inbound Email using a B2B Gateway Service

This pattern requires the B2B Module and is commonly used by customers who want to receive files from partners over email. This is done by having your partner send email with a file attached to an email address of your choosing; this address is accessible by the DataPower POP Poller which will consume the files from the email server. The files are routed to an internal partner destination configured in the internal profile defined by the business ID in the B2B payload or the ID set using the Document Routing Pre-processor in the B2B Gateway Service Advanced tab.

A sample Routing Pre-processor XSL is illustrated in Listing 5-7. This XSL reads the email subject header, and when the IDs are in the Subject line formatted like ReceiverID;SenderID, it will be able to find the profile in the B2B Gateway.

Listing 5-7 Document Routing Pre-processor

```xml
<?xml version="1.0" encoding="UTF-8"?>
<!--DataPower XB60 B2B Document Routing Preprocessor Stylesheet
Licensed Materials - Property of IBM
IBM WebSphere DataPower Appliances
Copyright IBM Corporation 2008. All Rights Reserved.
US Government Users Restricted Rights - Use, duplication or
disclosure
restricted by GSA ADP Schedule Contract with IBM Corp.-->
<xsl:stylesheet version="1.0"
xmlns:xsl="http://www.w3.org/1999/XSL/Transform"
xmlns:dp="http://www.datapower.com/extensions" extension-element-
prefixes="dp"> <xsl:template match="/">
        <xsl:variable name="protocol"
select="dp:variable('var://service/protocol')" />
        <xsl:variable name="Subject" select="dp:http-request-
header('Subject')"/>
    <xsl:choose>
        <xsl:when test="$protocol='pop' and
$Subject='mycompany;partner1'">
            <dp:set-variable name="'var://service/b2b-doc-type'"
value="'binary'"/>
  <dp:set-variable name="'var://service/b2b-partner-to'"
value="'mycompany'" />
  <dp:set-variable name="'var://service/b2b-partner-from'"
value="'partner1'" />
        </xsl:when>
        <xsl:when test="$protocol='pop' and
$Subject='zzmycompany;zzpartner1'">
```

```
<dp:set-variable name="'var://service/b2b-doc-type'"
value="'binary'"/>
                <dp:set-variable name="'var://service/b2b-partner-to'"
value="'zzmycompany'" />

<dp:set-variable name="'var://service/b2b-partner-from'"
value="'zzpartner1'" />
                </xsl:when>
                <xsl:otherwise>
<!-- By default, do nothing. This will autodetect the message type,
but binary messages will fail for lack of partner IDs. -->
                </xsl:otherwise>
        </xsl:choose>
</xsl:template>
</xsl:stylesheet>
```

A B2B Gateway Service is needed for this pattern. A POP Poller Front-side protocol handler can be added to a B2B gateway by creating it in the Document Routing section in the Main tab as seen in Figure 5-46.

Figure 5-46 Add POP Poller Front Side Handler – B2B Gateway.

The POP Poller Front Side Handler configuration screen in our example is shown in Figure 5-47. The POP Poller needs to be configured with the proper credentials to log on to the email server and retrieve the messages.

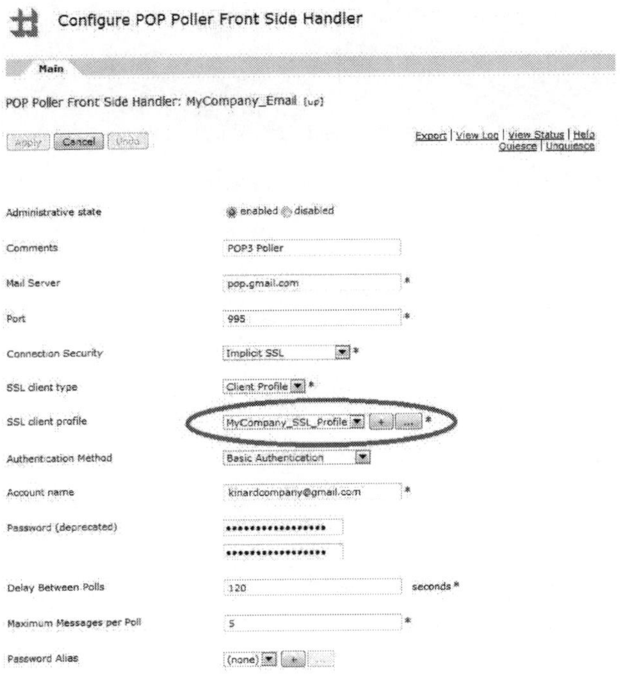

Figure 5-47 Configure POP Poller Front Side – B2B Gateway.

In our example we are using a Gmail account. Gmail requires a username, password and must use SSL when logging on. To do this we need to set the Authentication Method to Basic Authentication, the Account name to the email account used to log on to the email server and the password used with the account. We also need to set the Connection Security field to Implicit SSL, the SSL Client Type field to Client Profile, and then create a SSL Client Profile by clicking on the plus sign to the right of the field. Figure 5-48 shows an example of the SSL Client Profile configuration.

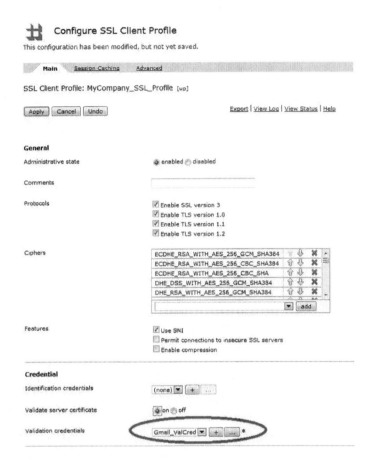

Figure 5-48 Configure SSL Client Profile.

In the Configure SSL Client Profile screen you can configure the Validation credentials to validate the server if you choose to do so. Figure 5-49 shows an example of what the Validation Credential configuration screen looks like.

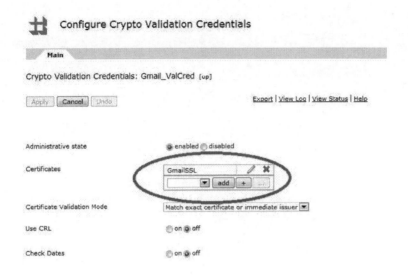

Figure 5-49 Configure Crypto Validation Credentials.

After applying the changes to the crypto validation credentials, SSL Client Profile and POP Poller Front Side Handler you must also click on Add in the Document Routing section of the B2B Gateway Service before applying the changes to the service.

After adding the POP Poller Front Side Handler to the B2B Gateway it will start to poll for files in the specified partner's SFTP server.

Figure 5-50 illustrates an example of this flow as seen in the B2B Transaction Viewer where the receiving partner is MyCompany.

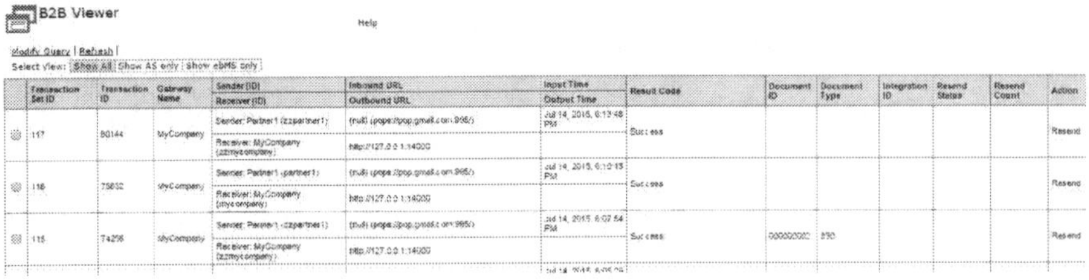

Figure 5-50 B2B Transaction Viewer – Inbound Email.

NOTE—POP Poller and Multiple Attachments

The POP poller will only process the first attachment in the email message that has multiple attachments. If you wish to process all attachments this can be accomplished by adding a processing policy with XSL or GatewayScript to detach each file and send them to the back-side.

---

2. Outbound Email to an External Partner using a B2B Gateway Service

This pattern requires the B2B Module and is used when you need to send files to your partner over email. This pattern could also be accomplished in a Multi-Protocol Gateway Service where the main difference is the outbound flows in a Multi-Protocol Gateway Service do not route based on partner profiles.

Unlike the Multi-Protocol Gateway Service the output of a B2B Gateway Service is through a partner profile. For files that are destined for a trading partner outside of your network, the profile type used is external.

This pattern requires an SMTP destination to be configured in an external profile. You can access the B2B Partner Profile manager from the GUI in the Control Panel, Left Navigation menu or from inside the B2B Gateway Service Main tab. Click on the profile to edit or create a new partner profile. In the Main tab of the Configure B2B Partner Profile we want to add email addresses to the Partner's E-mail Addresses field as seen in Figure 5-51.

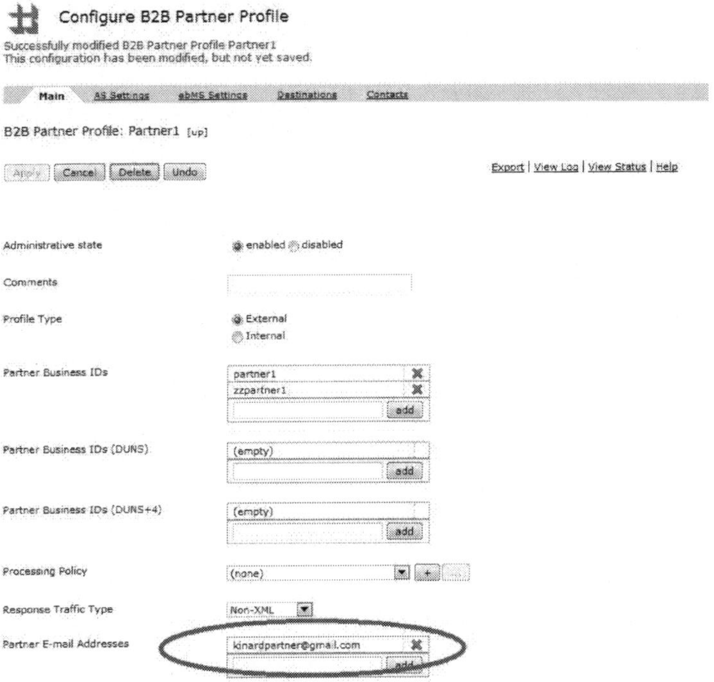

Figure 5-51 B2B Partner Profile SMTP Destination.

In the Destinations tab of the Configure B2B Partner Profile screen you can add the SMTP destination by clicking on the Add button to the far right in the Destination table and selecting //dpsmtp from the drop down in the Destination URL field. You also need to give the destination a name, provide the address for your SMTP server, provide the email address you want to send the file to and create or select a SMTP Server Connection object to use for outgoing mail.

Figure 5-52 shows an example of a configured Partner Profile with a SMTP Destination.

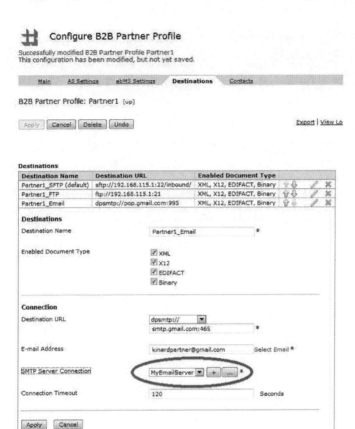

Figure 5-52 Configure Partner Profile – SMTP Destination.

To create an SMTP Server Connection you can click on the + (plus) sign to the right of the field. If the default SMTP connection is already configured you can select Default from the drop down.

Figure 5-53 illustrates what a configured SMTP Server Connection object looks like.

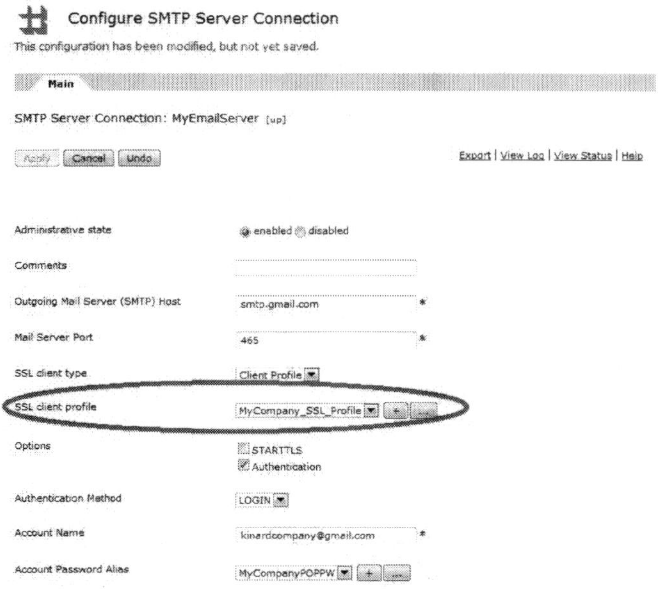

Figure 5-53 – Partner Destination – SMTP Server Connection.

In the Configure SMTP Server Connection screen you need provide the host name or IP address of the SMTP Outgoing Mail Server and its port number. If the server requires SSL and/or account authentication this information also needs to be provided in this screen. In our example we are using SSL and Account Authentication. An example of the SSL client profile we are using is seen in Figure 5-54.

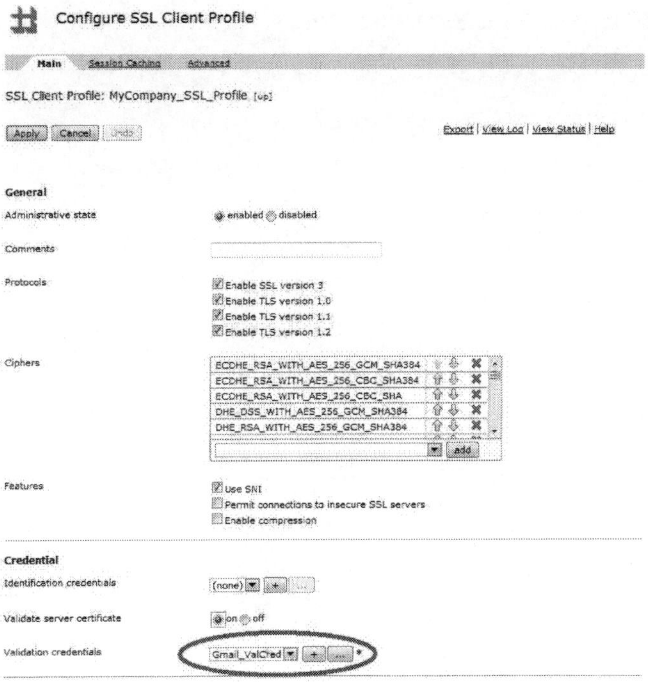

Figure 5-54 SMTP Destination SSL Client Profile.

You have the option of validating the SMTP Server certificate. If you choose not to validate the certificate it will accept the certificate presented by the server and use it for securing the connection. In our example we are validating the server certificate; an example of this configuration is seen in Figure 5-55.

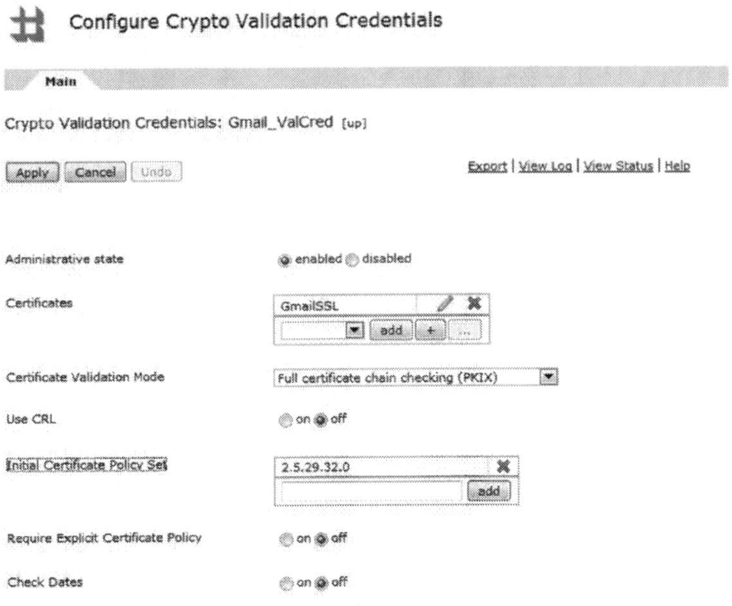

Configure Crypto Validation Credentials

Main

Crypto Validation Credentials: Gmail_ValCred [up]

[Apply] [Cancel] [Undo]   Export | View Log | View Status | Help

Administrative state	⦿ enabled ⦾ disabled
Certificates	GmailSSL ✏ ✖
	[▼] [add] [+] [...]
Certificate Validation Mode	Full certificate chain checking (PKIX) [▼]
Use CRL	⦾ on ⦿ off
Initial Certificate Policy Set	2.5.29.32.0 ✖
	[add]
Require Explicit Certificate Policy	⦾ on ⦿ off
Check Dates	⦾ on ⦿ off

Figure 5-55 SMTP Destination SSL Profile Crypto ValCred.

After configuring the SMTP Client profile you must apply the configuration in each screen to get back to the Destination Configuration screen. To save the destination, you need to click on the Apply button inside the destination configuration screen and then click on the Apply button again in the profile configuration screen after you have configured all of the required fields for the profile.

If you have multiple destinations configured as we do in the examples provided, you will need to move the SMTP destination to the default location at the top of the Destination list or make sure the B2B Gateway Service has it explicitly selected as seen in Figure 5-56.

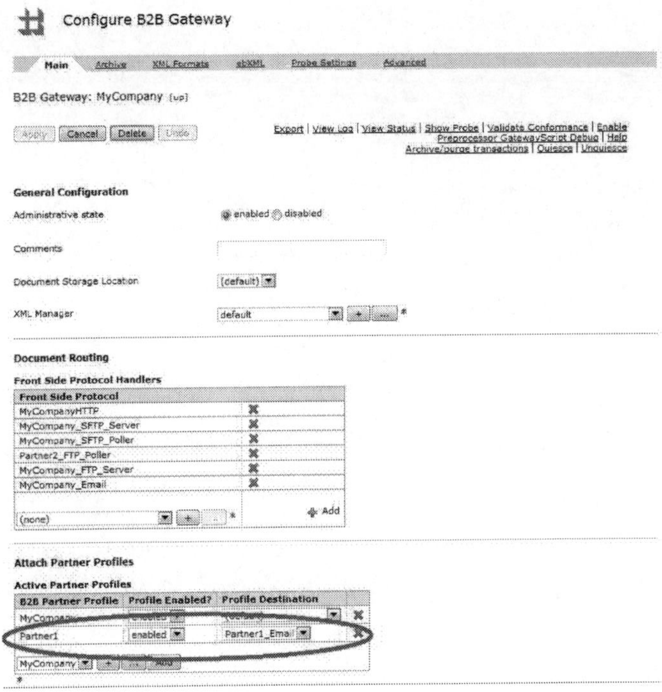

Figure 5-56 – B2B Gateway Service with Partner1 SMTP Destination.

When the file is picked up from the back-end location and determined to be destined for the external partner the B2B Gateway Service will email the file as an attachment to the partner based on the SMTP Destination we configured in the partner profile Destination tab.

Figure 5-57 illustrates an example of this flow as seen in the B2B Transaction Viewer where the receiving partner is Partner1.

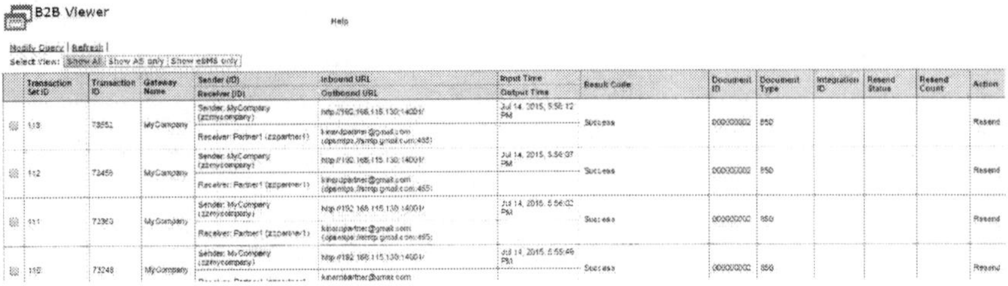

Figure 5-57 B2B Transaction Viewer – Outbound Email.

NOTE—MPGW and Sending Email

A Multi-protocol gateway can also be used to send and receive email messages. When used in conjunction with a B2B Gateway Service, the Multi-Protocol Gateway Server becomes either a pre or post process to the B2B Gateway, commonly known as service chaining.

DataPower B2B with MQ Managed File Transfer

DataPower B2B, when used with MQ Managed File Transfer (MQ MFT) (a.k.a MQ FTE), facilitates the secure, reliable and real-time transfer of files over the Internet between trading partners and systems inside the trusted network. MQ MFT is a manageable and auditable file transfer solution that provides greater visibility and control of file transfer activity over a MQ Network to your internal systems. This pattern is commonly used by customers who want to use a robust and fully auditable internal file transfer solution and would like to connect it securely to external trading partners using standards based protocols.

NOTE—IBM MQ Managed File Transfer (MFT)

Detailed information on IBM MQ Managed File Transfer can be found at the following URL: http://www-03.ibm.com/software/products/en/ibm-mq-managed-file-transfer

---

Our example uses DataPower B2B in the DMZ to trade AS2 (common AS2 patterns can be found in Chapter 4 of this book) transactions with trading partners while using DataPower's protocol bridging capabilities to integrate to the internal network over MQ MFT. Figure 5-58 illustrates the inbound and outbound flows used in the example; we are only showing the DataPower B2B Gateway and Partner configuration for this scenario. The MQ MFT configuration consisting of Queue Managers, Queues, Listeners, Monitoring, etc. should be completed on the MQ MFT servers following the MQ MFT documentation prior to configuring DataPower B2B.

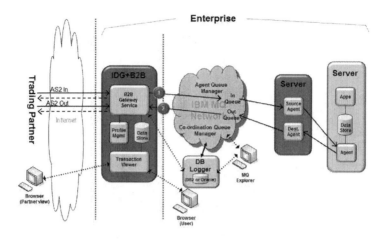

Figure 5-58 DataPower B2B with MQ MFT.

1. Inbound AS2 to MQ MFT Backside

This pattern requires the B2B Module and is used when you want your external communications with trading partners to benefit from using AS2 messaging for secured, non-repudiated file transfer over the Internet and need to integrate with your internal MQ MFT network for sending files to applications in the internal network.

NOTE—IBM MQ Managed File Transfer (MFT)

Files coming from partners can be any protocol DataPower supports. We are using AS2 in this example since it is the most widely used B2B Messaging protocol in use for file transfer across all industries.

The first step is to create a MQ Queue Manager Object in DataPower that links to the Queue Manager being used by MQ MFT. You can create the MQ Queue Manager object by navigating to the MQ Queue Manager link in the Left Navigation Menu and clicking on the Add button as seen in Figure 5-59.

Figure 5-59 MQ Queue Manager Creation.

There are multiple tabs in the MQ Queue Manager configuration screen. We are only interested in the Main tab and only need to configure the Name field with a descriptive name, Host Name field with the host name or IP address and port of your MQ Listener and the Queue Manager Name field which should match the MQ Queue Manager name you are using in IBM MQ MFT. Figure 5-60 illustrates what a configured MQ Queue Manager object looks like.

Figure 5-60 MQ Queue Manager Configuration.

To receive AS2 messages from trading partners, you need an AS2 Front Side Protocol Handler to be configured in your B2B Gateway Service. This AS2 Listener must be added to the Front Side Protocol Handlers table in the Document Routing section of the Main tab as seen in Figure 5-61.

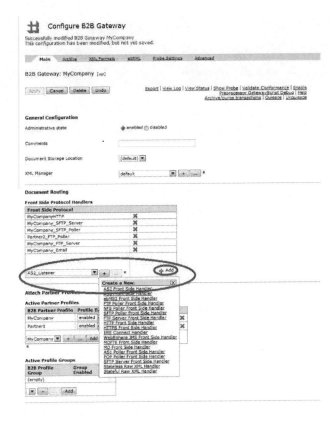

Figure 5-61 B2B Gateway - AS2 Front Side Handler.

Figure 5-62 illustrates what a configured AS2 Front Side Handler looks like. It is a simple HTTP Listener that has logic built in to process AS2 messages. For this example we only configured the Local IP Address and Port Number and took all of the defaults for the remaining fields.

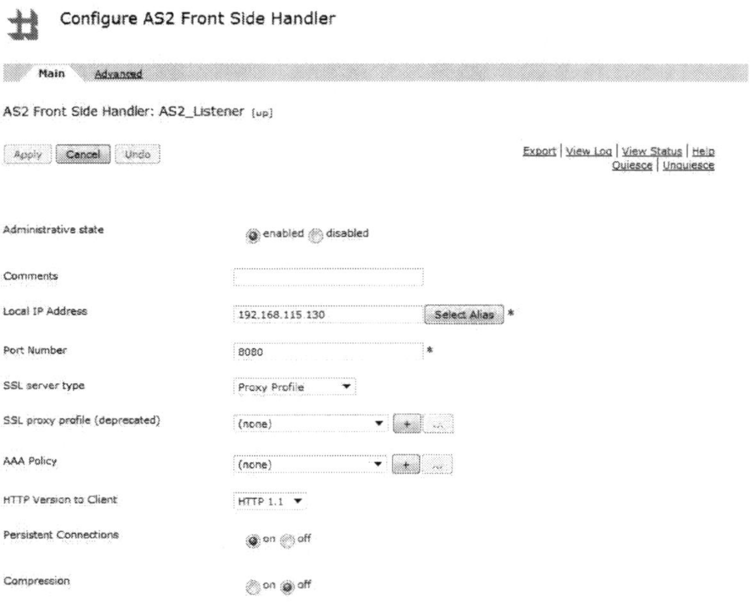

Configure AS2 Front Side Handler

Main	Advanced

AS2 Front Side Handler: AS2_Listener [up]

Apply Cancel Undo

Export | View Log | View Status | Help
Quiesce | Unquiesce

Administrative state	⦿ enabled ◯ disabled
Comments	[ ]
Local IP Address	192.168.115 130 Select Alias *
Port Number	8080 *
SSL server type	Proxy Profile ▾
SSL proxy profile (deprecated)	(none) ▾ [+] ...
AAA Policy	(none) ▾ [+] ...
HTTP Version to Client	HTTP 1.1 ▾
Persistent Connections	⦿ on ◯ off
Compression	◯ on ⦿ off

Figure 6-62 Configure AS2 Front Side Handler.

In addition to the AS2 Front Side Handler we also need a MQFTE Destination on the Internal Partner profile. For our example we added a MQFTE Destination to the MyCompany Profile as seen in Figure 5-63.

In the Destination table we click on Add button in the lower right side of the table and select dpmqfte:// from the drop down and type in a destination that corresponds with our MQ MFT configuration.

In our example we are using the following destination: dpmqfte://QM1/?RequestQueue=IDG_IN&DestAgent=QM1.AGENT&DestQM=QM1&DestFile=/tmp/fte/

- QM1 is the name of the MQ Queue Manager object we created, the RequestQueue is the name of the queue that is being monitored by MQ MFT.

- DestAgent is the MQ MFT Agent that is to receive this file.

- DestQM is the name of the Queue Manager servicing the queue and DestFile is the directory location where you want the file written to inside your network.

- You can also include a file name if you want the files to be written with a specific name; DataPower will create a filename if one is not present.

When Use Unique File Names is checked the handler will write out each file with a unique name.

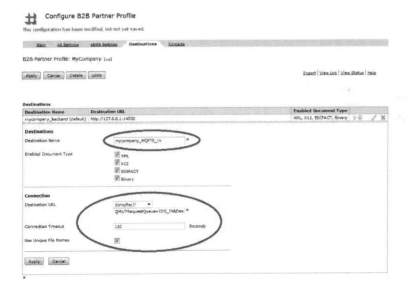

Figure 5-63 Configure MyCompany MQFTE Destination.

After completing the MyCompany MQFTE destination configuration, you can save it by clicking on the Apply button and then click on the Apply button again in the B2B Partner Configuration screen. Also, be sure to move the MQFTE destination to the default location in the destinations table by clicking on the up arrow to the right of the destination or go into the B2B Gateway Service and explicitly select the MQFTE destination in the Attach Partner Profiles table for the MyCompany profile.

When the AS2 message is received from the partner and determined to be destined for the internal partner, the B2B Gateway Service will process the AS2 message by verifying the profiles exist in the B2B Gateway, verifying the signature, decrypting the message and detaching the file and then sending the file to the internal partner's MQFTE destination.

Figure 5-64 illustrates an example of this flow as seen in the B2B Transaction Viewer where the receiving partner is MyCompany and the Outbound URL is the dpmqfte:// location set in the destination. Additionally, there is now an integration ID associated with the transaction.

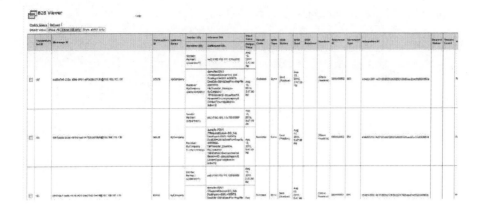

Figure 5-64 B2B Viewer Inbound AS2 to MQ MFT.

2. Outbound AS2 from MQ MFT Backside

This pattern requires the B2B Module and is used when you want to consume files from your internal MQ MFT network and send them to trading partners using AS2 to secure and non-repudiate the file transfers.

We need an MQFTE front side handler in the B2B Gateway Service to consume messages off of the queue where the MQ MFT Source Agent is dropping files for DataPower to pick up.

To create a MQFTE Front Side Handler, click on the plus sign to the right of the drop down field in the Front Side Protocol Handlers table and select MQFTE Front Side Handler as seen in Figure 5-65.

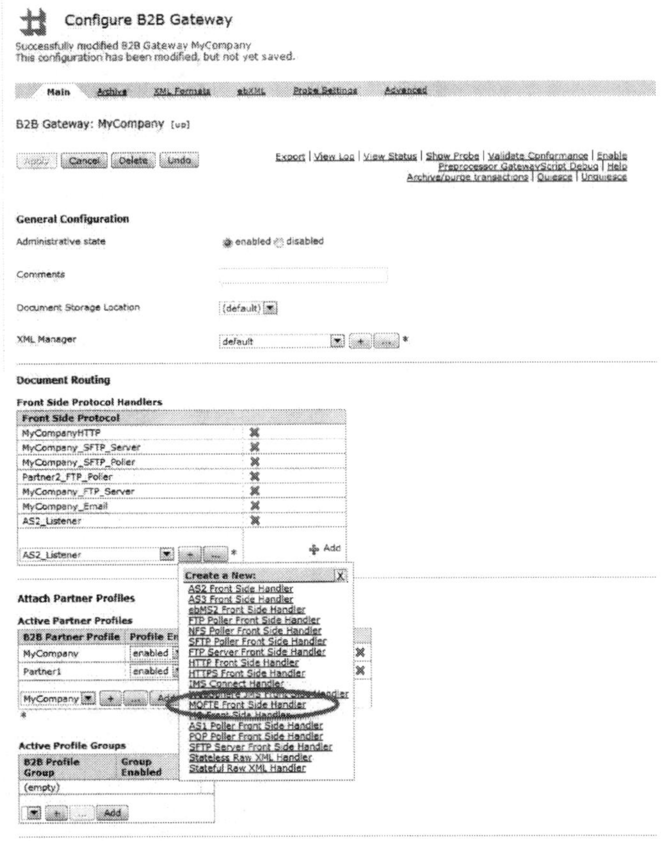

Figure 5-65 B2B Gateway - Create MQFTE Front Side Handler.

We need a MQFTE Front Side Handler to poll files from inside the network. We are using the same MQ Queue Manager object we created in the inbound MQ MFT pattern by selecting it from the drop down in the Queue Manager field. We are polling files every 30 seconds from the IDG_OUT queue. Figure 5-66 shows the MQFTE Front Side Handler configuration we used in this example.

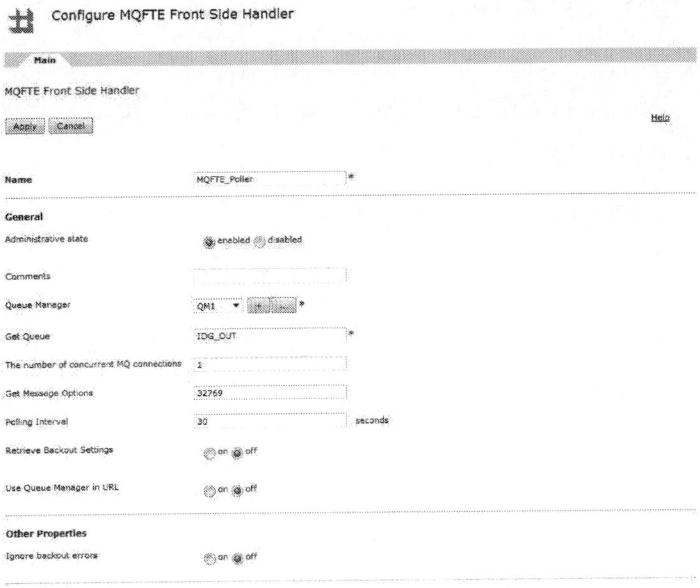

Figure 5-66 Configure MQFTE Front Side Handler.

After completing the MQFTE Front Side Handler configuration, you can save it by clicking on the Apply button. Be sure to click on the Add button in the far right bottom of the Front Side Handler table to add the handler to the B2B Gateway and then click on the Apply button in the B2B Gateway Service configuration screen.

The MQFTE Source Agent can optionally be configured with the following metadata when integrating with the DataPower B2B Module, when set the B2B Gateway will use the following information to match the right partner profile settings:

- DPMQFTESenderID is the business ID of internal partner

- DPMQFTEReceiverID is the business ID of external partner
- DPMQFTEContentType is the content type of message payload

When the file is received from the MQFTE Queue that is being polled by the MQFTE Front Side Handler, the business IDs are identified by looking in the payload or by looking at the MQ headers that contain the Business ID's. The file is routed based on the receiving partner's Destination.

In our example, that destination is an AS2 destination. Figure 5-67 illustrates what the AS2 Destination looks like for Partner1. After setting the destination in the profile be sure to move the AS2 destination to the default location in the destinations table by clicking on the up arrow to the right of the destination or go into the B2B Gateway Service and explicitly select the AS2 destination in the Attach Partner Profiles table for the Partner1 profile.

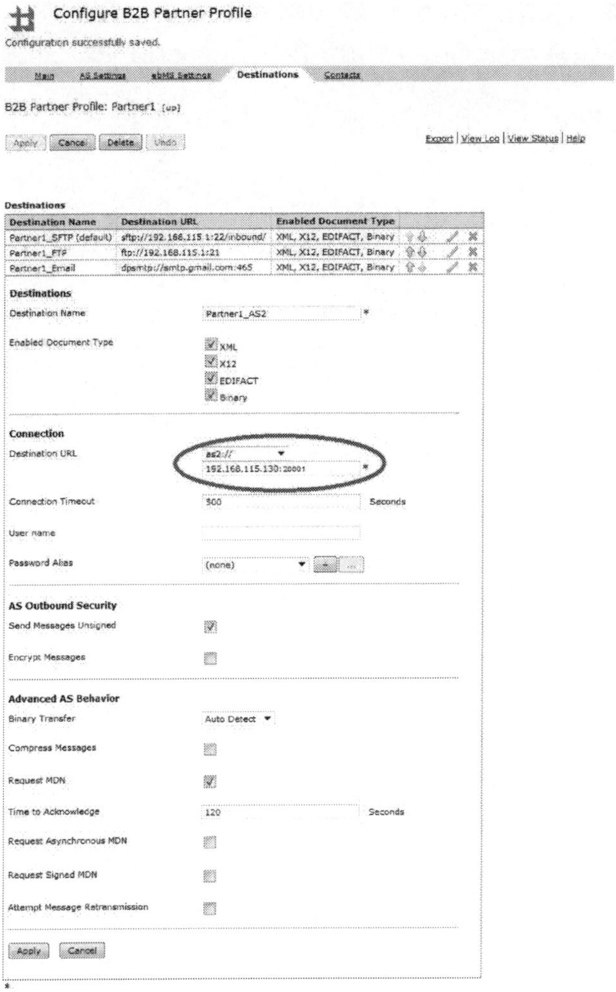

Figure 5-67 Partner1 AS2 Destination.

Figure 5-68 illustrates an example of this flow as seen in the B2B Transaction Viewer where the receiving partner is Partner1 and the Outbound URL is the AS2 location set in

, Partner1's destination. Additionally, there is now an integration ID associated with the transaction.

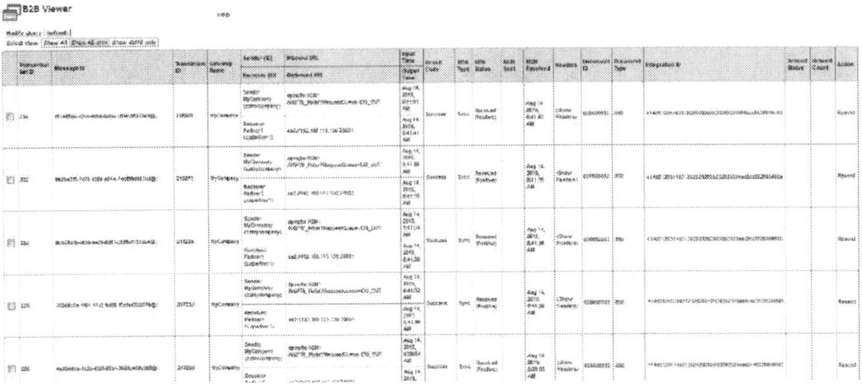

Figure 5-68 B2B Transaction Viewer – Outbound AS2 from MQ MFT.

Extending Transaction Visibility to MQ MFT Transactions

MQ FTE Handlers exist in both the Integration Module and B2B Module. However, one feature unique to the B2B Module when used with MQ MFT allows customers to use the B2B Viewer to see the status of transactions end-to-end. This is done by linking the B2B Gateway Service to the MQ MFT DBLogger database using the SQL Data Source configuration in the Advanced tab of the B2B Gateway Service. Figure 5-69 illustrates what the B2B Gateway SQL Data Source configuration looks like.

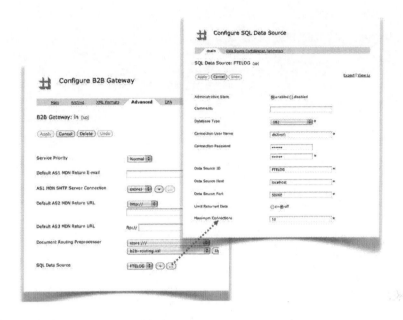

Figure 5-69 B2B Gateway SQL Data Source Configuration.

After configuring the DBLogger data source in the B2B Gateway Service the Integration ID link can be used to display the file transfer status through MQ MFT. Figure 5-70 illustrates how the file is viewed in DataPower when the Integration ID link is selected.

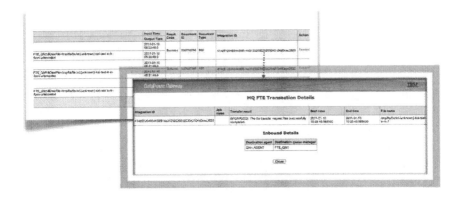

Figure 5-70 B2B Viewer – Linked to a MQ MFT transaction.

Summary

This chapter provided you with an overview of how DataPower is used for Managed File Transfer. There are two primary methods used in the examples; proxy of data using a Multi-Protocol Gateway Service and transferring data using a gateway pattern and profile management. This chapter demonstrates patterns for the most widely used file transfer protocols; FTP, SFTP, POP, SMTP and MQ FTE.

Chapter 6 DataPower OpenPGP Integration

This chapter presents a detailed description of how to configure DataPower to use OpenPGP encryption when sending files and OpenPGP decryption when receiving files from trading partners. It showcases an example of how we can use DataPower's Gateway Script functionality to make an external call to an instance of OpenPGP that resides on an external server for PGP encryption and decryption. If OpenPGP is not a requirement, we recommend the use of X.509 security which is already available on DataPower today.

History of PGP

In 1991, cryptography master Philip Zimmermann released version 1.0 of his Pretty Good Privacy (PGP), an email encryption software package, for free on the Internet. The release of Zimmermann's software triggered an investigation by the U.S. Attorney's Office, seeking prosecution for violations regarding the export of cryptography software outside of the United States. The case was dropped, leading Zimmermann to found a company called PGP Inc. Due to various license and patent issues that encumbered the software; a new, freely available standard was created. This new standard, based on PGP v5.3, is called OpenPGP and is the format of PGP that will be used in this book.

The OpenPGP Request for Comments (RFC) can be reviewed at the following URL:

http://www.ietf.org/rfc/rfc4880.txt

While an RFC is not officially a standard, it becomes the accepted authoritative format in practice once adopted by multiple users. If all vendors are compliant with the standard, logic dictates they should be interoperable. But, this is not always the case as not all implementations may fully support the standard or they may interpret the standard differently. Various implementations of OpenPGP exist including Bouncy Castle, OpenPGP.js and GNU Privacy Guard. For the purposes of this book, the Bouncy Castle implementation will be used.

Why OpenPGP?

The original intended use of PGP was to provide a mechanism to secure email messages. Since that time, its use has been expanded to secure files of any type. OpenPGP continues this expanded support and with it offers the following features:

- Digital signatures
- Encryption
- Compression
- Radix-64 conversion (Base64 with checksum)
- Key management and certificate services

OpenPGP does not dictate a mandatory transport. However, there is an additional RFC (http://www.ietf.org/rfc/rfc3156.txt) that describes how MIME can be used with it. This book will focus on encryption and decryption of embedded messages. These messages may be a standalone message from a FTP or SFTP server, the payload portion of an AS2 message, an HTTP POST, or just a single element in an XML message from any transport.

The Bouncy Castle implementation of OpenPGP supports both ASCII-armored and binary objects. This means that your keys, certificates and encryption outputs can be either ASCII-armored or binary. We will only be using ASCII-armored in this chapter as it makes the output easier to view, both in this book or when performing testing on your own. The actual payloads can be text (such as XML or EDI), or binary (such as a zip file or png image). Capacity planning is crucial to be sure there is enough memory available for the encrypt/decrypt process. Payload sizes will be limited by the amount of memory being used on the system by all processes.

Deployment of the OpenPGP Web Service and DataPower Configuration

DataPower can be configured, with a small helper application, to utilize OpenPGP in message exchanges with your trading partners. This chapter will present the use of the Bouncy Castle OpenPGP implementation running in a web service on a Windows server. DataPower will make a call to this web service when messages need to be encrypted or decrypted. All of the keys and certificates will be stored on the DataPower device and are passed to this web service with each call. Figure 6-1 shows DataPower making a call to the OpenPGP Web Service for encryption and decryption.

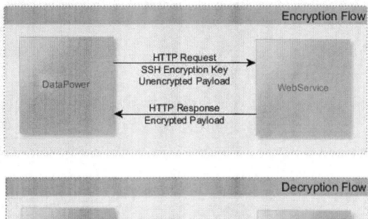

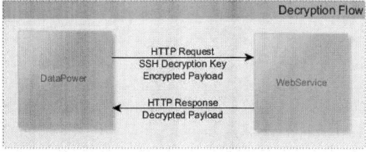

Figure 6-1 PGP Encryption/Decryption from DataPower.

Since private keys and unencrypted data will be going over the network, you should make sure the connection is secured. The use of SSL is the most common way to secure a connection. However, SSL is not foolproof and should be complemented with Access Control List capabilities of the inner firewall when running the OpenPGP Service in the trusted zone. For example, configure a firewall rule that only allows the IP address of the DataPower instance to access the system running the service. Another method that can be used is to deploy the OpenPGP Web Service system in the same rack as DataPower and use a crossover Ethernet cable to connect the OpenPGP web service system directly to one of

DataPower's Ethernet ports, thus creating a private two-system network.

Figure 6-2 depicts a deployment consistent with securing the OpenPGP web service system in the trusted zone and configuring a firewall rule to only allow access to the system from the DataPower IP address.

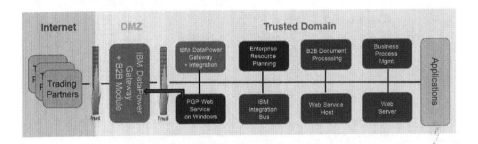

Figure 6-2 DataPower with PGP Web Service in the Trusted Zone.

Figure 6-3 depicts a deployment consistent with securing the OpenPGP web service system in the DMZ by directly connecting the DataPower System to the OpenPGP web service system on dedicated Ethernet adapters, thus creating a secure private network between the two devices.

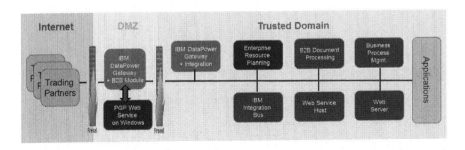

Figure 6-3 DataPower with PGP Web Service in DMZ on Private Network.

OpenPGP Web Service Deployment

The first step in utilizing the OpenPGP web service with DataPower is to ensure that Java 7 or 8 is installed on the system where the web service will be running. If the installed Java version does not include the unlimited Java Cryptography Extension (JCE) files, follow the instructions on Oracle's web site, shown below. Otherwise, you will receive key-size errors when processing files.

http://www.oracle.com/technetwork/java/javase/downloads/index.html

NOTE—Determining Your Java Version

You can determine what version of Java is installed by launching a command prompt and typing java –version; it should be JRE 1.7.0 or JRE 1.8.0. To check if the unlimited JCE is installed, navigate to the java/jre/lib/security directory, open the local_Policy.jar file in a Zip Application like 7-Zip and open the default_local.policy file in a text editor such as Notepad. If the policy file states there are no restrictions to any algorithms then you are using the unlimited JCE. There may be multiple versions of Java installed, ensure you are reviewing the Java version included in the path environment variable.

The example web service is written in Java and uses the Bouncy Castle Java implementation. The full source code and binary release of this implementation is available on the GitHub web site below:

https://github.com/CyberLinkComputing/openpgp-webservice

Default host and port numbers, a sample SSL certificate and sample OpenPGP keys are provided for testing. You can build the project using Apache Maven (http://maven.apache.org) or download a binary release version. The instructions below use the release version on Windows.

1. Download the openpgpwebservice-0.95-binary-release.zip file from the GitHub web site.

2. Unzip/expand the release zip version to the computer you are installing the OpenPGP web service on.

3. Open a command prompt to the expanded directory and launch the bin\openpgpwebservice.bat batch file from the current directory. When the program launches you will see a screen status like Figure 6-4.

This Java web service will need to be accessible from DataPower. By default it will listen on all IPv4 network addresses using port 8080 for unencrypted traffic and 8443 for SSL connections. The default IP address and port numbers can be overridden by executing the openpgpwebservices.bat file with additional parameters. The first parameter is for non-encrypted traffic and the second parameter is for SSL-encrypted traffic. For example, to change the default ports for this example start the script as shown in Listing 6-1.

Listing 6-1 Successful Launch of the PGP Web Service.

```
bin\openpgpwebservice.bat 8081 9443

C:\temp\pgptest\openpgpwebservice-0.95-binary-release>dir

 Volume in drive C is OS

 Volume Serial Number is C657-7CDC

 Directory of C:\temp\pgptest\openpgpwebservice-0.95-binary-release

01/07/2015  02:25 PM    <DIR>          .

01/07/2015  02:25 PM    <DIR>          ..

01/07/2015  02:25 PM    <DIR>          bin

01/07/2015  02:25 PM    <DIR>          certs

01/07/2015  02:25 PM    <DIR>          js

01/07/2015  02:25 PM    <DIR>          pgpkeys

01/07/2015  02:25 PM    <DIR>          repo

               0 File(s)              0 bytes

               7 Dir(s)  14,521,196,544 bytes free

C:\temp\pgptest\openpgpwebservice-0.95-binary-
release>bin\openpgpwebservice.bat 8081 9443

Jan 07, 2015 2:45:57 PM
com.sun.jersey.api.core.PackagesResourceConfig init

INFO: Scanning for root resource and provider classes in the
packages:

   com.clcomputing.openpgp.controllers

Jan 07, 2015 2:45:57 PM
com.sun.jersey.api.core.ScanningResourceConfig logClasses

INFO: Root resource classes found:

   class com.clcomputing.openpgp.controllers.PGPServiceController

Jan 07, 2015 2:45:57 PM
com.sun.jersey.api.core.ScanningResourceConfig init

INFO: No provider classes found.

Jan 07, 2015 2:45:57 PM
com.sun.jersey.server.impl.application.WebApplicationImpl _initiate

INFO: Initiating Jersey application, version 'Jersey: 1.18.1
02/19/2014 03:28 AM'

Jan 07, 2015 2:45:57 PM
org.glassfish.grizzly.http.server.NetworkListener start
```

```
INFO: Started listener bound to [0.0.0.0:8081]

Jan 07, 2015 2:45:57 PM org.glassfish.grizzly.http.server.HttpServer
start

INFO: [HttpServer] Started.

Jan 07, 2015 2:45:57 PM
com.sun.jersey.server.impl.application.WebApplicationImpl _initiate

INFO: Initiating Jersey application, version 'Jersey: 1.18.1
02/19/2014 03:28 AM'

Jan 07, 2015 2:45:58 PM
org.glassfish.grizzly.http.server.NetworkListener start

INFO: Started listener bound to [0.0.0.0:9443]

Jan 07, 2015 2:45:58 PM org.glassfish.grizzly.http.server.HttpServer
start

INFO: [HttpServer-1] Started.

Press enter to stop the server...
```

DataPower Deployment and Configuration

This section describes the steps required to prepare the DataPower system to support using the OpenPGP web service example. The DataPower deployment can be the physical DataPower appliance or the virtual DataPower appliance. In this book we are using the B2B Module and a B2B Gateway Service for the examples, but the OpenPGP web service will also work with a Multi-protocol Gateway Service. The two configurations, one for B2B and one for a Multi-protocol gateway are described below.

OpenPGP with B2B Gateway Service

Instead of providing every configuration step, a domain export has been supplied. The remainder of this section will describe the key touch points of the imported domain with respect to their usage for OpenPGP. For any information on general B2B Gateway Service configuration, refer to previous chapters in this book.

An export of a preconfigured domain, PGP_Example, is provided in the export\datapower directory of the OpenPGP web service project. The OpenPGP Example domain uses four partner profiles and two B2B Gateway Services to properly test this flow. In this example all of the information is configured in a single DataPower domain and each partner will have an internal and external profile representation. When you import this example, it uses ports 27000, 27001, 28000, 28001 and 29000 on the DataPower appliance and may conflict with existing ports when testing on your own appliance. The ports can be changed in each of the http FSPH's in each B2B Gateway Service and in the Partner Destinations. Import the PGP_Example domain and then review the configuration as described below.

Files

The import will create a series of files which can be viewed using DataPower File Management from the Control Panel (see Figure 6-4) under the local: directory.

Figure 6-4 DataPower File Management.

These files will be shown in the //local:pgp/js directory:

- decryptB2B.js

- encryptB2B.js
- decryptverifyB2B.js
- signencryptB2B.js
- es6-promise.js
- pgpservice.js

These files will be shown in the pgp/keys directory:

- zzmypartner.pub.asc
- zzmypartner.secret.asc
- zzmypartner.secret.passphrase

The files in the pgp/keys directory have a specific naming convention that is used by the scripts from the pgp/js. When adding new files to the directory the same naming convention must be followed.

Description	Filename
OpenPGP Public Key	identifier.pub.asc
OpenPGP Secret Key	identifier.secret.asc
OpenPGP Secret Key Passphrase	identifier.secret.passphrase

Simply replace the identifier portion of the filename with an ID, to associate keys with a particular ID. In this example the keys are preceded with an ID of zzmypartner.

URL Configuration

The pgpservice.js file will need to be edited with the URL to where the Java Web Service resides. E.g. pgpservice.baseurl = http://10.8.5.8:8081/pgpservice/. In this example the base url is changed to match the IP Address and port I am using on my machine running the web service.

NOTE—Selecting Certificates

The keys in this example are used for the external partner profile and the business identifier of the partner. The .js scripts for B2B dynamically select the certificate to use based on the B2B identifier used in the data flow instead of hard coding the value in the .js files. The B2B .js files use custom context variables that are set from an XSL transform action to reflect the "to" and "from" partner IDs.

To make use of these .js files a document flow was configured. Our sample domain contains a basic HTTP flow in a pair of B2B Gateway Services that encrypts and decrypts the entire payload.

In our example, the payload is EDI-X12 to make it easier to natively find the partner profiles to use. However, the payload can be any type of document of your choosing providing you configure your system to appropriately identify the profiles to use. The B2B Gateway Services being used in this example can natively find partner information in EDI-X12, EDIFACT and XML files. Binary files must use the routing pre-processor to set the appropriate partner ids for the sender and receiver. Figure 6-5 depicts the configuration being used to test the OpenPGP Service. Since we are using two B2B Gateway Services we can test both encryption and decryption at the same time.

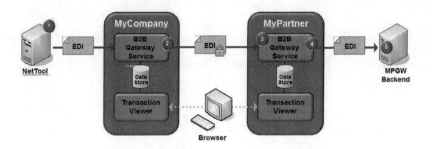

Figure 6-5 DataPower PGP_Example_Domain.

The Data flow for figure 6-5 is as follows:

1.   The EDI-X12 file is POSTed to HTTP port 27000 on the MyCompany B2B Gateway where the EDI-X12 file is parsed for sender and receiver information.

2.   The MyCompany B2B Gateway uses the processing policy in the external mypartner profile to encrypt the file using the PGP Web Service and sends it to the MyPartner B2B Gateway over http port 28000.

3.   Since the EDI-X12 file is encrypted the MyPartner B2B Gateway cannot parse the file for sender and receiver ID, so it will use the Routing pre-processor in the MyPartner B2B Gateway to set the partner profile IDs. We will match on the business ID's in the URL.   When the URL contains /zzmycompany/zzmypartner as the URI, the routing pre-processor policy in Listing 6-2 will extract the ID's from the URI.

Listing 6-2 Routing Pre-processor based on URI.

```
<?xml version="1.0" encoding="UTF-8"?>
```

```xml
<xsl:stylesheet exclude-result-prefixes="dp dpconfig" extension-
element-prefixes="dp regexp" version="1.0"
xmlns:dp="http://www.datapower.com/extensions"
xmlns:dpconfig="http://www.datapower.com/param/config"
xmlns:regexp="http://exslt.org/regular-expressions"
xmlns:xsl="http://www.w3.org/1999/XSL/Transform">


    <!-- =================================================== -->

    <!-- == Stylesheet: DataPower B2B Dynamic-->

    <!-- == Version:1.0-->

    <!-- =================================================== -->

    <!-- == History: -->

    <!-- == -->

    <!-- == Description:  Sets routing variables-->

    <!-- == Returns: N/A-->

    <!--
=================================================== -->
    <xsl:template match="/">

        <xsl:variable name="uri"
select="dp:variable('var://service/URI')" />

        <xsl:variable name="path"
select="dp:variable('var://service/URL-in')" />

        <xsl:variable name="beforeSlash">

            <xsl:value-of select="regexp:replace($uri,'^\/([A-Za-
z0-9\-]+)\/([A-Za-z0-9\-]+)','','$1')"/>

        </xsl:variable>

        <xsl:variable name="afterSlash">

            <xsl:value-of select="regexp:replace($uri,'^\/([A-Za-
z0-9\-]+)\/([A-Za-z0-9\-]+)','','$2')"/>

        </xsl:variable>

        <xsl:choose>

            <xsl:when test="contains($path,
'http://127.0.0.1:28000')">

                <dp:set-variable name="'var://service/b2b-doc-type'"
value="binary" />

                <dp:set-variable name="'var://service/b2b-partner-
from'" value="$beforeSlash" />

                <dp:set-variable name="'var://service/b2b-partner-
to'" value="$afterSlash" />

            </xsl:when>
```

```
    <xsl:otherwise>
        <!-- Autodetect -->
    </xsl:otherwise>
    </xsl:choose>
    </xsl:template>
</xsl:stylesheet>
```

4. After the trading partner relationship has been identified, the MyPartner B2B Gateway will use the processing policy in the internal mypartner profile to decrypt the file and will route the unencrypted EDI-X12 file to the simulated back-end MPGW.

5. The Back-end MPGW will throw away the request. We do not need it to properly test this scenario.

For the OpenPGP web service to be called, a GatewayScript action was added to a Processing Policy. In our example, we created an encrypt policy for the MyPartner external profile which is used in the MyCompany B2B Gateway and a decrypt policy for the internal MyPartner profile which is used in the MyPartner B2B Gateway.

Figure 6-6 shows what the encrypt policy looks like in our example. Listings 6-3 and 6-4 show what the xsl in the transform action and .js in GatewayScript action looks like respectively.

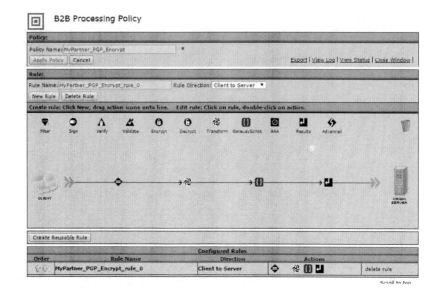

Figure 6-6 MyPartner PGP Encrypt Policy.

Listing 6-3 B2BIds.xsl - copies partner ID's to a context variable.

```
<?xml version="1.0" encoding="UTF-8"?>
<xsl:stylesheet version="2.0"
    xmlns:xsl="http://www.w3.org/1999/XSL/Transform"
    xmlns:dp="http://www.datapower.com/extensions"
    xmlns:dpconfig="http://www.datapower.com/param/config"
    extension-element-prefixes="dp" exclude-result-prefixes="dp
dpconfig">
    <xsl:output method="xml"/>


    <!-- ========================================================= -->
    <!-- == Stylesheet: DataPower B2B To and From IDs-->
    <!-- == Version:     1.0-->
    <!-- ========================================================= -->
    <!-- == History: -->
    <!-- ==-->
```

```
    <!-- == Description:  Captures sender and receiver details to
custom variables     -->

    <!-- == Returns: N/A-->

    <!-- =================================================== -->

      <xsl:template match="/">

          <!-- Source Data -->

      <xsl:variable name="from"
select="dp:variable('var://service/b2b-partner-from')"/>

      <xsl:variable name="to"
select="dp:variable('var://service/b2b-partner-to')"/>

          <!-- Write custom variables -->

      <dp:set-variable name="'var://context/message/b2bto'"
value="$to"/>

      <dp:set-variable name="'var://context/message/b2bfrom'"
value="$from"/>

    </xsl:template>
</xsl:stylesheet>
```

Listing 6-4 encryptB2B.js - uses the OpenPGP web service to encrypt.

```javascript
var pgpservice = require('pgp/js/pgpservice');
session.input.readAsBuffer(function (error, buffer) {
    if (error) {
        throw error;
    }
    var ctx = session.name('message');
    var toID = ctx.getVar('b2bto');

    pgpservice.encryptData(toID, buffer)
        .then(function (response) {
            session.output.write(response);
        })
        .catch(function (error) {
            throw error;
        });
});
```

Figure 6-7 shows what the decrypt policy looks like in our example and Listing 6-5 shows what the .js in GatewayScript action looks like, respectively. The xsl transform is identical to Listing 6-3.

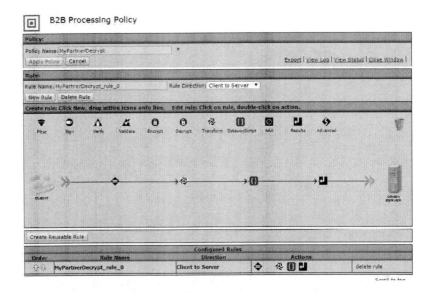

Figure 6-7 MyPartner PGP Decrypt Policy.

Listing 6-5 decryptB2B.js – uses the OpenPGP web service to decrypt.

```
var pgpservice = require('pgp/js/pgpservice');
session.input.readAsBuffer(function (error, buffer) {
    if (error) {
        throw error;
    }

    var ctx = session.name('message');
    var toID = ctx.getVar('b2bto');
```

```
pgpservice.decryptData(toID, buffer)
    .then(function (response) {
        session.output.write(response);
    })
    .catch(function (error) {
        throw error;
    });
});
```

Testing

We are using the NetTool Utility to send a sample EDI-X12 to the MyCompany B2B Gateway Service at HTTP port 27000 to test the PGP encryption and decryption service. NetTool can be downloaded from the following URL:

http://sourceforge.net/projects/nettool/

To test the example presented in this chapter all you need to do is the following:

1.   Start up the OpenPGP Web Service on a machine DataPower can access.

2.   Successfully import the PGP_Example domain into a DataPower device from the of the datapower\exports directory located in OpenPGP web service project.

3.   Change into the PGP_Example domain and edit the pgpservice.js file in the //local:pgp/js directory to point to the IP of the machine used in step 1 and the port number of the OpenPGP web service.

4.   Using NetTool, POST the pgptest.edi file to the IP of the DataPower device on port 27000 as seen in Figure 6-8. The sample EDI-X12 test file is found in

the payloads directory of OpenPGP web service project.

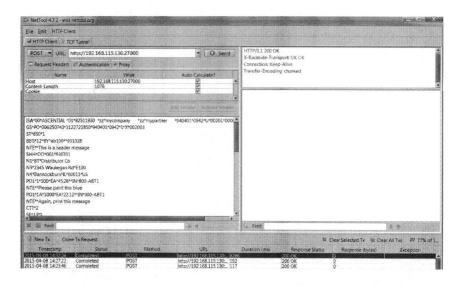

Figure 6-8 NetTool Post of PGPTest.edi to DataPower.

5.   Look at the B2B Viewer and verify you have successfully sent and received the file. It will look similar to Figure 6-9.   The latest transaction is always at the top.

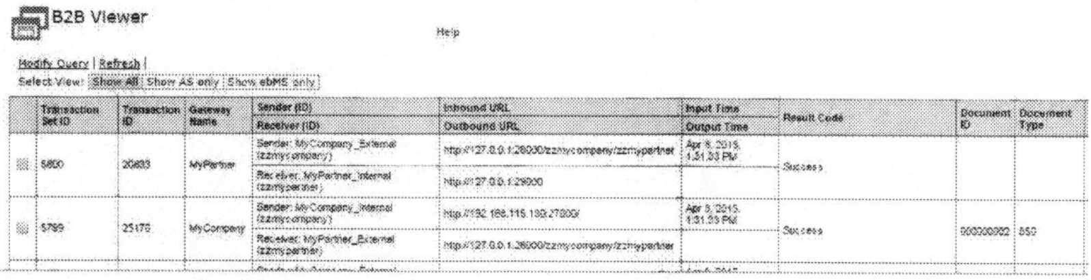

Figure 6-9 – B2B Viewer.

In this example you can see in transaction 5799 that the file was sent from mycompany to mypartner through the MyCompany B2B Gateway and it has a state of Success.

If you click on the 5799 Transaction Set ID a small menu will appear. Click on the content link and open the resulting output file. You can see that the content is PGP encrypted similar to Figure 6-10.

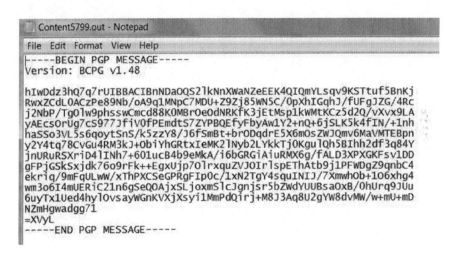

Figure 6-10 – PGP encrypted outbound file sent to zzmypartner.

You can also see in transaction 5800 that the file was received by mypartner from mycompany through the MyPartner B2B Gateway and it has a state of Success.

If you click on the 5800 Transaction Set ID a small menu will appear. Click on the content link and open the resulting output file. You can see that the content is now decrypted similar to Figure 6-11.

```
Content5800.out - Notepad
File  Edit  Format  View  Help
ISA*00*ASCENTIAL *01*92511930  *zz*mycompany      *zz*mypartner
*940401*0942*U*00201*000000002*0*T*>
GS*PO*006250740*3122721850*940401*0942*1*X*002003ST*850*1
BEG*12*BY*ab100**931028NTE**This is a header messageSHH*DD*001*930701
N1*BT*Distributor CoN3*2345 Waukegan Rd*E100N4*Bannockburn*IL*60015*US
PO1*1*500*EA*45.26**IN*800-ABT1NTE**Please paint this blue
PO1*1A*1000*EA*22.12**IN*900-ABT1NTE**Again, print this messageCTT*2SE*13*1
ST*850*2   BEG*12*BY*ab100**931028NTE**This is a header messageSHH*DD*001*930701
N1*BT*Distributor CoN3*2345 Waukegan Rd*E100N4*Bannockburn*IL*60015*US
PO1*1*500*EA*45.26**IN*800-ABT1NTE**Please paint this blue
PO1*1A*1000*EA*22.12**IN*900-ABT1NTE**Again, print this messageCTT*2SE*13*2
ST*850*3   BEG*12*BY*ab100**931028NTE**This is a header messageSHH*DD*001*930701
N1*BT*Distributor CoN3*2345 Waukegan Rd*E100N4*Bannockburn*IL*60015*US
PO1*1*500*EA*45.26**IN*800-ABT1NTE**Please paint this blue
PO1*1A*1000*EA*22.12**IN*900-ABT1NTE**Again, print this messageCTT*2SE*13*3
GE*3*1IEA*1*000000002
```

Figure 6-11 Inbound file received by zzmypartner after decryption.

OpenPGP with Multi-protocol Gateway Service

You may not have the B2B Module or simply do not wish to use profile management with your binary flows. In this case you would use the non-B2B scripts in a Multi-Protocol Gateway service, similarly to what was described in the B2B section. Here are some basic steps to follow for a simple HTTP flow that encrypts the entire payload. No domain import is needed for this flow.

- Create the //local:pgp/js and //local:pgp/keys directories for your domain. Upload the files for the js and keys directories from the source code found on the GitHub website.
  - These files should be added to the pgp/js directory: encrypt.js (for encryption), decrypt.js (for decryption), es6-promise.js, pgpservice.js.
  - These sample files should be added to the pgp/keys directory: zzmypartner.pub.asc,

zzmypartner.secret.asc,

zzmypartner.secret.passphrase

- Edit the pgpservice.js file in the //local:pgp/js directory to point to the IP and port number of the of the OpenPGP web service.

- Edit the encrypt.js file to use the partner id of the encryption key.

- Configure a Multi-Protocol Gateway, using an HTTP front side handler.

- Add a processing policy with a GatewayScript action to the Multi-Protocol Gateway that was just created. To perform an encryption of the payload, specify the encrypt.js file as shown in figure 6-12.

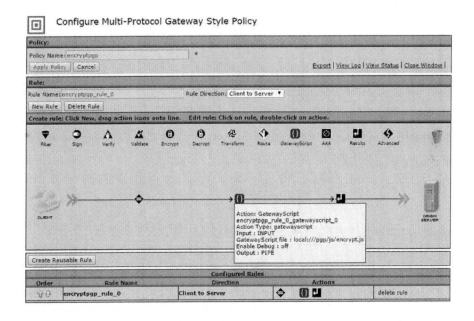

Figure 6-12 Multi-protocol gateway policy.

Note that our example script uses the ID of "zzmypartner". This means that all messages will be encrypted with the "zzmypartner" encryption key. This ID value is what correlates to the identifier section of the filenames in the pgp/keys directory. See the B2B section above for more details on the files in the pgp/keys directory.

To perform OpenPGP decryption, simply replace the encrypt.js with the decrypt.js file in the processing policy.

Testing

Send a test document, with NetTool, or other program, to the HTTP front-side handler. Using the probe to view the intermediate files, the content will be similar to what is described in the B2B section above. See figure 6-13 and 6-14 for the test results.

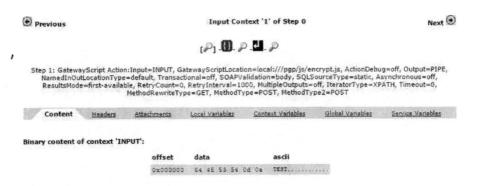

Figure 6-13 Test result showing plain text in probe.

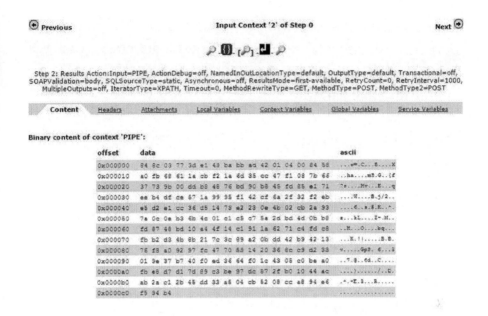

Figure 6-14 Test result showing encrypted text in probe.

Additional Document Flows

There are several ways to use the OpenPGP service. Below are two alternative use cases supplied with the sample code.

Sign and Encrypt Case

It may be desirable to do both encryption and signing of the document. In this case you would also provide your public, private and passphrase files for your profile (zzmycompany) and place them in the //local:pgp/keys directory. Use the signencryptB2B.js script for B2B or signencrypt.js script for a multi-protocol gateway.

Decrypt and Verify Case

It may be desirable to do both decryption and verification of the document. In this case you would also provide your public, private and passphrase files for your profile (zzmycompany) and place them in the //local:pgp/keys directory. Use the decryptverifyB2B.js script for B2B or decryptverify.js script for a multi-protocol gateway.

Summary

This chapter has provided an application, scripts, sample encryption runs and knowledge necessary to use OpenPGP with DataPower. Some customizations may be required to allow the use of the provided artifacts in your environment. Our example used unencrypted connections, but enabling SSL for the HTTP web service is essential before implementing this OpenPGP solution for production usage. When enabling SSL, replace any sample certificates provided with DataPower and the OpenPGP Web Service. In addition to SSL, follow the recommended securing techniques for the server connections.

Chapter 7 DataPower B2B with IBM Sterling B2B and IBM Systems Integration

This chapter describes how DataPower B2B can be used as a security gateway in front of IBM Integration Bus (IIB) as well as IBM Sterling B2B Integrator (B2Bi). The most common way to integrate DataPower B2B to IBM Integration Bus and IBM Sterling B2B Integrator is by using IBM MQ or MQ Managed File Transfer as an intermediary. DataPower B2B provides consolidation of proxy, FTP and SFTP servers in the DMZ and secure connections to partners outside of the trusted network. This chapter is not intended to give the reader detailed configuration steps for any of the products, but rather provide you with information to help you understand how IBM DataPower Gateway (IDG) with the B2B Module supports the proxy and gateway patterns used with IBM Systems Middleware and IBM Sterling solutions. This chapter assumes the reader already understands how to create standard DataPower objects, like MQ queue manager objects, crypto objects, AAA policy objects, SSL proxy objects, SSH client objects and front-side and back-side protocol handlers.

This chapter also does not show the configuration for IBM Integration Bus, The Standards Processing Engine nor the IBM Sterling solutions. When using MQ or MQMFT to communicate between DataPower and IBM Integration Bus or IBM Sterling B2B Integrator, the down-stream solution will poll the queue where DataPower is placing the files. When using FTP to communicate between DataPower and Sterling File Gateway, the Sterling solution will consume files with a FTP listener configured in Sterling File Gateway.

Value of DataPower B2B with IBM Integration Products

DataPower B2B with Sterling B2B

With the acquisition of Sterling Commerce, IBM quickly established itself as the top vendor in the B2B space. The Sterling portfolio provides a full suite of B2B products for both on-premise and off-premise deployment methods. Sterling also provides managed services on their Collaboration Network which was formerly called the Sterling Value Added Network (VAN). DataPower is best positioned as a security gateway in the DMZ in front of Sterling B2B Integrator or Sterling File Gateway. In this pattern both Sterling products would sit in the trusted network. In many cases, WebSphere MQ is used as an intermediary and persistence layer between DataPower and Sterling Integrator. Additionally, DataPower can be used to securely exchange data between the IBM Sterling Collaboration Network and your company.

By using DataPower B2B with Sterling B2B Integrator and/or Sterling File Gateway you get DataPower's market leading security and integration gateway capabilities for mobile, Web, API, B2B, SOA, and cloud workloads. You also get the market leading B2B processing capabilities of the Sterling B2B products.

DataPower B2B with IBM Integration Bus with the Standard Processing Engine

With the introduction of SPE module for IIB, this now provides an IIB customer support for B2B trading partner management, validation and transformation of EDI files, as well as acknowledgement support between them and their partners. IIB/SPE does not come with a security gateway at the edge of your network to address B2B messaging standards such as AS1, AS2, AS3, and ebMS. This is where utilizing DataPower B2B as your security gateway in the DMZ then integrating with IIB/SPE in the trusted zone would provide a complete B2B solution.

NOTE—DataPower B2B/IIB vs Sterling B2B

This solution is not intended to replace Sterling B2B solution but rather provide DataPower and IBM Integration Bus customers with a B2B solution if they do not have one today. This solution now provides the option to now use modules to extend their current investment in DataPower and IIB to support an end-to-end B2B Solution.

Key Benefits of using DataPower B2B in the DMZ

Each of these products has their own benefits individually. However, when used together, either of the combined solutions provides the other key benefits listed below:

- Moves B2B governance and security closer to the edge of the network. This rejects unwanted external connections before passing any data into the trusted network. It also means that partner traffic and profile configuration can be done without allowing partners to connect to the back-end trusted zone.

- Provides a reliable, robust and scalable architecture that is optimized to avoid bottlenecks on the back-end. This can reduce transaction loads on downstream systems by allowing DataPower to manage all external connections and routing decisions.

- Improves edge security by using a smart security gateway appliance in the DMZ, instead of a proxy server solution.

- Isolates trading partners from downstream system outages/issues by allowing DataPower to persist data to a queue where downstream systems can retrieve data when the network is available.

- Provides access to new channels of business by using DataPower's ability to support API Management, web services, B2B, SOA, cloud and mobile gateway patterns.

- Increases performance and efficiency of your B2B and file transfer flows.

- When using DataPower's hardware appliance, the B2B flows are optimized through hardware acceleration and gain the physical security provided by the IDG platform. This improves both security

and performance with B2B transaction volumes that
can be measured in the thousands per second.

AS2/EDI Pattern with DataPower B2B and IBM Integration Bus using SPE

This section describes the pattern most typically used with
DataPower B2B and IIB with SPE. As you already read in
Chapter 4 of this book, DataPower Gateway with the B2B
module provides the ability to support B2B messaging
protocols like AS1, AS2, AS3, and ebMS. However, if your need
is to also address B2B processing (validation of EDI structures,
transformation of EDI structures, generation of EDI functional
acknowledgement, EDI enveloping, EDI de-enveloping, control
number checking and generation), DataPower would require
IIB with SPE to fully support this requirement.

SPE is an optional module running on IIB. It consists of 3
nodes:

- Envelope Node
- De-Envelope Node
- Transformation Node

There is an additional SPE component for EDI Trading
Partner Management that can run on IIB. These partner
profiles hold the settings specific to EDI processing. The
settings are needed for generating EDI Functional
Acknowledgements, EDI enveloping, EDI de-enveloping, and
for generating and maintaining EDI Control numbers among
other things.

The Transformation Node comes with IBM Transformation Extender (ITX) (a.k.a. WTX) which is IBM's universal transformation engine for any-to-any transformation of messages and files. It consists of an Eclipse-based map design interface and Industry Packs for X12, EDIFACT, and HIPAA data formats. Industry packs are libraries of EDI and HIPAA data structures, valid code sets, and pre-defined validation rules.

Figure 7-1 depicts is an example architecture drawing showing an inbound AS2/EDI-X12 flow.

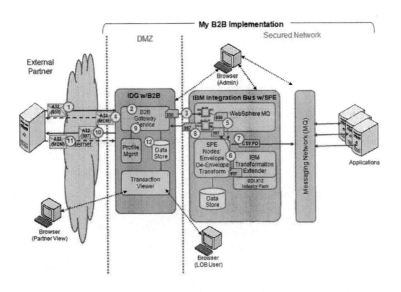

Fig 7-1 IDG+B2B with IIB+SPE data flow.

1. An X12-850 payload is wrapped in an AS2 message envelope and sent to IBM Datapower Gateway (IDG) with B2B Module sitting in the DMZ.

2.   The IDG receives the AS2 message, verifies the partner information, and unpackages the AS2 envelope.

3.   The B2B Gateway routes the X12-850 to the MQ queue defined in the internal partner profile's destination setting.

4.   After the X12-850 is successfully written to the MQ queue the B2B Gateway generates and sends an AS2 message disposition notification (MDN) back to the sending partner's system to inform it that the message was successfully received and the B2B Gateway marks the X12-850 transaction as complete.

5.   IBM Integration Bus (IIB) picks up the X12-850 from the q.in queue.

6.   IIB processes the X12-850 using Standards Processing Engine (SPE) and its nodes. The De-Envelope node parses the X12-850 and generates an X12-997 Functional Acknowledgement, routes the X12-997 to an out queue that is monitored by IDG B2B Gateway.

7.   SPE transformation node uses the ITX X12 industry pack to transform the X12-850 to CSV-PO.

8.   The IDB B2B Gateway picks up the X12-997 from the out queue.

9.   The B2B Gateway identifies the sending and receiving partner from the ISA header in the EDI payload, applies the attributes as defined in the receiving partner profile and wraps the X12-997 in

an AS2 messaging envelope as defined in the external partner profile's destination setting.

10. The B2B Gateway routes the AS2 message carrying the X12-997 payload to the external trading partner's configured destination.

11. The external trading partner sends a message disposition notification (MDN) to the B2B Gateway to inform it that the message was successfully received.

12. The B2B Gateway correlates the MDN to the original AS2 message and logs the X12-997 transaction as complete.

This is a gateway pattern where we are terminating the AS2 message in DataPower and responding back to the partner with the MDN. It requires a minimum of one external partner profile to represent the AS2 trading partner, an internal partner profile that represents the location or application where the EDI files need to go inside the trusted network (in this example we are using a MQ queue), and a B2B Gateway to process the AS2 messages and route the files. The As2 configuration for this pattern is similar to the AS2 configurations you have seen in Chapters 4 and 5. For this reason we are not repeating the configuration steps in this chapter. Please refer to the "DataPower B2B with MQ Managed File Transfer" section of Chapter 5 which demonstrates how to use MQ MFT to integrate to any downstream integration platform. If MQ is preferred you would use a MQ Front Side Protocol Handler in the B2B Gateway and MQ Destination in the internal profile which is described in the

"IBM Sterling Collaboration Network" pattern #1 in this chapter.

DataPower Patterns with Sterling Solutions

This section describes the patterns most typically used with Sterling solutions. In Figure 7-1, patterns 1 and 2 represent B2B messaging gateway patterns and patterns 3 and 4 represent proxy patterns. These patterns are described in detail in this section. DataPower does not currently support the Sterling Connect:Direct Protocol nor the PeSit protocol (a file transfer protocol developed in the 1980's by the French Interbank Teleclearing System Economic Interest Grouping). When using these protocols, Sterling Secure Proxy should be used in the DMZ to send the data to downstream Sterling applications.

Figure 7-2 illustrates the three typical DataPower patterns that can be used in DataPower B2B with Sterling File Gateway, Sterling B2B Integrator and the Sterling Collaboration Network (a.k.a. Sterling VAN).

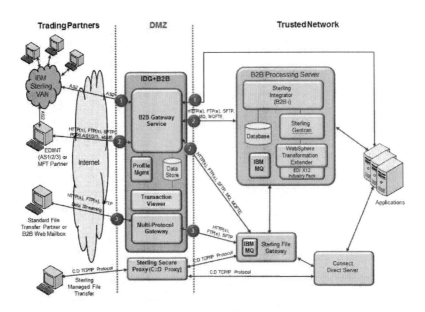

Figure 7-2 DataPower B2B with Sterling Solutions.

1. Integration with the IBM Sterling Collaboration Network

This gateway pattern is commonly used by customers who have many trading partners that also subscribe to the IBM Sterling Collaboration Network and wish to exchange B2B documents with them. The most common protocol of choice to communicate between your on-premise gateway and the Sterling Collaboration Network is AS2. However, DataPower can communicate with the IBM Sterling Collaboration Network over any protocol that is mutually supported by the services and DataPower.

Figure 7-3 illustrates this pattern in more detail. The IBM
Sterling Collaboration Network is not only providing a secure
connection to our trading partners, it is also validating and
transforming the EDI files into XML before sending the files to
the DataPower B2B Gateway Service.

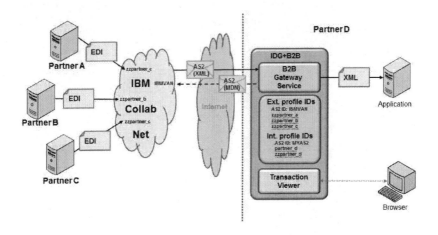

Figure 7-3 Connection to IBM Sterling Collaboration Network.

This is a gateway pattern where we are terminating the
AS2 message in DataPower and responding back to the partner
with the MDN. It requires 1) an external partner profile to
represent the IBM Sterling Collaboration Network, 2) an
internal partner profile that represents the location or
application where the files need to go inside the trusted
network and 3) a B2B Gateway to process the AS2 messages
and route the files.   The As2 configuration for this pattern is
similar to the AS2 configurations you have seen in previous
chapters of this book. The primary exception is the setting to

override AS2 IDs in the profiles to allow the payloads and AS2 messages to have different business IDs. It is a best practice to use a separate B2B Gateway for this scenario since it will handle traffic from multiple partners. In this way, it is easier to distinguish between point-to-point connections and VAN connections when looking at the B2B Transaction Viewer.

The key to supporting VAN patterns is being sure your VAN profile represents all partners that reside on the other side of the VAN. This means all of the business IDs for each VAN partner must be present in the external profile as seen in Figure 7-4.

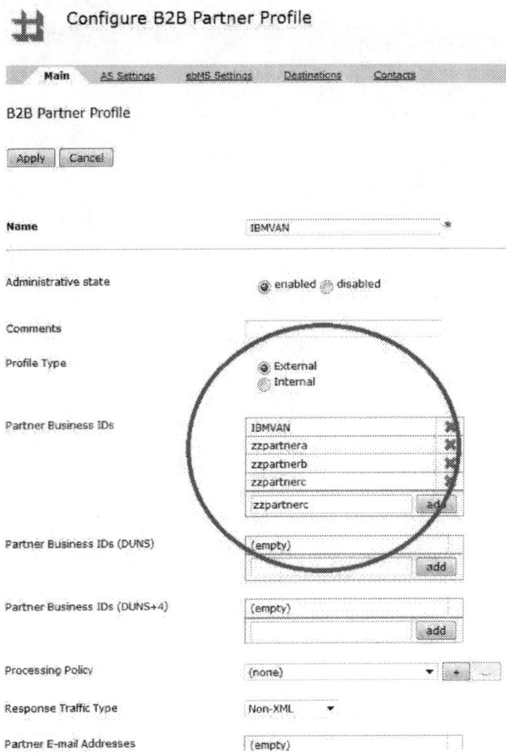

Figure 7-4 IBMVAN Partner Profile Configuration.

In addition to having all of the business IDs in the VAN
profile, you must tell the profile that you expect the files to
come in or go out with a single specific AS2 ID. This is done by
setting the Override AS ID field to the AS2 ID being used as
seen in Figure 7-5.

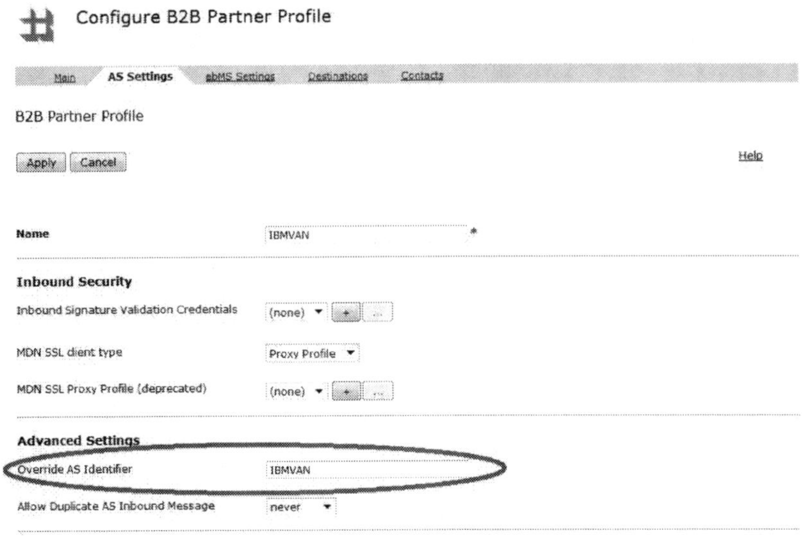

Configure B2B Partner Profile

Main | **AS Settings** | sbMS Settings | Destinations | Contacts

B2B Partner Profile

[Apply] [Cancel]

Help

Name   IBMVAN   *

Inbound Security

Inbound Signature Validation Credentials   (none) ▼ [+] [...]

MDN SSL client type   Proxy Profile ▼

MDN SSL Proxy Profile (deprecated)   (none) ▼ [+] [...]

Advanced Settings

Override AS Identifier   IBMVAN

Allow Duplicate AS Inbound Message   never ▼

Figure 7-5 IBMVAN Partner Profile – AS2 ID.

The last mandatory information to configure is to set the AS2 destination of the IBM Collaboration Network in the Destinations tab of the profile similar to Figure 7-6. Be sure to apply and then save the configuration.

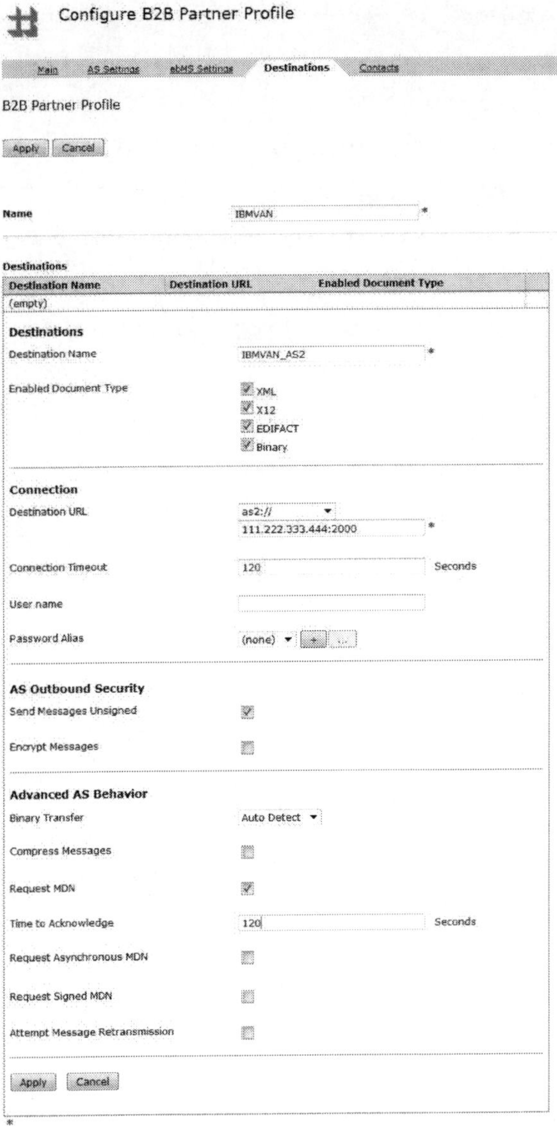

Configure B2B Partner Profile

Main   AS Settings   ebMS Settings   **Destinations**   Contacts

B2B Partner Profile

[Apply] [Cancel]   Help

Name   IBMVAN   *

Destinations

Destination Name	Destination URL	Enabled Document Type
(empty)		

Destinations

Destination Name   IBMVAN_AS2   *

Enabled Document Type   ☑ XML
                                ☑ X12
                                ☑ EDIFACT
                                ☑ Binary

Connection

Destination URL   as2://   ▼
                                111.222.333.444:2000   *

Connection Timeout   120   Seconds

User name

Password Alias   (none) ▼ [ ] [ ]

AS Outbound Security

Send Messages Unsigned   ☑

Encrypt Messages   ☐

Advanced AS Behavior

Binary Transfer   Auto Detect ▼

Compress Messages   ☐

Request MDN   ☑

Time to Acknowledge   120   Seconds

Request Asynchronous MDN   ☐

Request Signed MDN   ☐

Attempt Message Retransmission ☐

[Apply] [Cancel]

*

Figure 7-6 IBMVAN Partner Profile – AS2 Destination.

After completing the configuration of the IBMVAN external profile, we need to create the internal profile if one does not exist. When setting explicit AS2 IDs in the profile, we use a separate internal profile so as not to impact the point-to-point AS2 connections. In this example, since we are accepting AS2 and the payloads are in XML, the Business IDs need to reflect the XML file and the Override AS ID needs to reflect the AS2 relationship with the VAN. Figure 7-7 illustrates the Main tab configuration used in the internal partner profile.

Figure 7-7 MyCompany Partner Profile Configuration.

Just like in the external profile, you must configure the internal profile expect the files to come in or go out with a specific AS2 ID. This is done by setting the Override AS Identifier field to the AS2 ID being used as shown in Figure 7-8.

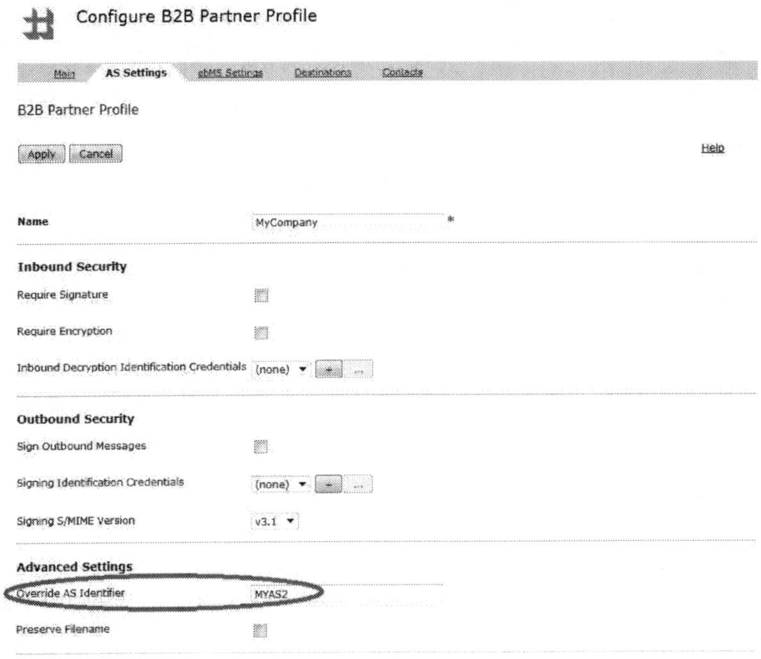

Figure 7-8 MyCompany Partner Profile – AS2 ID.

In this example, the internal profile is using MQ as the destination for transferring data into the trusted network and ultimately to the application that will consume the XML files. This configuration assumes you have already created a MQ Queue Manager Object. Details for creating a MQ Queue

Manager object can be found in Chapter 5, "DataPower B2B File Transfer Patterns."

Figure 7-9 illustrates the Destination configuration used in this example.

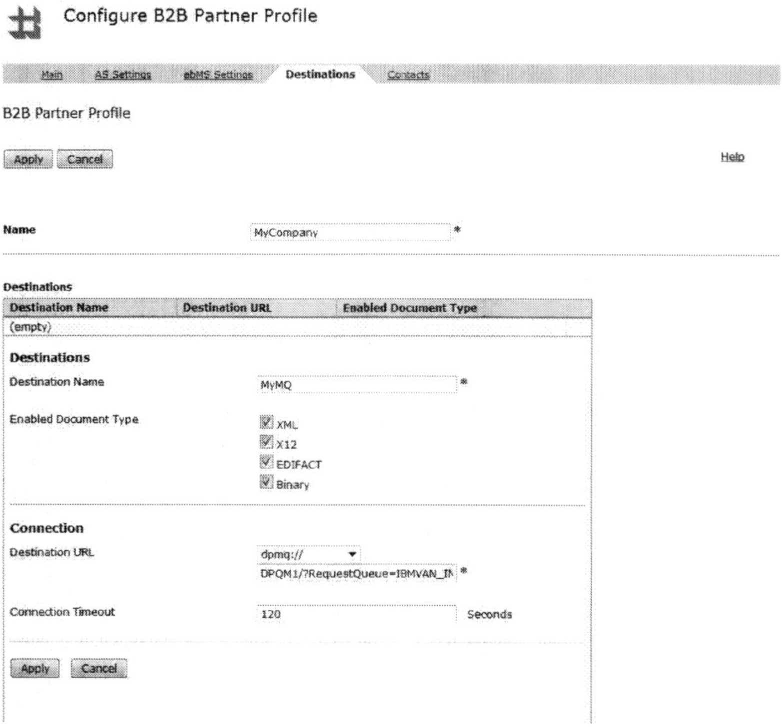

Figure 7-9 MyCompany Partner Profile Destination.

After completing and applying the configuration of the MyCompany internal profile, we need to create a B2B Gateway to consume and produce the AS2 files as well as route XML files received from the backend to the VAN.

In the Document Routing section we need an AS2 listener
with the IP address and port we will be listening on in the B2B
Gateway. We will also need a MQ Poller to consume the XML
files from backend applications in the trusted network. In the
Attach Partner Profiles section we use the drop down and
select both the IBMVAN and MyCompany partner profiles to
be used in this gateway. In addition to the Main tab, the
Archive tab must be configured to allow for the archive and
purge of metadata and files to prevent hard drive space issues.
The XML Formats tab must contain the XML Path Language
(XPATH) statements to extract the sending and receiving
partner IDs from the input files.

Figure 7-10 illustrates the B2B Gateway Service we used in
this example.

Figure 7-10 IBM Van Gateway Configuration.

When all of the mandatory fields and tabs are configured in the B2B Gateway service, save by clicking on the Apply button. It is also a good idea to save your configuration, so remember to click the Save Configuration link.

You are now ready to receive files from and send files to the VAN. The back-side in this case is using MQ to connect to the application that is going to consume the XML files. However, it could be transported over any protocol that

DataPower and the application mutually support. The Archive tab and XML Formats tab are not shown in this section since details about configuring each can be found elsewhere in this book.

Figure 7-11 illustrates an example of what the B2B Transaction Viewer looks like for transactions received using this pattern.

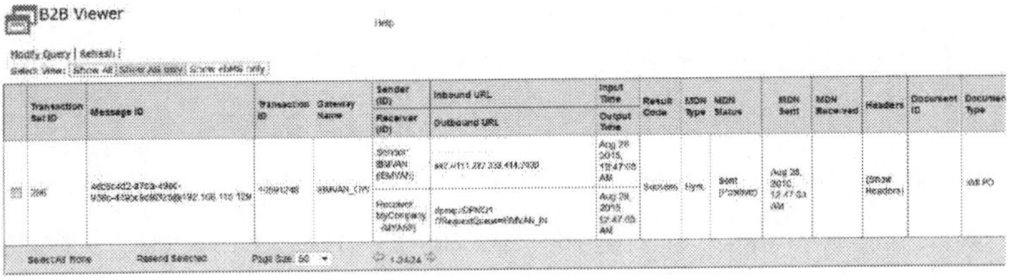

Figure 7-11 B2B Transaction Viewer – VAN Pattern.

NOTE—AS2 Security Sign/Encrypt

We did not configure AS2 security to keep it simple for this example. However, in the real world you would likely use both signing and encryption for your AS2 connections.

2. DataPower B2B with payload processing in Sterling Integrator or Sterling File Gateway

This gateway pattern is commonly used by customers who have the following three requirements:

- Wish to use the B2B Gateway in the DMZ to exchange files with partners over supported transport protocols or B2B messaging protocols
- Wish to use profile management and the B2B Transaction Viewer to identify, secure and monitor each connection.
- Wish to have Sterling route or process files internally.

Unlike a proxy pattern this pattern allows files to be passed through the service over a different front-side and back-side connection. This pattern natively bridges protocols on the fly. This is useful when you want to do something like check files for viruses, route files based on content, payload transformation or even apply and act on a service level monitor. This can all occur while the file is in transit. The result is then sent to your back-end over one standard protocol like MQ.

The key value to customers with this pattern is it allows them to use a single multi-channel gateway to support not only the B2B channel but also the API, mobile, cloud and web channels. The B2B module allows the customer to move their B2B security and governance into the DMZ using the IBM's market leading security gateway to reject unwanted connections or malicious data before it gets into the trusted network. It also acts as buffer to the downstream systems due to its ability to consume transactions faster than traditional software. This gateway can throttle those transactions to the back-side preventing an overrun condition on the downstream systems.

Figure 7-12 illustrates this pattern in more detail. In this example we are using a SFTP Server on the front-side to consume inbound EDI files, FTP on the back-side for Sterling File Gateway and MQ on the back-side for Sterling B2B Integrator. This demonstrates DataPower's flexibility in bridging common file transfer protocols. To make things even more interesting we are using a processing policy to dynamically route all EDI files to Sterling B2B Integrator and all non-EDI files to Sterling File Gateway. This is called dynamic destination routing.

NOTE—Secure Backside Connections

In this example we are securing the connection by using SFTP between the partner and DataPower. On the back-side between DataPower and the systems in the trusted network we are not securing the connection. However, SSL should be used to secure connection between the DMZ and the trusted network in a real-world deployment.

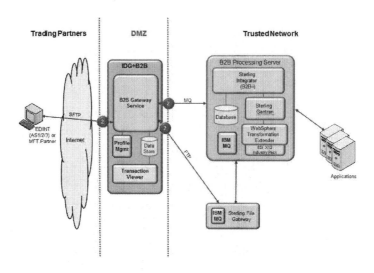

Figure 7-12 DataPower DMZ to Sterling Solutions.

This gateway pattern uses an external profile to represent the trading partner, an internal profile to represent both Sterling B2B Integrator and Sterling File Gateway and finally a DataPower B2B Gateway to process the files.

Figure 7-13 and 7-14 illustrate an example of what the external trading partner profile configuration looks like. Since we are not using AS or ebMS protocols, we only need to configure the Main and Destinations tabs in the profile.

In the Main tab we only need to set the partner to external and provide the business ID being used for this partner. The zz is the qualifier part of the x12 ISA header and the partner1 is the identifier part. An additional business ID that represents the XML file is also added.

7-13 Partner1 Profile Configuration – Main tab.

In Destinations tab we create a destination by clicking on the Add button in the destination table as seen in Figure 7-14 and use the drop down to select SFTP as the protocol of choice. We also need to create a SSH client connection for this partner. Details on what the SSH client connection configuration looks like can be found in the SFTP patterns section of Chapter 5, "DataPower B2B File Transfer Patterns."

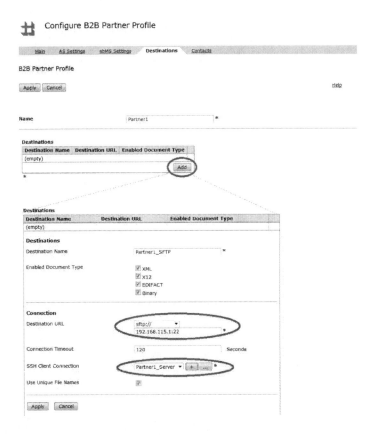

Figure 7-14 Partner1 Profile Configuration – Destination.

After completing and saving the configuration of the Partner1 external profile, we need to create the internal profile for this pattern. The Sterling internal profile example is illustrated in figures 7-15 and 7-16.

In the Main tab as seen in Figure 7-15 we set the business IDs to reflect the sender and receiver information in the EDI and XML files. We created a processing policy to dynamically

route EDI files to Sterling B2B Integrator over MQ and to route
all other file types to Sterling File Gateway over FTP.

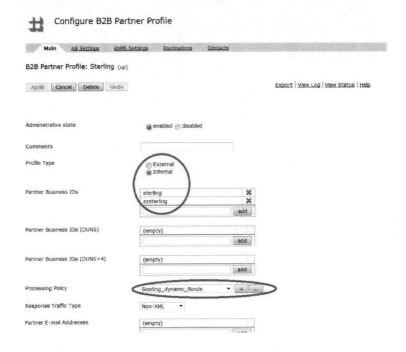

Figure 7-15 Sterling Partner Profile – Main tab.

The processing policy created for this pattern is shown in
Figure 7-16. It only has a single rule consisting of a match
action. This action has a rule that will match on all data
destined for this profile. The Transform action uses an XSL
stylesheet to facilitate the dynamic route and finally a results
action to complete the rule.

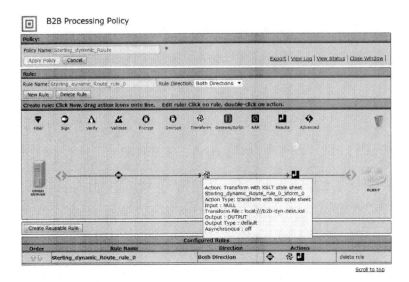

Figure 7-16 Sterling Profile – Processing Policy.

The example b2b-dyn-dest.xsl stylesheet is used to dynamically route to the destination, based on B2B document type, is shown in Listing 7-1.

Listing 7-1 Stylesheet used for dynamic routing.

```
<?xml version="1.0" encoding="utf-8"?>
<!--

  Licensed Materials - Property of IBM

  IBM WebSphere DataPower Appliances

  Copyright IBM Corporation 2007. All Rights Reserved.

  US Government Users Restricted Rights - Use, duplication or
disclosure

  restricted by GSA ADP Schedule Contract with IBM Corp.

-->
<xsl:stylesheet version="1.0"

    xmlns:xsl="http://www.w3.org/1999/XSL/Transform"
```

```
xmlns:dp="http://www.datapower.com/extensions"
xmlns:dpconfig="http://www.datapower.com/param/config"
extension-element-prefixes="dp"
exclude-result-prefixes="dp dpconfig">
  <xsl:template match="/">
 <!-- Determine and display b2b-doc-type in the logs -->
    <xsl:variable name="doctype"
select="dp:variable('var://service/b2b-doc-type')"/>
    <xsl:message dp:priority="warn"> Document Type = <xsl:value-of
select="$doctype"/>
    </xsl:message>
      <!-- When Content-type is x12 set the destination to Sterling
Integrator
      otherwise set the destination to Sterling File Gateway -->
    <xsl:choose>
      <xsl:when test="$doctype='x12'">
        <xsl:message dp:priority="warn"> Set Dynamic Destination to
B2B-i</xsl:message>
        <dp:set-variable name="'var://service/b2b-partner-
destination'" value="'B2B-i'"/>
      </xsl:when>
      <xsl:otherwise>
        <xsl:message dp:priority="warn"> Set Dynamic Destination to
SFG.</xsl:message>
        <dp:set-variable name="'var://service/b2b-partner-
destination'" value="'SFG'"/>
      </xsl:otherwise>
    </xsl:choose>
  </xsl:template>
</xsl:stylesheet>
```

By setting the 'var://service/b2b-partner-destination' variable we are overriding the default destination, as set in the GUI, by specifying the destination in this file. The value for this variable must be the name of a destination in the profile's destination list.

Figure 7-17 shows what the destination list looks like for the Sterling internal profile. We are not showing the details of the destinations since there are examples of both elsewhere in this book.

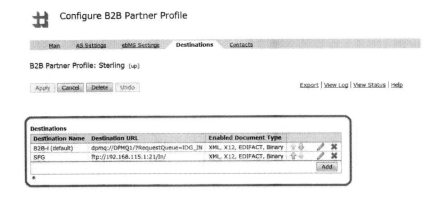

Figure 7-17 Sterling Profile – Destinations List.

After completing and applying the configuration of the Sterling internal profile, we need to create a B2B Gateway to process and route the files between the partners and ultimately Sterling B2B Integrator and Sterling File Gateway.

In the Document Routing section we need an SFTP listener with the IP address and port to listen on in the B2B Gateway. We also need a MQ Poller to consume files from Sterling B2B Integrator and a FTP Listener to consume files from Sterling File Gateway. In the Attach Partner Profiles section, we use

the drop-down and select the Partner1 and Sterling partner
profiles for this gateway. In addition to the Main tab, the
Archive tab must be configured and the XML Formats tab
must contain the XML XPATH to extract the information from
the files we need to route.

Figure 7-18 illustrates the B2B Gateway Service we used in
this example.

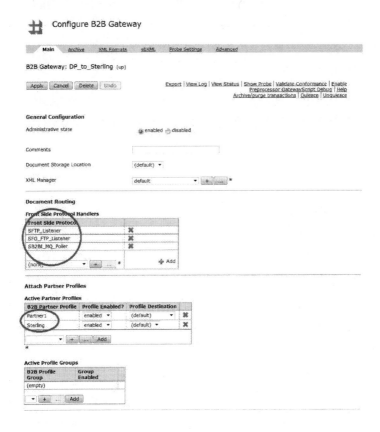

Figure 7-18 DP_to_Sterling B2B Gateway Configuration- Main tab.

When all of the mandatory fields and tabs are configured in the B2B Gateway service, and saved by clicking on the Apply button, you are ready to receive files from and send files to the trading partners. In this pattern there is one SFTP front-side connection for receiving files and two back-side connections; one using MQ and the other using FTP. These connections are selected based on what document type is being received. Any protocol can be used on both the front-side and back-side that DataPower and the Sterling solutions mutually support. The Archive tab and XML Formats tab are not shown in this section since details about configuring each can be found elsewhere in this book.

Figure 7-19 illustrates an example of what the B2B Transaction Viewer looks like for transactions received using this pattern.

| | B2B Viewer | | | | Help | | | | | |

Modify Query | Refresh |
Select View: Show All Show AS only Show ebMS only

	Transaction Set ID	Transaction ID	Gateway Name	Sender (ID)	Inbound URL	Input Time	Result Code	Document ID	Document Type	In
				Receiver (ID)	Outbound URL	Output Time				ID
☑	259	10748126	DP_to_Sterling	Sender: Partner1 (partner1)	sftp://[...]:22822/NotEDI.xml	Aug 28, 2015, 4:12:37 AM	Success		CustomXML	
				Receiver: Sterling (sterling)	ftp://192.168.115.1:21/in/0000000 Cbapter8-DP_to_Sterling-259					
☑	258	10747488	DP_to_Sterling	Sender: Partner1 (zzpartner1)	sftp://[...]:22822/editest.edi	Aug 28, 2015, 4:12:21 AM	Success	000000002	850	
				Receiver: Sterling (zzsterling)	dpmq://DPMQ1/?RequestQueue=IDG_IN					

Figure 7-19 B2B Transaction Viewer – DP to Sterling Pattern.

When Sterling B2B Integrator receives the EDI files it will validate the EDI, send a Functional Acknowledgment back through DataPower to the partner, and transform the EDI message into any format supported by Sterling B2Bi. When Sterling File Gateway receives the non-EDI files it will use

Sterling B2B Integrator for processing the payload and route the files to their final destination.

3. DataPower Proxy to Sterling

This gateway pattern is commonly used by customers who wish to use DataPower in the DMZ to proxy files to Sterling solutions that are sitting in the trusted network. The difference between this pattern and the Gateway patterns above is in this pattern the files are streamed through the front-side to the back-side using the same protocol. This allows us to pass files of unlimited size from the front to the back. Protocols HTTP(S), FTP(S) and SFTP are the most commonly used in this pattern. The SFTP and FTP(S) Proxy pattern configuration details can be found in Chapter 5, "DataPower B2B File Transfer Patterns," so we will only describe the HTTP(S) Proxy pattern in this section.

Figure 7-20 illustrates the HTTP(S) Proxy pattern used to proxy AS2 through DataPower to Sterling B2B Integrator. The same HTTP(S) pattern can be used to proxy any type of file to Sterling File Gateway or even to allow a secure connection to Web Mailboxes managed in Sterling.

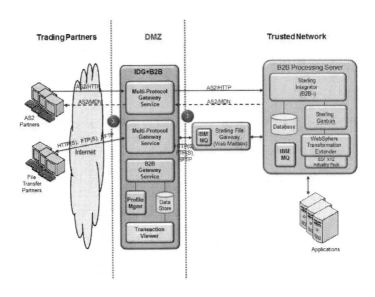

Figure 7-20 DataPower HTTP Proxy to SFG.

Proxy patterns are created using a Multi-Protocol Gateway Service. A Multi-Protocol Gateway Service can be created from the Control Panel by clicking on the Multi-Protocol Gateway icon or by navigating to it in the left navigation menu. There are many tabs in the Multi-Protocol Gateway. However, we only need to configure a few fields in the Main tab to meet the minimum configuration requirements.

In our example, we provide a descriptive name for the gateway and set the Processing Policy to default. The backend URL is the IP Address that Sterling B2B Integrator is using as an AS2 Listener, the Front Side Protocol is set to an IP address and port where external partners will send their AS2 files. Since we are not using a processing policy we can set both the Response Type and Request Type to Pass-through. We finally need to set the Streaming setting to stream output to both front and back. We took the defaults for all other fields and tabs. However, you can add SSL Proxy settings to secure the connection and also add a processing policy to affect routing of the files.

Figure 7-21 illustrates an example of how the HTTP proxy pattern can be achieved in a Multi-Protocol Gateway.

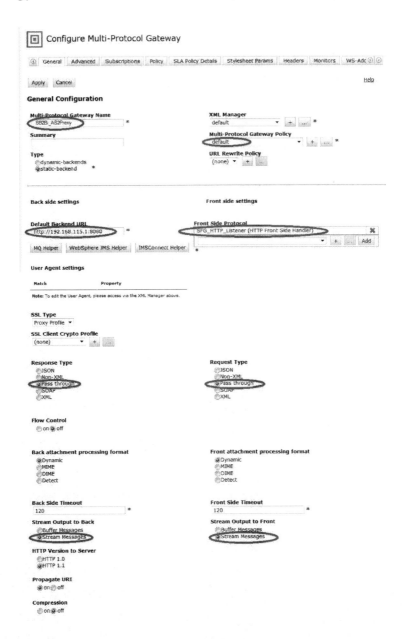

Figure 7-21 Multi-Protocol Gateway - HTTP Proxy Pattern.

After all of the mandatory fields have been configured and the Multi-Protocol Gateway has been applied, you can save the configuration and start using the service to proxy HTTP requests from DataPower to Sterling B2B Integrator or Sterling File Gateway.

NOTE—Service Does Not Use B2B Gateway

Since this service is not tied to the B2B Gateway Service it will not use profile management, nor will it display transaction state in the B2B Transaction Viewer. A Processing policy in the Multi-Protocol Gateway can be used to capture metadata about the transaction. This metadata can be sent to the B2B Gateway for the sole purpose of populating the B2B Transaction Viewer with an entry representative of the file transfer. A processing policy can also be used to provide Authentication, Authorization, and Auditing and also pass metadata to Sterling B2B Integrator or Sterling File Gateway if needed.

Summary

This chapter provided you with an overview and benefits of using DataPower B2B as a multi-channel gateway in the DMZ to secure access to IBM Integration Bus and multiple Sterling solutions deployed in the trusted network. Some customers run both IIB and Sterling B2Bi in the trusted zone and let DataPower in the DMZ make a routing decision to either product depending on their data flow requirements. This example also illustrated how DataPower B2B can be used as a secure cloud connector to the IBM Collaboration Network.

Appendix A:
Acronyms Glossary

A2A	Application to Application
AAA	Authentication Authorization and Audit
ACK	Acknowledgment
ACL	Access Control List
AES	Advanced Encryption Standard
API	Application Programming Interface
APOP	Authenticated Post Office Protocol
AS	Applicability Statement
AS1	Applicability Statement over SMTP/POP3
AS2	Applicability Statement over HTTP
AS3	Applicability Statement over FTP
B2B	Business to Business
B2BGW	B2B Gateway
B2C	Business to Consumer
BPSS	Business Process Specification Schema
CPA	Collaboration Protocol Agreement (ebXML)
CPP	Collaboration Protocol Profile
CPPA (ebXML)	Collaboration-Protocol Profile and Agreement
DHCP	Dynamic Host Configuration Protocol

DMZ	Demilitarized Zone
DUNS	Data Universal Numbering System
DUNS+4	Data Universal Numbering System + Affiliate or Subsidiary ID
EBMS	ebXML Messaging Service
EBXML	Electronic Business XML
EDI	Electronic Data Interchange
EDI-X12	
EDIFACT	Electronic Data Interchange For Administration, Commerce and Transport
EDIINT	Electronic Data Interchange – Internet Integration
FSPH	Front-Side Protocol Handler
FA	Functional Acknowledgement
FTP	File Transfer Protocol
GUI	Graphical User Interface
GZIP	GNU ZIP
HA	High Availability
HTTP	Hypertext Transfer Protocol
HTTPS	Hypertext Transfer Protocol with Secure Socket Layer
HSM	Hardware Security Module
ICAP	Internet Content Adaptation Protocol

ID	Identifier
IDG	IBM DataPower Gateway
IETF	Internet Engineering Task Force
IIB	IBM Integration Bus
IMS	Information Management Service
IP	Internet Protocol
ISAM	IBM Security Access Manager
ISSW	IBM Software Services for WebSphere
JCE	Java Cryptography Extension
KB	Kilobyte
LAN	Local Area Network
LDAP	Lightweight Directory Access Protocol
MB	Megabyte
MDN	Message Disposition Notification
MFT	Managed File Transfer
MIME	Multipurpose Internet Mail Extensions
MPGW	Multi-Protocol Gateway
MQ	Message Queue (IBM)
MSH	Message Service Handler (ebXML)
MSI	Message Service Interface (ebXML)
NAT	Network Address Translation
NFS	Network File System

OASIS Organization for the Advancement of Structured Information Standards

OWASP	Open Web Application Security Project
PAT	Port Address Translation
PCI	Payment Card Industry
PCRE	Perl Compatible Regular Expressions
PGP	Pretty Good Privacy
POP3	Post Office Protocol 3
RAID	Redundant Array of Independent Disks
RBM	Role Based Management
RFC	Request for Comment
S/MIME	Secure/Multipurpose Internet Mail Extensions
SDK	Software Development Kit
SFTP	Secure File Transfer Protocol
SHA-2	Secure Hash Algorithm 2
SLM	Service Level Management
SMTP	Simple Mail Transfer Protocol
SNMP	Simple Network Management Protocol
SOA	Service Orientated Architecture
SOAP	Simple Object Access Protocol
SOMA	SOAP Configuration Management
SPE	Standards Processing Engine
SQL	Structured Query Language

SSH	Secure Shell
SSL	Secure Sockets Layer
STARTTLS	Start Transport Layer Security
TCP	Transmission Control Protocol
TLS	Transport Layer Security
TPS	Transactions per Second
UN/CEFACT	United Nations Centre for Trade Facilitation and Electronic Business
URI	Uniform Resource Identifier
URL	Uniform Resource Locator
VAN	Value Added Network
VIP	Virtual IP (address)
WTX	WebSphere Transformation Extender
XML	Extensible Markup Language
XPATH	XML Path Language
XSL	Extensible Stylesheet Language

Appendix B:
DataPower Resources

IBM DataPower Handbooks:

Volume I: DataPower Intro & Setup:

http://amzn.to/1ljrEBb

Volume II: DataPower Networking:

http://amzn.to/1Ijrzh3

Volume III: DataPower Development:

Should be available on by January 2015

IBM DataPower Knowledge Center:

http://www-01.ibm.com/support/knowledgecenter/SS9H2Y/welcome

IBM DataPower Information Center:

http://www.ibm.com/software/integration/datapower/library/documentation

IBM DataPower Internet/WWW Main Product Page:

http://www.ibm.com/datapower

DataPower GitHub:

https://github.com/ibm-datapower

Twitter:

https://twitter.com/IBMGateways

YouTube:

https://www.youtube.com/channel/UCV2_-gdea5LM58S-E3WCqew

LinkedIn:

https://www.linkedin.com/groups?home=&gid=4820454

developerWorks Discussion Forum:

https://www.ibm.com/developerworks/community/forums/html/forum?id=11111111-0000-0000-0000-000000001198

Weekly DataPower Webcast:

https://www14.software.ibm.com/webapp/iwm/web/signup.do?source=swg-wdwfw

SlideShare:

http://www.slideshare.net/ibmdatapower/

How-to find appropriate DataPower product information:

http://www-01.ibm.com/support/docview.wss?uid=swg21377654

DataPower Product Support Website:

Contains firmware, documentation, support procedure, technotes and other helpful material:

http://www.ibm.com/software/integration/datapower/support/

Redbooks:

http://www.redbooks.ibm.com/cgi-bin/searchsite.cgi?query=datapower

Software Services for WebSphere:

Top-notch DataPower consulting from IBM WebSphere.

http://www.ibm.com/developerworks/websphere/services/fin
dbykeyword.html?q1=DataPower

Hermann Stamm-Wilbrandt's Blog:

Hermann is one of the brightest minds in DataPower-land, and
his blog on development topics is incredibly valuable, featuring
tips and techniques that can't be found elsewhere.

https://www.ibm.com/developerworks/community/blogs
/HermannSW/?lang=en

WebSphere Global Community DataPower Group:

http://www.websphereusergroup.org/datapower

IBM WebSphere DataPower Support:

http://www.ibm.com/software/integration/datapower/suppor
t/

Support Flashes RSS Feed:

http://www-
947.ibm.com/systems/support/myfeed/xmlfeeder.wss?feeder.
requid=feeder.create_public_feed&feeder.feedtype=RSS&feed
er.maxfeed=25&OC=SS9H2Y&feeder.subdefkey=swgws&feede
r.channel.title=WebSphere%20DataPower%20SOA%20Applia
nces&feeder.channel.descr=The%20latest%20updates%20abo
ut%20WebSphere%20DataPower%20SOA%20Appliances

IBM DataPower Support Technotes:

http://www.ibm.com/search/csass/search?q=&sn=spe&lang=en&filter=collection:stgsysx,dblue,ic,pubs,devrel1&prod=U692969C82819Q63

IBM Education Assistant DataPower Modules:

http://www-01.ibm.com/support/knowledgecenter/websphere_iea/com.ibm.iea.wdatapower/plugin_coverpage.dita

WAMC Technote:

http://www-01.ibm.com/support/docview.wss?uid=swg24032265

DataPower Feature Grid:

We consider the Feature Grid to be an invaluable resource, and we are excited to provide it to you. It yields the answers to the most commonly asked questions about DataPower ("Is feature/protocol/spec X supported on my Y appliance?") We had initially included the entire table here, spread across several pages. However, due to its density, it was hard to read, and it was literally changing under us as product management made changes for the impending announcements.

We debated and felt that the best thing we could do for our readers would be to provide a URL hyperlink, so that the most up to date information (and not stale or incorrect information!) is available to you. There are detriments to this approach, such as the dreaded 'busted URL', but in this day and age it's likely that you are reading this on a device with an Internet connection, or have one within reach, and as well we have the capability to update this book as soon as we find that something is amiss. You can find the features grid at:

http://www.slideshare.net/ibmdatapower/ibm-data-power-gateways-features-comparison

Acknowledgements

The Author Team:

The Author Team would like to thank the following people for technical contributions, clarifications, and suggestions for much of the content in this book: Bill Hines, Jeffrey Liu, Johnson Chiang, Tony Ffrench, Neal Alewine, and Tim Baker.

Richard Kinard:

I'd like thank Ajay Kadakia, Steven Cawn, Thomas Infantino and Sid Antflick for being exceptional role models and mentoring me throughout my time in IBM Product Management and Sales. I'd like to especially thank my friends and family for their support and understanding throughout my life and career. Finally, I'd like to thank my author team for the exceptional work they did on this book and for forgiving me when I applied a little too much pressure on them to fine tune and finish their chapters. You should all be very proud of the job we have done on this book; I know I am.

Andre Manriquez:

I'd like to thank Rich Kinard for inviting me to participate in writing this book and being the glue on our team. I'd also like to acknowledge Bill Hines for all his efforts and time on this book. Finally I'd like to also acknowledge and thank Tim Baker, Kaleb MeKonnen, and Ozair Sheikh for all their assistance and input.

Steven Koehler:

I'd like to thank Rich Kinard for giving me the opportunity to collaborate and work with him on the writing of this DataPower Book.

Charlie Sumner:

I'd like to thank Rich Kinard for putting some much needed polish on my chapter, and to Bill Hines and Rich for leading the author team to a final version that we are all very proud of.

About the Authors

Richard Kinard

Rich Kinard is a Worldwide Competitive Sales Leader for DataPower, API Management and Cast Iron in IBM Systems Middleware. He is a subject matter expert in business-to-business (B2B) and integration technologies with over 15 years of B2B experience and 14 years of network engineering experience designing, developing, and implementing integration solutions all over the world in many industries. Mr. Kinard has worked on many initiatives with Internet standards organizations to promote B2B interoperability and security and has written a total of nine IBM Redbooks publications covering best practices for IBM B2B and Managed File Transfer. Rich is a United States Air Force veteran and has several certifications from the Community College of the Air Force in Satellite Computer Control Systems and Electronics.

Andre Manriquez

Andre Manriquez is a Systems Middleware Sr. Technical Sales Specialist and B2B SME for IBM. He has been with IBM for 9 years supporting SOA, API Management, Integration, and B2B. Prior to IBM he spent 16 years working with a handful of B2B and Managed File Transfer software vendors, including Premenos, Harbinger, IPNet Solutions, and Cyclone Commerce. He has held roles in Support, Education Services, Professional Services, and Technical Sales with primary focus on B2B. He has been supporting and evangelizing B2B since he started his career 25 years ago. Andre attended Contra Costa College where he majored in Computer Science and received various certifications around Cobol and Assembler programming, as well TCP/IP Communications at SE College from IBM.

Steven Koehler

Steven Koehler is an owner of CyberLink Computing, LLC (www.clcomputing.com), a consulting company he founded in 2009. Steven holds a Bachelor of Science degree in Business Management from North Carolina State University. Programming since the early 1980's, Steven began working with B2B software in 2002. He has traveled world-wide developing IBM WebSphere Partner Gateway Java user exits and was a co-creator of the IBM DataPower B2B appliance. CyberLink Computing, LLC is an IBM Business Partner that specializes in B2B solutions including WebSphere Partner Gateway and Data Power. Steven is currently developing new applications for the B2B marketplace, including cloud and mobile solutions. He resides in Cave Creek, Arizona with his wife Paula. You can reach him at skoehler@clcomputing.com.

Charlie Sumner

Charles Sumner is a Senior Managing Consultant in the IBM Systems Middleware organization. He is a subject matter expert in the IBM DataPower Gateway technology and has over 37 years of experience in various areas of software development, test and support. Mr. Sumner has worked on the product implementation of many of IBM's leading technologies including speech recognition where he was the Senior Test and Support Manager for the IBM WebSphere Voice products. He has also contributed to a number of patents and published works and to the development of product certification tests.

Afterword

Afterword by Eugene Kuznetsov

"The proper planning of any job is the first requirement. With limited knowledge of a trade, the job of planning is doubly hard, but there are certain steps that any person can take towards proper planning if he only will."

—Robert Oakes Jordan, Masonry

I founded a company called DataPower® in the spring of 1999 to build products based on several distinct ideas. The first idea involved applying reconfigurable computing and dynamic code generation to the problem of integrating disparate applications. The second idea centered on the concept of data-oriented programming (DOP) as the means to achieve direct and robust data interchange. The third idea involved delivering middleware as a network function, enabled by the DOP technology and inspired by the successful models of ubiquitous connectivity. The product's journey since has been remarkable, and this great book is another milestone for the entire team behind DataPower. Before more discussion of the book itself, a few words on these three ideas.

Rapidly adapting to change is key for everything and everyone in today's world, and IBM appliances are no exception. Whether it's a policy, a transformation map, a schema, or a security rule, DataPower will try to put it into effect with as little delay and interruption as possible. Popular methods for maintaining this kind of flexibility come with a large performance penalty. However, by dynamically generating code and reconfiguring hardware based on the current message flow, it became possible to achieve both flexibility and near-optimal performance. At any given point, the device operates as a custom engine for a particular task, but when the task changes, it can rapidly become a different custom engine underneath the covers.

This dynamic adaptability is especially useful when combined with DOP. Stated briefly, DOP emphasizes formally documenting data formats and using them directly, instead of encapsulation or abstraction, to integrate or secure different modules or systems. Today, XML is probably one of the most successful and readily recognized examples of DOP, but the principles are more universal than any particular technology. Another example of DOP is the way DataPower XI52 processes binary data, by using high-level format descriptors instead of adaptors.

These, in turn, enable the creation of network hardware (also known as appliance) products that operate on whole application messages (rather than network packets) to integrate, secure, or control applications. Greater simplicity, performance, security, and cost-effectiveness were envisioned—and are now proven—with the appliance approach. Beyond the appliance design discipline, the success of IP & Ethernet networking in achieving universal connectivity has much to teach about the best way to achieve radically simplified and near-universal application integration.

Reading this book will enable you to benefit from the previous three ideas in their concrete form: the award-winning IBM products they became. From basic setup to the most powerful advanced features, it covers DataPower appliances in a readable tone with a solid balance of theory and examples. For example, Chapter 6 does a great job in explaining the big-picture view of device operation, and Chapter 22 gives a detailed how-to on extending its capabilities. With some of the most experienced hands-on DataPower practitioners among its authors, it provides the kind of real-world advice that is essential to learning any craft.

When learning IBM DataPower, there is one thing that may be more helpful and rewarding than remembering every particular detail, and that is developing an internal "mental model" of how the devices are meant to operate and fit into the environment. Especially when troubleshooting or learning new features, this "mental model" can make device behavior intuitive. Reading the following pages with an eye toward not just the details but also this mental model will speed both productivity and enjoyment.

In conclusion, I would like to use this occasion to thank the entire team, past and present, who made and continues to make DataPower possible. Their work and the passion of DataPower users is an inspiring example of how great people and a powerful idea can change the world for the better.

—*Eugene Kuznetsov, Cambridge, MA Founder of DataPower Technology, Inc. served as President, Chairman, and CTO at various points in the company's history, and then served as director of Product Management and Marketing, SOA Appliances at IBM Corporation.*

DataPower's first office is on the right. Photo courtesy of Merryman Design.

Afterword by Jerry Cuomo

It all started when I was asked to co-host an IBM Academy Conference on "Accelerators and Off-Loading" in 2004. I was feeling a little out of my element, so I decided to take some of the focus off me and put it on others. I had been reading about some of the new XML-centered hardware devices and was intrigued. I have always been interested in system performance. With XML dominating our emerging workloads (e.g., Service Oriented Architecture), the impact of XML performance on system performance was becoming increasingly important. Hence, I thought it would be a good idea to invite a handful of these XML vendors to our conference.

At the conference, the DataPower presentation was quite different from the others. It wasn't about ASICs or transistors; it was about improving time to value and total cost of operation. The DataPower presentation focused on topics that were also near and dear to me, such as systems integration, configuration over programming, and the merits of built-for-purpose systems. In essence, Eugene Kuznetsov, the DataPower founder and presenter, was talking about the value of appliances. While very intriguing, I couldn't help but feel curious about whether the claims were accurate. So, after the conference I invited Eugene to come to our lab in Research Triangle Park in North Carolina to run some tests.

I have to admit now that in the back of my mind, I operated on the principle of "keeping your friends close and your enemies closer." Behind my intrigue was a feeling of wanting to understand their capabilities so that we could outperform vendors with WebSphere® Application Server. The tests went well; however, the DataPower team was somewhat reluctant to dwell on the raw XML performance capabilities of their appliance. Feeling a little suspicious, I had my team run some raw performance experiments. The results were off the charts. Why wasn't the DataPower team flaunting this capability? This is when I had my "ah-ha" moment. While performance measured in transactions per second is important and part of the value equation, the overall performance metrics found while assessing time to value and overall cost of operation and ownership are the most critical performance metrics to a business. This is where the DataPower appliances outperform. I read a paper, written by Jim Barton, CTO and co-founder of Tivo, called "Tivo-lution." The paper was inspiring as it confirmed the motivations and aspirations that I've had ever since I led IBM's acquisition of DataPower in 2005. In the paper, Barton describes the challenges of making complex systems usable and how "purpose-built" computer systems are one answer to the challenge:

"One of the greatest challenges of designing a computer system is in making sure the system itself is 'invisible' to the user. The system should simply be a conduit to the desired result. There are many examples of such purpose-built systems, ranging from modern automobiles to mobile phones."

The concept of purpose-built systems is deeply engrained in our DNA at IBM. The name of our company implies this concept: International Business Machines.

IBM has a long history of building purposed machines, such as the 1933 Type 285, an electric bookkeeping and accounting machine. I can imagine this machine being delivered to an accountant, plugging it in, immediately followed by number crunching. The accountant didn't have to worry about hard drive capacity, operating system levels, compatibility between middleware vendors, or application functionality. It just did the job. I can also imagine it followed the 80/20 rule. It probably didn't do 100% of what all accountants needed. But it probably did 80% of what all accountants needed very well. Users just dealt with the remaining 20%, or learned to live without it.

"Business Machines, Again" is my inspiration. Our customers respond positively to the re-emergence of this approach to engineering products. It's all about time-to-value and total cost of operation and ownership. Appliances such as our WebSphere DataPower are leading the way in delivering on these attributes.

At the extreme, purpose-built systems, such as a Tivo DVR and an XI52, are built from the ground up for their purposes. While they might use off-the-shelf parts, such as an embedded Linux® OS, it is important that all parts are "right sized" for the job. Right-sizing source code in a hardware appliance is more like firmware (with strong affinity to the underlying hardware) than it is software. As such, the Tivo-lution paper describes the need to own every line of source code to ensure the highest level of integration and quality:

"...by having control of each and every line of source code...

Tivo would have full control of product quality and development schedules. When the big bug hunt occurred, as it always does, we needed the ability to follow every lead, understand every path, and track every problem down to its source."

The Tivo team even modified the GNU C++ compiler to eliminate the use of exceptions (which generate a lot of code that is seldom used) in favor of rigid checking of return code usage in the firmware. DataPower similarly contains a custom XML compiler that generates standard executable code for its general-purpose CPUs, as well as custom code for the (XG4) XML coprocessor card.

A physical appliance has the unparalleled benefit of being hardened for security. Jim talks about this in his Tivo paper:

"Security must be fundamental to the design...We wanted to make it as difficult as possible, within the economics of the DVR platform, to corrupt the security of any particular DVR."

The DataPower team has taught me the meaning of "tamper-proof" appliances, or more precisely "tamper-evident." Like the 1982 Tylenol scare, we can't stop you from opening the box, but we can protect you, if someone does open it. In fact, the physical security characteristics of DataPower make it one of the only technologies some of our most stringent customers will put on their network Demilitarized Zone (DMZ). If a DataPower box is compromised and opened, it basically stops working. An encrypted flash drive makes any configuration data, including security keys, difficult to exploit. "DP is like the roach motel; private keys go in, but never come out" is the way we sometimes describe the tamper-proof qualities of DataPower.

But the truth is, DataPower is not a DVR. DataPower is a middleware appliance. Middleware is a tricky thing to make an appliance out of. Middleware is enabling technology and by its nature is not specific to any application or vendor. The Tivo appliance is a specific application (TV and guide) that makes it somewhat easier to constrain:

"Remember, it's television. Everybody knows how television works."

"Television never stops, even when you turn off the TV set. Televisions never crash."

Hence, the challenge (and the art) in building a middleware appliance involves providing the right amount of constraint, without rendering the appliance useless. For example, DataPower does not run Java™ code (which is the primary means of customizing much of the WebSphere portfolio); instead, it uses XML as the primary mode of behavior customization. So, at some level, DP is not programmed, but instead it is configured. Now, for those who have used XML (and its cousin XSLT), you know that it's more than configuration; however, it is a constraint over Java programming, which has unbounded levels of customizability. The combined team of IBM and DataPower have been bridging this gap (of special to general purpose) effectively. We have recently added features to DP to allow it to seamlessly connect to IBM mainframe software (IMS™ and DB2®) as well as capabilities to manage a collection of appliances as if they were one.

IBM has a healthy general-purpose software business. Our WebSphere, Java-based middleware is the poster child for general-purpose middleware (write once, run almost everywhere). However, there is a place for business machines that are purposed built and focus on providing the 80 part of the 80/20 rule. We are heading down this path in a Big Blue way.

This book represents an important milestone in the adoption of DataPower into the IBM family. The authors of this book represent some of IBM's most skilled practitioners of Service Oriented Architecture (SOA). This team is a customer facing team and has a great deal of experience in helping our customers quickly realize value from our products. They have also been among the most passionate within IBM of adopting the appliance approach to rapidly illustrating the value of SOA to our customers. The authors have unparalleled experience in using DataPower to solve some of our customers' most stringent systems integration problems. This book captures their experiences and best practices and is a valuable tool for deriving the most out of your WebSphere DataPower appliance.

—*Jerry Cuomo, IBM Fellow, WebSphere CTO*

Afterword by Kyle Brown

I can still remember the day in late 2005 when Jerry Cuomo first called me into his office to tell me about an acquisition (then pending) of a small Massachusetts company that manufactured hardware devices.

"Wait a minute. Hardware??!?"

That's the first incredulous thought that went through my mind. Jerry was the CTO of the WebSphere brand in IBM, which had become the industry-leading brand of middleware based on Java. Why were we looking at a company that made hardware? Echoing the immortal words of Dr. "Bones" McCoy from the classic Star Trek series, I then thought,

"I'm a software engineer, not a hardware engineer, dang it!"

But as I sat in his office, Jerry wove me a story (as he had for our executives) that soon had me convinced that this acquisition did, in fact, make sense for WebSphere as a brand and for IBM as a whole. Jerry had the vision of a whole new way of looking at SOA middleware—a vision that encompassed efficient, special-purpose appliances that could be used to build many of the parts of an SOA. Key to this vision was the acquisition of DataPower, which gave us not only a wealth of smart people with deep experience in Networking, XML, and SOA, but an entry into this field with the DataPower family of appliances—notably the Integration appliance.

Since that day, I've never regretted our decision to branch out the WebSphere brand well beyond its Java roots. The market response to the introduction of the DataPower appliances to the brand has been nothing short of phenomenal. Far from distracting us, the ability to provide our customers with an easy-to-use, easy-to-install, and remarkably efficient hardware-based option for their ESB and security needs has turned out to be an asset that created synergy with our other product lines and made the brand stronger as a whole. It's been an incredible journey, and as we begin to bring out new appliances in the DataPower line, we're only now beginning to see the fundamental shift in thinking that appliance-based approaches can give us.

On this journey, I've been accompanied by a fantastic group of people—some who came to us through the DataPower acquisition and some who were already part of the WebSphere family—who have helped our customers make use of these new technologies. Bill, John, and the rest of the author team are the true experts in this technology, and their expertise and experience show in this book.

This book provides a wealth of practical information for people who are either novices with the DataPower appliances, or who want to learn how to get the most from their appliances. It provides comprehensive coverage of all the topics that are necessary to master the DataPower appliance, from basic networking and security concepts, through advanced configuration of the Appliance's features. It provides copious, detailed examples of how the features of the appliances work, and provides debugging help and tips for helping you determine how to make those examples (and your own projects) work. But what's most helpful about this book is the way in which the team has given you not just an explanation of how you would use each feature, but also why the features are built the way they are. Understanding the thinking behind the approaches taken is an enormous help in fully mastering these appliances. The team provides that, and provides you with a wealth of hints, tips, and time-saving advice not just for using and configuring devices, but also for how to structure your work with the devices.

This book is something the DataPower community has needed for a long time, and I'm glad that the authors have now provided it to the community. So sit back, crack open the book, open up the admin console (unless you have yet to take the appliance out of the box—the book will help you there, too!) and begin. Your work with the appliances is about to get a whole lot easier, more comprehensible, and enjoyable as well.

—*Kyle Brown, Distinguished Engineer, IBM Software Services and Support*